795
R587

Margaret Leighton
The Elusive Pimpernel.

Gérard
Philipe
La Beauté du
Diable.

Michel Simon
La Beauté
du Diable.

Ann Sheridan
Woman On The
Run.

Joseph Cotten

PUNCH
AT THE
CINEMA

FIRST PUBLISHED IN GREAT BRITAIN IN 1981
BY ROBSON BOOKS LTD., BOLSOVER HOUSE,
5-6 CLIPSTONE STREET. LONDON W1P 7EB.
COPYRIGHT © 1981 PUNCH PUBLICATIONS LTD.

British Library Cataloguing in Publication Data

Powell, Dilys
    Punch at the cinema.
    1. Moving-pictures — Anecdotes, facetiae
satire, etc.
    I. Title
    827.908'0355   PN6231.M7

    ISBN 0-86051-145-6

Designed by Glyn Rees
Edited by Susan Jeffreys

Printed in Hungary

PUNCH AT THE CINEMA

Presented by Dilys Powell

ⵍⵍ Robson Books

CONTENTS

"Two next to a loud-mouth who read the book."

"Attention, fellow citizens: the following is the Fenton T. Armbrewster list of the ten best movies of all time."

INTRODUCTION
Dilys Powell

Images moving in black and white or colour on a screen at the end of a darkened room: that is the cinema. The images are shadows of a reality which is itself a fake. But they talk, sing, dance, fight, suffer, make love and die. And they stir the spectator. They excite rage and delight, pity, terror, grief, affection, nausea, revulsion, adulation and hilarity. They inhabit a world which is intangible; we watch but cannot enter it. Only on rare occasions can we meet, can we converse with its inhabitants or its creators when they float down to our level.

This book, drawn from the pages of PUNCH—and the pages of PUNCH, entertaining, witty, critically amused, are basically far more serious, when seriousness is needed, than they are given credit for—this book is a record of reactions to the cinema; you will find some of the reactions listed above. Silent movies are not really covered and so some famous figures are absent: no study, for instance, of the exquisite Lillian Gish (though she moved without diminution into the sound cinema). Chaplin of course is here, belonging as he did to both silents and talkies; but the great Buster Keaton scrapes in with only a reference. Garbo is here (a critic writing about her betrays a preference for Dietrich); John Gilbert survives not as the great lover but as the star whose voice—squeaky, lacking in the resonance of amorous fervour—when the talkies arrived destroyed him. But then PUNCH does not go to the cinema to provide a handbook for historians, and the pieces here selected very properly keep a balance between assessment, appreciation and fun.

Professional interest leads me to look first at the reviews of individual films: at Richard Mallett extolling the qualities of *Brief Encounter* and Barry Took expressing a preference for *Star Wars* over *Close Encounters of the Third Kind*. I am struck by the differences—a matter of period, perhaps—in approach: the well-bred remoteness of E. V. Lucas, toying with *Kid Galahad*, and the immediacy, the contemporary feeling of Benny Green—a feeling which makes him relate the character played by Jack Lemmon in *Save the Tiger* to his own view of life—makes him, rightly in my opinion, admire the film. Critics nowadays take a more deeply personal attitude: sometimes a deeply exasperated one. But I am indulging myself. I am neglecting the main drive of a book which is full of pleasures: the occasional excursions, for example, into another kind of personal experience: a heart-felt cry from a writer hired and sacked and hired again, and once required to rewrite his script not because it did not do the job but because a different star had been engaged. And I treasure Barry Humphries's account of the struggle, in filming *The Adventures of Barry McKenzie*, to get the riches of Australian speech past the delicacy of the British censor.

These practical experiences indeed are the blood and bones of the book. And speaking of blood and bones I think of Carl Foreman, writer of *High Noon*, and his answer, good manners veiling bitterness, to John Wayne, who in the McCarthy days did his best to see that Mr Foreman and a good many other gifted people never worked again. I once met John Wayne at lunch in a Hollywood studio canteen. He clanked in, all spurs and frontier air; with astonishment, for I knew nothing about Hollywood politics, I listened to his opinions on a film which allowed its hero to throw his sheriff's badge on the ground. I have never been able to dislike John Wayne, politics or no; I have for too long been seduced by his bluff good looks and the grandeur of the westerns he adorned. He was, after all, one of the great figures of the American cinema and today one can look back on him as merely contributing, misguidedly and obstinately, a tiny fragment to a malignant passage of history. But it is worth noting that PUNCH, laughing PUNCH, joky PUNCH was ready to offer a serious comment on a lethal chapter.

This book, then, offers roughly half a century of those images on the screen: a selection of what films people saw and what some people thought about them—thrillers and tales of adventure, tragedy, comedy, domestic drama, science fiction, reflections of war and the complexities of espionage. Sometimes the human creatures who cast those shadows manifest themselves; curious that we know the shadows so much better than the living man or woman. In conversation with David Taylor, Rod Steiger lets you know that for an actor it is painful hearing people in an elevator discussing why they aren't going to see his movie. Turning to the manipulators of those frail shadows we hear Hitchcock talking about frustration: he wasn't allowed, in *North By North-West*, to let his players cavort over the heads, the actual monumental heads of the Presidents on Mount Rushmore. And then, balancing fact with the parody which is itself a criticism, there is Alan Coren's spoof autobiography of Elizabeth Taylor or Stanley Reynolds's spoof enquiry into the life behind the public face of Raquel Welch. Shifting the balance back again, there are the accounts of the practical business which makes the cinema work—the job of a projectionist, a manager, an usherette.

The cinema has changed since the earliest of these pieces appeared. It has grown more brutal and more extravagant; its fantasies today are more remote, its enigmas have deepened. Confronted with a movie which nowadays is routine, an audience of the 1930s would be lost. The early Orson Welles, remember, was received with suspicion, sometimes with derision. Today's spectators are acclimatised; experiments no longer infuriate. If people don't like a film they don't throw things at the screen, as the politically perceptive French threw things at Renoir's *La Règle du Jeu*: they just walk out. And a new sophistication takes hold. The work of the film societies and such institutions as the National Film Theatre has taught a new generation to recognise and appreciate the simple sincerities of the silent cinema. People don't laugh at, say, *Tol'able David*. In the 1930s the young enthusiasts of the cinema were politically conscious. They followed the lead of the British documentary movement, still more the campaigns of the great Russians. Today there has been a swing to formal experiments. Political conviction is apt to be veiled by aesthetic experiments.

The audience, in fact, has become much more knowledgeable than its predecessors. It knows about camerawork and composition and the tricks of technique. Naturally enough, a critic is expected to show an understanding of the screen unheard of forty or fifty years ago. The cinema has become a serious matter. The old jokes about its absurdities—and the absurdities are still there, all right—no longer raise a laugh; for, parallel with the idiocies, there is a new concern with a relation to human experience. The cinema still speaks to the adventurer in all of us. But, because people know more, a serious film calls for a deeper response. And the new generation really do know the cinema more intimately, more independently. And the embroiderers on the themes of the screen, the fantasy-writers and the creators of brilliant comment do really know the cinema. None of your old-fashioned patronage; these are writers who have observed and assimilated the essence of the most popular of the arts. Occasionally, a note of condescension, but that is rare. And perhaps the important thing is that all but an obstinate defector or two really like the cinema. You can't parody something unless you know it in your bones. But the best parodies, the best jokes proceed from more than knowledge, they proceed from something like affection. I can't believe that Alan Coren *really* doesn't like, for example, *Casablanca*—not in my opinion a good film, but like many middling movies thoroughly enjoyable.

An entertainment and an industry, an art which began not with the graphic precisions of cave drawings but with a circus-tent peep-show, with what the butler saw. If you read the histories you will find that it pretty soon got on to something which is still among its main assets—the kiss. Today it has become international, a matter for government subsidies. It is at once low-brow and high-brow, commercial and the goal of the uncommercially creative. It is obscure and fortunes are lavished on its production; it is the medium of pornography, but a Graham Greene writes for it, a Picasso, his marvellous hand tracing audacious patterns, has lent himself to its

performance. And in its train an army from other arts follows: writers, designers, critics, cartoonists (whom in my particular field I have often found better critics than the writers).

The critic, it seems to me, has a perilous job. Ideally, a review should take into account not only the players and their direction, not only the writer and the impact of narrative and character, but the cameraman, the composer, the designer of sets and costumes, an army of skilled technicians. What is more, nowadays, when a movie puts its trust in superhuman acrobatics and the horrors of space, the reviewer must not overlook either the creators of special effects or the stuntmen, those leapers from heights, those swimmers in the impossible void. But the critic hasn't the space. Nobody reads a catalogue of contributors to a movie—except, or course, the contributors themselves. And the reviewer hopes to be read.

The writers in this book are impeccably readable: they don't make catalogues. Nevertheless, one gives a faint cheer when a critic of an individual film mentions, say, the music. Not that he necessarily likes it. He may say, for instance, that in *Top Hat* Fred Astaire's songs are ''deplorable''. I know *Dancing cheek to cheek* isn't Brahms: I should have thought, though, that in its context it would do. Even so, a mere mention is encouraging. We have all been brought up in a literary tradition. I am, of course, including myself when I remark that critics—well, most of them—judge a film on its narrative and dramatic qualities; and to do that is to disregard the extraordinary gifts brought to the screen by artists and craftsmen whose names are almost unknown to the general public. But we can't help it. Upbringing, tradition and the steel walls of column and page imprison us. The compositions of sound and silence which mean pace and urgency, repose or the tension of waiting; the elaborate structure of the seen and the heard—it has to be taken for granted. And probably if it weren't, if in writing about a movie we tried to assess its value, nobody would care.

I am not, naturally, speaking of the screen musical, which more often than not is a translation from the stage; here the audience wants especially the music. There are even cases where a non-musical movie is loved for its musical theme: Addinzell's *Warsaw Concerto* it was which made the war-time *Dangerous Moonlight* popular. The visual effect is more insidious, though goodness knows it is the very basis of the cinema. The spectator may whistle the tunes; he is unlikely to mention the name of the cameraman. Yet it is in the visual that the spell of the cinema resides: the spell of a painter. True that now and then a movie may be too beautiful for its own good. Kubrick's *Barry Lyndon* with its warmly lit interiors and the lovely distances of its landscapes had an art-gallery fascination; but the narrative, for me at any rate, is lost in the brush-work.

For the cinema has its own way of telling a story: the speed, the duration of those shifting images, their position on the screen, their entry and departure and their relation one to another. You can see it at work with the fugitives and the pursuers in the Monument Valley of *Stagecoach*; in the stillness of the watchers and the turmoil of the fighters in *Kagemusha*; in the concentration within the frame of Buster Keaton's *The General*; in the isolation within the vast baronial hall of the bored wife in *Citizen Kane*. You may not think of it as you watch; but it holds you, manoeuvres you. For a moment or two it obliterates everything except the scene, the figures, the gestures in your line of vision.

And it is magic.

Quentin Blake

Here Comes,
There Goes,
You Know Who!
Alan Coren

"You're nobody till somebody cares"—*F. A. Sinatra*

A Gala Film Premiere, as anyone over the age of Baby LeRoy knows, is always put on in aid of charity. The charity it's always put on in aid of is the company that made the movie. The Illegitimate Offspring Of Distressed Starlets' Fund, or whichever other deserving cause happens to be specified in the advance publicity, does, of course, pick up a few bob along the way; but the whole object of the exercise is that, under the snug cover of philanthropy, Big Names get drawn to the film's first showing, big newspapers get drawn to the Big Names, and big newspapers make for big box-offices. If it all works smoothly.

There's not much in the way of spontaneous pocket-dipping. As soon as the film is in the can, if not sooner, the producer goes off to find a Royal; having found one, he invites it to grace his premiere and give it that without which no public relations stunt

would be complete, in return for which his company will fork out a large bale of negotiable hay to any charity nominated by the Royal. With the Royal in the bag, the premiere is under way, and Stage II of the operation is launched: this is to fill the two thousand unRoyal seats with luminaries of as bright a corona as can be drawn to Leicester Square for a free film and the chance of being photo-graphed in the neighbourhood of a tiara. So the big stars come, and the little stars come to be near the big stars, and in the comet-trail of the little stars follows a Milky, or perhaps Ginny, Way composed of ever-weenier asteroids, them-selves bombarded by those brief meteorites categorised under the general heading of The London Scene.

Occasionally, you also get nonentities.

"Who are you, then?" said the cab driver, nudging his mud-guards into the motorcade waiting

to discharge its glittering contents into the foyer of the Leicester Square Odeon.

I ignored this. It's a hard enough question to answer at the best of times, let alone at a moment when the car in front is visibly packed with Big Names all aligning their toupees prior to launching themselves on their slavering fans. The cab driver insisted.

"He's Freddie Bartholomew," said my wife.

"Where's his hair?" said the cabdriver. "It was all over his face in *Little Lord Fauntleroy*."

"That was thirty years ago," said my wife. She can be very loyal at times. Not that this was one of them. "You can't be a child star all your life."

I watched the cab driver's eyes focus on me in his driving mirror.

"What is he now, then?" he said. That's one of the things about being a Big Name: bystanders talk about you in the third person, or rather third object, since that's what you are.

"He's going to make a comeback," she said, "aren't you, darling? He's going to be in *Big Lord Fauntleroy*."

A commissionaire sprang to the door, and the night rushed in. Mobs strained against the crash-barriers as the arc-lights hit my shirtfront, and looked away again, disgusted; autograph-books snapped shut, and more than one raspberry echoed across the drizzled Square. The appearance of my wife, who is value for money in any stargazer's lens, went some way towards making up for the apparent loathliness of her escort, so I tried to look like the sort of money that could afford to buy her, and we went inside, unpelted.

The foyer was packed with people straining to recognise one another while at the same time trying to appear nonchalant about not being recognised themselves. The trick, I observed, is to rise on tip-toe above the heads of the crowd, pivot gently through 360° wearing a fixed smile, and gradually sink back again into the throng. With upwards of five hundred well-oiled skulls engaged in this activity, the effect is

10

reminiscent of all those movies about the *Titanic*: a seaful of brave, dinner-jacketed smiles bobbing evenly on the regular swell, before going down without trace.

All around us, people were murmuring "Isn't that whatsisname?" and being told it wasn't, and there was a considerable amount of high shrill laughter for no observable cause. At one moment, not yet having recognised anyone at all, I had the terrible feeling that by some awful error of the two-tier post, or perhaps some nauseous practical joke, everybody here was Nobody, people belonging to a different do; these were all members of the Worshipful Company of Something, gathered together for their annual beanfeast and prizegiving, and down in the City, at some Monger's Hall, a thousand film stars were currently shaking the Lord Mayor's hand and wondering why he wasn't being played by Robert Morley. It was only the arrival of the Royals which scotched this fear in the nick of time; there was much relieved sighing of the kind you won't hear in a republic—*They* were here, and it was all going to be all right, like King George going down to Bethnal Green to examine the bomb-damage. Sadly, the Royals involved were a short (though much-loved) couple, and we didn't actually *see* them; though she had her hair up, which helped, and I caught sight of a few stately strands, passing by, several heads away. Brunette, in case you're interested.

We all pressed into the auditorium after that, but it took a hell of a time for the crowd to sit down, since the whole foyer bit was repeated, i.e. everybody wanted to remain standing because of the vantage point it gave them to see who was sitting down, and those already sitting down kept getting up in order to see who was standing around. Even when the film came on, the odd half-recognised silhouette was still pottering about the aisle, hoping to engrave his image on the attendant retinas. Nothing much happened during the first half of the film itself, except that a disc-jockey on my wife's right kept

engaging her in witty banter, which kept one of them highly amused; no one, of course, leaned over and said Shut up, some people have come here to see the film, because none of them had.

What they'd come for was the intermission. I didn't realise this, and was coolly strolling up the aisle in search of air when the Welsh pack caught me full between the shoulder-blades. They were all wearing busts and giggling, but they couldn't fool me; I saw them seconds later in a scrum round Michael Caine, and if you want my opinion, their trainer ought to take them aside for a quiet word. I passed the interval pleasantly enough, pressed against a radiator with Stirling Moss who'd been planning to buy an ice-cream but hadn't had room to get at his change. We didn't talk, just stared at one another, breathing alternately.

The second half of the film went by without incident; as the critics have since pointed out. And in no time, the heaving mob had us both back in the dread foyer again;

outside the cinema, the white faces of the fans were bobbing once more between the linked police elbows, while the rain belted down and a uniformed character with a loud-hailer walked about on the pavement shouting "LAST BUS FOR CLARIDGES." Which, no doubt, was where the post-premiere party was being held; either that, or he was announcing a forthcoming attraction: you have to admit, it's a great title. It was at this point that I felt an iron grip on my left forearm, and found myself staring into the open mouth of an unknown face. The arc-lights winked briefly off his fillings.

"I say!" he cried, in a voice which had the heads swivelling. "Are you by any chance Alan Coren?"

I dropped my eyes with the sort of humility I am rarely called upon to show, and nodded tolerantly. The crowd paused, watching what was clearly a devoted fan for further exposition. He shook my hand.

"I used to know your father," he said.

"Your acting's fine, but you failed the medical."

MY DOCUMENTARY FILM
Anthony Carson

Quite a long time ago I worked for a film company. Cosmos Pictures Ltd. I was in the scenario department, lodged in a fake Elizabethan manor house, examining scripts written by hysterical housewives. They had titles like "Hold Back To-morrow" or "But For December?" The department was full of baronets, and there was even a duchess in a bogus keep. After a time I came to the conclusion that my work was unneccessary.

A man who was supposed to be descended from Shakespeare was the head of the department, and all he did was to file my work. Sir Hector Engelbrecht, the owner of Cosmos never came near the scenario department at all, and hired his real staff in enormous hotels crammed with flowers. *Peter Pan* directed by Eisenstein with music by Schönberg starring Rita Hayworth and Sir Laurence Olivier.

So I spent most of my time reclining under a tree near an ornamental pond containing three contract swans. Time went by, and one day I was joined by an introspective, bald-headed man. We sat together for weeks watching the swans. His name was Albertini. "I am under contract to Engelbrecht," he said moodily. "I am supposed to be directing a film about the Theory of Relativity starring Margaret Lockwood. I know nothing about the Theory of Relativity." "But why make it?" "Engelbrecht is turning intellectual," said Albertini. "I am documentary director, and he feels we are getting fashionable." He sighed. More months went by, and one day he arrived at the pond to say good-bye to me and the swans. "Engelbrecht has forgotten about me," he said, "I can't see him. I can't get past the duchess. It has been nice to meet somebody like you who appreciates the meaning of Film. Come and see me?" He handed me his card.

One day I called in at the department to get some bread for the swans, when I was met by my chief. He was in tears. "I have bad news," he said. "The scenario department has ceased to exist." It took some time for me to absorb this information. The world outside was a cruel place. "Engelbrecht has thanked us for all we have done. It appears there is a crisis. Even the duchess has been liquidated." Shakespeare's descendant looked at me miserably. He had six children. We shook hands and dispersed.

It was a bad winter. My wife left me, and fog chloroformed the last asters in the front garden. I moved to lodgings near the hooting vault of Paddington Station and locked up old happy summers in my heart. Then I remembered Albertini and called at his office. "Delighted to see you," he said, rising from his desk. "I knew this would happen. That is the way they treat you and me in the commercial film world. You want a job?" "Yes," I said. "I will get you one. The pay is not very high in the Documentary field, I am afraid. Only four pounds a week. And you will start on rather routine stuff, of course. But a man of your intelligence will rise high." I began work the next week.

It was the time when Documentary makers were employed by the GPO. All their films had to be about postmen, telephones, directories and telegraph wire. But privately they were interested in Reality, which had just been discovered. This meant showing to the public how ordinary life was, and how dull conversation could be. It was a revelation. You saw postmen getting up in the morning, coughing, getting on their bicycles, sorting letters and knocking at doors. You heard them talking to each other. Naturally. "Hullo, Bill, how's the chilblains?" "Something shocking. Will you do the 4.30 collection?" You saw them going home, taking off their boots, and talking to their wives. "I delivered two letters wrong this morning. Wasn't half a row." "Go on Bert, you're a caution. Ready for your cocoa?" But there were variations on the theme. Postmen were also used symbolically with poetic commentary snapping at their heels and their heads in a cloud of atonal. It was a far cry from the days when people thought of them as automatons in peaked caps who got bitten by dogs. In fact they began to give themselves airs.

The studio was at Blackheath. Albertini found me a chair stuck between a moviola and a pile of cans. The room was bombarded with noise from sound tracks. There was morse, atonal music, trains, and TIM. Postman stars marched through to the stage. "Hold the letter so that we can see it, Mr. Todman." Albertini found me some work connected with titling. "For films shown at Rest Homes for Aged Postmen," said Albertini. "You've just got to make the words simple." I went on with this job for six months until one day I cornered Albertini and told him I wanted to get my teeth into something bigger. "All I've got is an old film which the GPO want to scrap," he said. "You can have a shot at reconstituting it, if you like." He ran it through for me in the projection room. It was about a village with a postman, but no other means of communication. So the villagers decided to have telephones installed, and there is a frenzy of building, telegraph poles, and Post Office technicians measuring everything. Then it is spring, and with a flourish of daffodils a telephone exchange is born, and hundreds of people are coiling in smiles, lifting their receivers, and gabbling. "A bit pedestrian, possibly dull," said Albertini, "but efficient. See what you can do with it."

This was my chance. From now on I was a film director. I wrote a poetic commentary and drove out into the country in a van and shot millions of leaves and insects, and then hired guitarists, drummers and extras. Then I got hold of old library film stock, containing shots of telegraph wire, telegraph poles, washing, and postmen. I strung all this together with my sound track (Elizabethan madrigals) and hired an out-of-work actor to speak my commentary. By now the film ran for an hour and a half. The original went twenty minutes. My version had poetry, rhythm, supermontage, chiaroscuro and sex. I got hold of Albertini and invited him into the projection theatre.

As the film unwound itself I felt a terrible hollow in the pit of my stomach. It was quite clear that the commentator had adenoids and you could hear his false teeth click above the madrigals. The journey out into the country became so prolonged I kept on lighting cigarettes and throwing them away. There seemed an infinity of telegraph poles and washing, and all my extras loomed forward with ghastly grins like holiday snaps at Shoreham-on-Sea. After an hour of it Albertini suddenly got up and burst into tears. I stopped the projection, and looked at him in the empty theatre. In the distance we could hear someone running TIM backwards on the moviola. "My God," cried Albertini, putting his hand on my shoulder, "what has Engelbrecht done to you, my boy?" He waved his hand towards the screen and tottered out of the room. I was put back to titling. But I threw up films and became an actor.

I am still ready to have another go.

The Home Office plans to develop prison industries
and make an international bid to sell the stuff
they make. It is bound to affect the life
in gaol that every film-goer knows . . .

After tense negotiations lasting twelve years with remission, the Dartmoor (Holdings) salesmen team assembles for a briefing on the latest market trends. In this gripping sequence from Polanski's *Life on the Run*, an affinity-group charter flight is laid on to the Dusseldorf Inmates Fair and against some fierce competition with a team from the Isle of Wight, they struggle to sell their merchandise on behalf of Pentonville. The gaily-striped uniforms and the ball-and-chain motif is a triumph for the wardrobe men and there's a highly-comical scene in which they each try to pick up their samples bag.

Edward G. Robinson as the hard-bitten governor, "Productivity" Hopkinson, in a dramatic episode from *Nobody Leaves* in which he finds that his prison-tailored overcoat does not fit him in the sleeve. Against an atmosphere of industrial unrest, he works on the hunch that a mob from over the wall has somehow tampered with the sewing shop but, before he can reach a settlement, a gang of frenzied luddites peppers the prison pottery (right) with a Wormwood bazooka as part of a promotion stunt. After a long and meaningful interlude, as the governor reflects that rising crime will double his wages bill, the dispute is resolved by a merger with "J" block fancy-goods.

A poignant sequence from *Doing Time-and-a-half* as Number 49566 shows the management over his hand-crafted closet and matching walnut clock, shortly before he learns that he is condemned to a stretch in the after-sales service wing. This moving film is a warm and sensitive study of one man's struggle against restrictive practices and to rid himself of the stigma of a record of assembly faults and consequent losses to the export drive. In a sudden and tense down-tools towards the end, he unmasks the crooked shop-steward, Pee-Wee Weatherby (left), and has him hived off into solitary docket work.

On Her Majesty's Quality Merchandise tells the touching story of what happens when a rep. on parole meets with Holloway's "Twister" Olive and they talk about the old days sewing mailbags in their cells. This romantic clip shows them sharing a workshop spiritual as he comes to mend her mixer which he made the week before. Together, they go to business school and then a life of crime sends them apart to the world they know. Mimi dies after an accident on the polishing lathe and her lover leads the tool-room in a bid for better conditions and pay. There's a spectacular finale when they storm the varnishing shed.

TORCH SONG
Jo Packer

Some of the Truth about the Cinema

Contact with the public is the usherette's curse, but it has its compensations. "Which seats, please?" you ask each arrival. One person will push past without a word, stamp down the gangway, and slump into his seat with a crash of springs. It is then you remember that a torch can give more than a light. It can give a splitting headache. You turn to the next patron, and find you are being offered a chocolate from a newly-opened box. Life tastes of Parma violets once more.

In between these extremes flow the tractable thousands who blink as they enter and disrobe, asking "Is it warmer inside?" or "How long has it been on?" or "Is is good?" in addition to telling you whether they are one-and-sixes or two shillings.

When I carried a torch for J. Arthur Rank the one-and-sixes were at the front, near the screen. Our manager, fond of the alliterative sound of "Watch your one-and-sixes, girls," would constantly repeat it. So a conscientious usherette felt duty bound to accompany all one-and-sixes as far as the white line, to make sure they didn't slide into the two shilling section. I did that at first, but soon discovered that the denizens of the front stalls were a regular bunch who knew their job. Or rather, knew their white line. A flash of the torch down the gangway met the need, and for an experienced one-and-sixer even this was unnecessary.

Now and then one of them would creep into a two shilling seat, but I always left him there. I admire the cold self-possession it takes to do it, and besides, I used to do it myself when I was very much younger. But the other girls always weeded these opportunists out, admonished them, and generally tried to keep them cinema-trained.

Upstairs it was just the opposite. The two-and-sixpenny seats were at the back, and the three shillings at the front of the circle. Many folk paid three shillings and went into the two-and-sixes. They preferred the back seats and imagined them to be the most expensive. On busy nights this led to congestion as the two-and-sixpennies would fill rapidly with people, of whom about half had paid three shillings. Then I wouldn't know where to put the genuine two-and-sixers.

Being "on seating" is a frustrating duty. Most people have their favourite seat in a cinema—dead centre, next to the gangway, over at the side, or up in the corner—and they'll go there whether you show them to another place or not. Nothing is so amusing to an usherette as to see one of her colleagues marching the length of the gangway with what she thinks is a whole string of people following her, when all the time they are busy camping down on the back row. This proves that usherettes are not really essential; the cinema industry could save money by reducing their numbers.

"On tickets" is far more satisfying. No one is allowed through the inner doors without a ticket, and the usherette in charge feels of some consequence. Tear-ing tickets in two is a pleasing occupation at which one gets more nimble as the evening progresses. The patron who spoils everything is the one who sweeps through and does not wait for his torn half. You find you are handing it to the empty air. Feelings can be relieved by throwing it after him in pellet form, but the damage has been done, the rhythm upset.

The candy kiosk by the pay-box in the foyer complicates matters for the girl on tickets. People stream out of the cinema to get supplies of dental decay some three or four times per evening. Those that don't bother to tell you they are kiosk-bound cause panic on their return for they fail to hand you a ticket. I often chase some-one half-way down the aisle crying "Can I have your ticket please?" only to find that the answer is a tube of clear gums.

More helpful are those who tell you where they are going. The very nicest almost put their hands up to ask for permission, and state what they are hoping to buy. When they show you, on their return, the purchase as a proof of legitimacy, a ticket-collector's life becomes really worth living.

Another useful clan is composed of signallers. They are usually young men aspiring to slickness, and they jerk their thumbs in the direction of the kiosk as they stride zestfully through the swing doors. They help to give the cinema that smooth and efficient look beloved of managers, except when they collide on the far side of the door with incoming patrons.

Two of my regular re-entrants were old men who cared not for the smooth look. One of them used to make an ear-whispered arrangement for me to re-admit him in fifteen minutes' time, so his destination was farther than the kiosk. He would return half-drunk, all the better in his opinion to enjoy "the big fillum". The other man mumbled "Argus" in my ear. The first time I thought it was a new brand of sweet, but I learnt better when he returned with a gleamy look and a pink sports paper. After the performance I found it with the racing results marked off, so he had made good use of the interval.

These were the only two

examples I knew of riotous living on the old age pension. All the other pensioners lashed out in frugal fashion at the matinées. During the afternoon they were admitted for sevenpence. Consequently between one-thirty and five we had a quiet and dependable audience. Also a familiar one since many of them came two, three or even four times a week. ''For a warm,'' they would explain on the fourth visit, or ''For a sleep''. Ice-cream sales slumped during these matinées, the best customers being the usherettes.

If the cinema became packed during the Last Complete Performance (or Last Round-up as the staff called it) a couple of usherettes were taken off gangways and put on sales. When the lights went up small fighting boys appeared underneath my tray and around my milkmaid skirts, followed by larger boys who were terribly rich and paid for everything with half-crowns. As soon as the tray was empty I ran to the refrigerator for fresh supplies, one word beating in my brain like stereophonic sound: Commission, Commission.

The final showing of the big film was always the most chafing part of the evening. If you felt courageous you could quell a few Teddy Boys, or fetch the manager and set him loose to prowl the aisles, or watch the film for the tenth time. Then the peculiarities of the audience would reveal themselves. There could be deafening gunfire on the screen, a stampede, an avalanche, a noisy comedy sequence and no one would move. But let there be a quiet scene, with the camera in close-up, every word counting, and the actors playing for an Oscar, and you could bet your life a dozen seats would go bash and four exit doors crash. Desecration, I told myself, and the cinema trying so hard to become an art, too.

But all is forgotten when at last you are tipping up the seats, wondering who brought in three bottles of pop. Your wonder increases when you find this month's *Film Review* on one seat, an unopened box of liquorice allsorts on another, and nothing on another, not even a seat.

Alfred Hitchcock
talks to David Taylor

I had my doubts, if not the shivers, from the minute we stepped in. Less than five minutes' walk away, across the carpeted field of a Claridge's high-class suite, sat Hitchcock, motionless, a perfectly studied profile, like a sphere going runny at the edge, with the light flooding in from behind. His agent, in a pretty shirt and with a warm and friendly grin, led us across the furnished gap to where the master sat, mysterious, a familiar grotesque, with his pyjamas on. It is mid-morning. There are no papers, no correspondence, no drinks, no smoke. Only a basket of grapes sits on the side, with a cellophane top. ''Good morning,'' Alfred Hitchcock said, and I shook him with a clammy hand.

If you happen to want to know about the scripting of a horror film of how it's shot and how it's edited, about the crop-sprayer, say, which he used in *North By North-West* or the shower scene in *Psycho*, Hitchcock is a non-stop source. I asked him what else he did. ''Well, I suppose reading mostly.'' Like? ''Not fiction. Biography.'' Then he coughed for a very long time. I asked him what, apart from reading, he might do on an idle afternoon. ''Er, very little else. Travel, maybe, but not much else.'' Was he interested in other people? ''No.'' Sport? ''No.'' Did he get easily bored? ''No. I've a very placid temperament.'' Would he say, perhaps, that his waking life was totally absorbed by films? ''Yes.'' Ah! So we talked about films.

Hitchcock, 73, has been making his films for over fifty years now. He never looks through the camera, "What's the point?" People think that he's an ogre, he says, "but everything that I film doesn't relate to me personally whatsoever. I get no pleasure from putting a rape scene on the screen; it's a sort of job of work." And in talking about that job of work, Hitchcock is blessed with an absorbing total recall. *Psycho*, shot in black-and-white, to avoid the tasteless rivers of red blood, he described in perfect detail, how the knife never touched the girl's body at any stage, how it was partially shot in slow motion so that movements were controlled and the nipples didn't show. He remembers how he was thwarted, during the shooting of *North By North-West*, because the Department of the Interior wouldn't let cinema chases be filmed across the hallowed surfaces of the Mount Rushmore presidential monuments. Hitchcock still believes he should *use* the available locations. "I wanted Cary Grant to slide down Lincoln's nose and then hide in the nostril. Then he gets the sneezes. Cary Grant does, not Lincoln."

Of other people's films, we didn't talk too much, because "there's very little genuine cinematic work done these days. Most of the films I see are what I call photographs of people talking". In sharp contrast, "I believe in using the visual as much as possible, I am more or less a puritan. The avoidance of the cliché is the main preoccupation". And we covered some more examples in order to stress this point. I asked him if he ever got tired of talking about his films and he said, No, he rather enjoyed it in fact.

His latest film, called *Frenzy*, is the reason he's in town. The film is set in London and it opens with a body that is floating down the Thames, face-down, strangled by a neck-tie. "Then I cut to a picture of a man putting his neck-tie on." Hitchcock likes the Thames. Once he found a little place called All Hallows on Sea and he liked the name. Another time, he sailed down the Thames, almost alone on a giant steamer, in November, in the drizzle, in the dark. "I found that very interesting."

Everything he sees, he does, in terms of the visually dramatic. Near to his home in northern California, there's a wood that he frequents that is wooded with enormous trees. Trees that are so big, he says, "that the base of one of them is almost as big as this room," which is far from poky. "If you go and stand in a clump of these trees, it's very gothic, like being in a black cathedral." He finds that interesting, too.

Hitchcock is a gadget man. His kitchen at home, "in birch-wood and stainless steel, has any number in. It has everything. Of course, it doesn't go as far as having drapes and a piano in". Favourite of his push-button toys is a digital clock he's brought with him on this London trip. Now he wants one which, when you press it, there's a voice that tells the time. "I think that's very amusing," he said.

But films are Alfred Hitchcock and, with infinite patience, he can discuss them by the hour. Everything else soon bores him. "Where do you most like working?" he says people ask him and he answers that "When the studio doors close, it's like asking which coal-mine does a miner like working in. They're all the same. You don't even know what the weather's like outside".

Hitchcock doesn't want to know. Filming totally absorbs him. "I'll be what Churchill said of Hitler," he said, "an enigma within an enigma."

"I'm sort of Woody Allen without the humour."

STORM OF PROTEST OVER "RELIGIOUS LIFE OF CHRIST" PLAN: STOP THIS FILM NOW! PLEA

Miles Kington reports

THIS IS A MATTER FOR RECONSIDERATION

says The Times

In a message to the nation today, reprinted in full exclusively in *The Times,* Fr. William Rees Mogg condemns the project of the Danish film maker Thor Amundsen to make a full-length feature on the life of Christ from the religious angle.

"We gather," says Fr. Rees Mogg, presumably by "we" meaning himself and Bernard Levin, "that Mr. Amundsen intends to concentrate entirely on the moral message given by Christ. If by this he meant only that he intended to promote a general feeling of co-operation and good will on the part of all sections of the community, thus leading to a renewed programme of investment by industry and trade union moderation, well and good. But we gather that Mr. Amundsen has every intention of concentrating on such controversial statements as 'sell all thou hast and give unto the poor' and 'blessed are the meek, for they shall inherit the earth'.

"In a state of full employment and growing production there would be room for such wild slogans, perhaps, though even that is doubtful. In our present state of recession and painful under-investment, such pre-Keynesian naïvety is little short of disastrous. Can one imagine the effect of the average man in middle management, earning perhaps £7,000 a year and doing his best to revive British industry, suddenly selling his house and car, giving the proceeds to Oxfam and going on Social Security? Is there any other role at the moment for the meek than to be outsold and outmanoeuvred by the Japanese and Germans?

"No, Mr. Amundsen. A religious life of Christ may be filmed one day, but not yet. The last qualities we want in Britain today are meekness and asceticism. Love thy neighbour by all means, but sell him a British car first. Then we can love him. If you really want to make a film about Christ, Mr. Amundsen, for heaven's sake confine yourself to some uncontroversial and harmless aspect, such as his sex life."

THIS IS TOTALLY WRONG-HEADED

declares the Bishop of Peckham

Methvin Lambert, Bishop of Peckham, explained last night why he disapproves of Thor Amundsen's plans to film Christ's life. Methvin Lambert, who was just about to appear on the Parkinson Show to talk about famous stars he has known, is most familiar, perhaps, as one of the most progressive talkers and sometimes thinkers in the Church today.

"By all means let Mr. Amundsen come here and make his film. The less restrictions on human thought and behaviour the better. But, you know, I wonder what purpose will be served by a picture of Christ as an old-fashioned speaker and preacher? All those well-turned phrases so familiar to us, familiar to the point of nausea—what good will they do?

"If you get below the surface of the New Testament, you see, you will find that Christ was not a simple bringer of messages. He was much much more than that. He was a drop-out. He was in a single-child situation. He was at one and the same time very humble and conscious of a divine mission. Schizophrenic perhaps? In very real Laingian sense, yes. We must not listen to Christ's words for what he was saying but for what he was trying to say; and underneath all those fine phrases, yes, underneath the Sermon on the Mount, is a loud and very real cry for help. I have come here, Christ is saying, for you to help save *me*!

"So, you see, it is a great mistake to take Christ's words literally.What we must do is to see them as right for *him*! But a great deal has changed since then, and we must now listen to other teachers, other thinkers. Make a film by all means. But I would have thought there were people alive today who would make more provoking subjects for a life story. More I cannot say."

18

THIS IS FANTASTICALLY CONTROVERSIAL

says Thor Amundsen

After the storm of controversy which has burst over his head following announcement of his plans to film a simple, based-on-the-book life of Christ, Mr. Amundsen said today:

"Things are coming along nicely. I had hoped to get a little publicity but nothing like this. You see, I knew that people were uncomfortably aware that their lives did not correspond to Christian standards any more, but I had no idea that they cared about it. Myself, for instance, I do not care about it. Basically I am making this film to try to shock myself into leading a better life. So far, it has not worked as, if anything, I am a worse person now than when I started writing the film, having been tempted by visions of riches far beyond what I have ever owned. However, it may happen that before the film is finished. I might decide to give away all the profits to the poor. I do not think it is likely. I think it is more possible I shall give away all the profits to the British tax people. Will they give it to the poor for me? I do hope so, but I think it is not probable.

"By the way, please make sure to spell my name properly. I am a little vain in these things. Yes, I know what Christ said, but we cannot all be meek."

THIS IS A DIABOLICAL LIBERTY

claims the TUC

The TUC today came out very strongly against the idea of Mr. Amundsen's film of Christ's life and teachings. Pulling no punches and mincing no words, it plainly condemned Christ's thought as "Muddle-headed and playing into the hands of the employers".

"Look, we'll admit that Christ himself was a law-abiding citizen, at least, until his last clash with the law where he was unfairly victimised for leading an ill-fated demo," said TUC spokesman Len Brisket. "But let's face it, Christ was a political naïve, a fly in the ointment, a barrier to free collective bargaining. He was sincere, maybe, but he was politically unaware, and that kind represents the worst threat to the trade union movement.

"I'll tell you who he reminds me of. Solzhenitsyn. Both of them basically decent blokes, coming along from a backward country and shooting their mouth off about what they don't really understand. 'The labourer is worthy of his hire,' says Christ. Fair enough. But what about 'from him that hath not, shall be taken away even what he has'? Even Enoch Powell wouldn't say that! He hadn't thought things out, had he?

"See, Christ is another of these old-fashioned self-employed, go-it-alone, craftsman types who just don't get in with the modern union scene. He was for the underdog, yes, but he had no conception of getting the underdog organised. If we return to the teachings of Christ, that's a hundred years of union progress down the drain. I'm sorry, but I can't see us allowing a life of Christ into this country."

THIS IS OBNOXIOUS

says the Queen

Millions of telegrams have arrived at Buckingham Palace from ordinary people, to protest against the Christ life film plan, pointing out that Christ had on one occasion said, "There is no king but God." This they felt, was an unambiguous insult to all earthly monarchs and especially Her Majesty.

In a standard reply, her Press Secretary has said that the Queen feels that if the New Testament does indeed include an attack on the British monarchy's role in the world today, then it does seem obnoxious.

More comment from around Britain

"My solicitors are looking into any possible disadvantageous implications of the reported script"
—MR. JIMMY GOLDSMITH

"...On the other hand..."   —THE GUARDIAN

"This is going to be a complete travesty, so to speak, of the brave stance of a very aware guy"   —GAY LIBERATION FRONT

"Not having thought of the idea first, I can only condemn it out of hand"   —MR. DAVID FROST

THE HEROES
BY CHARLES KINGSLEY

MANNERS AND MODES
Hero-worship:Distractions of the Film World

The Cricklewood Greats
Alan Coren

Why not build film studios there? After all, to many people, Cricklewood is a vibrant, cosmopolitan, glamorous place.
Evening Standard

I love this crazy town.

I came here a long time ago, the way a lot of people did who had stars in their eyes, and it still has the old magic. That wonderful wacky feeling of waking up in the morning and knowing that anything could happen, and probably will! Maybe there'll be a refuse strike, and we'll have to haul our garbage right over to Dollis Hill, Rovers and Volvos and chirpy little Hondas with their seats piled high with bulging black plastic bags, and behind the wheel famous faces from the shoe industry, from the world of quantity surveying and army surplus, from the tobacconist profession, driving along just like ordinary men and women, pulling their weight for the community. Or maybe the milkman will be out of cherry yoghourt, and you'll hear kids' voices raised above the busy clatter of breaking crockery. It could be that the traffic lights will blow again, the way they do in this anything-goes-town, at the glittering junction of Cricklewood Lane and Hendon Way, and the colourful juggernauts will be backed up as far as Cricklewood Broadway, many of them hooting. Or I might just take an ordinary thing, such as a stroll, down to the famous mailbox in West End Lane and meet one of Cricklewood's real old-timers, like Nat Selby, say, the former blouse factor now sadly retired, who's been here so long he'll walk right past me without saying anything. That's the kind of town Cricklewood is.

I came out here soon after I was married, a green kid from nearly three miles away; that was in the days before there was a flyover at Staples Corner bringing, as it inevitably did, the Edgware Road into the raucous, sizzling, tinsel world of the Twentieth Century. In the old days of which I speak, you could actually drive right past the Staples Mattress Factory itself, look up at the windows, and almost see the people making the interior springing destined to travel from there to countless parts of the Home Counties. Now there is only the flyover: tourists can roar in from Colindale and Burnt Oak right to the very heart of Cricklewood itself, even missing the bus garage at Gladstone Park where the big Number Sixteens turn round in their dozens, under the ever-watchful eyes of top-name Inspectors.

They had the studio system, then. It was run by a handful of moguls who had become legends in their own lifetime. They hadn't always been moguls, most of them had come over here as ragged kids from Poland and Russia and Latvia; they came to this wide open town, and even if they couldn't speak English too well, they knew the studio business. The way it worked was, you would go into one of their famous estate offices, and you would ask if they had any flats at around eight pounds a week, and they would look at you and come out with one of their now-legendary wisecracks, such as

"Flats at around *eight pounds a week*? You're asking me if we've got any *flats* at around eight pounds a week? At eight pounds a week, you're asking *me* if we've got any flats?"

And then, just as you were about to apologise and leave, the mogul would riffle through his papers and say: "How about a studio?"

And you, because you were young and romantic and naive and remembered Cornel Wilde composing his Unfinished Symphony in a sun-filled atelier, you would turn and cry: "A studio?"

And the mogul would quip, "Have *I* got a studio for you!"

And within an hour you would be sitting in your own basement bedsitter in Definitely Not Kilburn, hoping someone would come and drive the removal van away from your air-vent and let enough light in for you to swat the rats. It was a large area, Definitely Not Kilburn, a mile or so from downtown Cricklewood; it received its name from estate agents' handouts, and a lot of us lived there, underneath Kilburn High Road. But by the time you realised, it was too late: you had signed the contract; you were bound to the studio for years.

But you made good, in time, because a lot of people did, and if they didn't, you didn't get to hear about it, because Cricklewood wasn't about failure. The ones who didn't make it just quietly packed up and went back to Limerick and Hyderabad and Lower Volta.

And yet, for those who did make it, success often came at incalculable personal cost. I talked, just a day or so ago, to Bernie Schwartz, a man who has been a star for as long as anybody can remember and whose name is a household word wherever pickle-jars are opened; not, of course, that the name was always Bernie Schwartz; he was born humble Tony Curtis, but there was a lot of prejudice in Cricklewood in the early days, and as he so frankly puts it, "Who'd buy delicatessen from someone called Curtis?"

We were sitting in the manicured grounds of his elegant nearly-detached Brondesbury Hills mansion, beside his pool, and watching his children inflate it from an expensive-looking foot-pump, when I said to him: "You've come a long way, Bernie, from that one little shop in Fortune Green Road. You now have two little shops in Fortune Green Road. You must be a happy man."

"*Nihil est ab omni parte beatum*," he murmured, in the rich Middle Etonian accent of his people, which he has never quite lost. "Nothing ·is all good, old sport. It cost me my wife, remember. Ambition is a cruel taskmaster. Putting her in charge of the second shop was a terrible mistake."

I looked away. I had, of course, heard rumours. In a town like Cricklewood, gossip runs rife; and stars have many enemies.

"I understand," I said, quietly, "that she couldn't keep her hands off the stock?"

"It was the pumpernickel that finally got her," he said, nodding. "She weighs twenty-eight stone now, you know. She may have to spend the rest of her life at a health farm."

There are many personal tragedies like that in Cricklewood. As the song says, a million hearts beat quicker there,* and it is a pace to which many of those bright hearts fall victim. Marriages and a Cricklewood career rarely mix: take, for example, the star-cros't, ill-matched Sidney and Doreen Brill, whose tempestuous relationship came to its dreadful but inevitable end in that summer of 1971 that none of us will ever forget.

Sidney, at 44, was at the height of his career as a traveller in bathroom sundries. His work naturally took him away from home much of the time, driven on as he was by the dream not only of becoming Area Sales Manager (NW London), but also of earning enough to convert his toolshed into a sauna. Doreen was left alone, drinking advocaat and wondering when he was going to put the shelf up in the kitchen. One evening in late July, after he had returned worn out in his sleek Mini Clubman, she put that question to him, for the twentieth time. "I don't bloody know," he replied; and she hit him with the bottle. It was the end of his career; after the blow, he could never remember how to get out onto the North Circular from Willesden Lane. They were forced to sell Dunscreamin, and moved away. We never heard of them again. Just two more casualties of the battle for wealth and stardom.

But there were heroes, too; and none more worthy of the name than that tiny, courageous, persecuted group who became known as The Cricklewood Ten. Now, two decades on, it is almost impossible to convey the terror that the name of McCarthy could evoke in all but the stoutest breasts. He was nothing much to look at, short, balding, only the tiny paranoid eyes betraying what lay in the addled brain behind, but when his council truck rumbled down the opulent Cricklewood streets every November, and McCarthy would hammer at each pastel door and cry his fearful cry of "Happy Christmas from the dustmen!", people coughed up. It was more than your life was worth to ignore him; but ten householders did, and paid the dreadful penalty. Pleading the Fifth Amendment, which states that all council dustvans must bear clearly on their doors the legend *No gratuities,* they turned him from their teakette porch extensions, and faced a year not only of boot-crunched geraniums, fishheads in the hedge, and a tin-filled front lawn, but also of the opprobrium and ostracism of their colleagues and neighbours who stared bitterly out from their trim John Lewis curtains at the litter-

strewn streets and asked one another what the neighbourhood was coming to. Even now, long years afterwards with the old battles fought and won, some simmering rancour remains; only the other day, veteran member of the Ten, Dennis Bagley, told me: "Hardly a night goes past without old Mrs Simmonds letting her collie widdle on my bumper."

But if many of the old attitudes haven't changed, Cricklewood itself has. Time and economics have caught it up; the wildness, and the crazy hopes, and the crazier buccaneering are long gone. The days when a raw good-looking kid could blow in from Tipperary and begin digging holes in the hope of making a fortune are past. Big international agglomerates do the roadworks, now. The little unostentatious seeming-tatty garment shops where men became legends in their own lifetimes, if only with their tax inspectors, have made way for rank upon rank of anonymous chain-stores. And television, of course, has taken its drear toll of Cricklewood: stroll down the Broadway now, and every third window belongs to a TV-rental company, its glimmering sets stared at by groups of expatriate Provisionals trying to follow the test card.

True, there are still parties where you can get cheddar and pineapple on the same stick, but they don't go on beyond ten pm any more; there are still wacky people doing wacky stunts, but they're not in the same league as the time old Big Bill Hooper came to a Guy Fawkes celebration in his wife's raincoat; there is still a strange smell at the corner of Frodwych Road, but it doesn't make the head-lines any more.

Yet to many of us who remember the great days, Crickle-wood remains a very special place, even if, perhaps, the glamour is today compounded largely of nostalgia. There is still that special something in the air, even if we've all come a long and not always happy way from that bright morning long ago when I put my hand-print in the fresh cement outside the Ding Dong Chinese Takeaway, and was chased almost to Swiss Cottage by a screaming Mr Ding and a cleaver-waving Mrs Dong.

But what that special something is, who can say? When you begin to analyse it, it just, well, sort of comes apart in your hands, leaving nothing behind.

*©Cricklewood Broadway Melody of 1933.

"I think they've spotted the hide, Neville."

SILENCE
WAS GOLDEN
Benny Green

When I arrived outside the residence of Pandro S. Berman, it was still early morning, the mercury was up in the mid-eighties and the water sprinklers were describing drought-defying parabolas down every avenue in Beverly Hills. Apparently there is a city ordinance making garden maintenance compulsory, and I was glad to see that a citizen as eminent as Mr Berman was abiding by it so conscientiously. One of his menials, a wizened little fellow in a denim suit, was standing on the sidewalk outside the house, jingling the small change in his pocket and gazing down at the grass with that expression of baleful disenchantment you will sometimes find in those who tend the earth all their lives without expecting much back in return.

It was a good start; such signs of control and organisation are only fitting in a mogul whose track record conjures visions of cirrus clouds of Havana cigar smoke, and whose ambiance was nailed once and for all many moons ago by Wodehouse when he created a studio called Perfecto-Fishbein.

While these romantic thoughts were running through my mind, the gardener spotted me and, evidently unmindful of his resemblance to Edward G. Robinson and mine to Goofy, led me down a side alley and into the house, sat me down on a sofa and asked me what questions I wished to ask him. This was very forward behaviour in an agricultural labourer, even for California, so there was nothing for it but to assume that this was neither the gardener nor Mr Robinson's kid brother, but Pandro S. Berman himself, the man who all my life I had bracketed with Nosmo King and Cosmo Topper as the pos-

sessor of one of the three most dapper Christian names in the book, but who now loomed before me as the mastermind who produced all eight of the classic Astaire-Rogers musicals.

We hear a great deal about characters like John Gilbert whose burgeoning virility was snatched away when the Talkies arrived. The Great Heart-throb opened his beautiful mouth to speak, out came a noise like the squeak of a church mouse, and in no time at all a great career was in ruins. But some of the traffic was moving the other way. Had not the invention of sound led inevitably to the movie musical, Berman might never have imposed that exotic Christian name on the annals of the industry at all. In silent days he had been an underling, working for the studio he was destined to rescue. "When we started making the Astaire-Rogers pictures, the receivers were in. *Top Hat* cost under six hundred thousand and grossed over three million. I got ten per cent of the profits. So did Irving Berlin. Berlin only thought of himself. A real egocentric. One time I lent him a brand new overcoat. When I asked for it back he said he lost it. That guy was only thinking of himself all the time."

Later that day, out at Malibu, where the Pacific breakers look like the back-drop to *From Here to Eternity* where Deborah Kerr wrestles with Burt Lancaster, and the dusk comes and goes in about five minutes, I listened to Joan Blondell, who had once marched to the orders of Busby Berkeley. "Jimmy Cagney and I had been playing opposite each other in a play, so they brought us out here together. First day on the lot, Cagney and me did a dialogue scene, and when the rushes came in and they saw how fast we were

throwing the lines to each other, they signed us there and then for five years. You see, the silent players couldn't do that sort of thing. It was the Depression, and it was great to be working." Blondell made over a hundred movies, taking whatever the studio threw at her. "Cagney was more selective. One day he came to me and he said, 'Joanie, it's time for you to walk,' but I never did. I did whatever parts they asked me to."

As you listened to her chatting, it was not hard to imagine how impressed by her incisive delivery Warners must have been. Such a style must have been a revelation to casting directors driven to distraction by dumb broads who sounded like Jean Hagen in *Singing in the Rain*, able

"I shall not return."

25

to make a simple statement like "I can't stand him," sound like the squeaking of a rusty hinge. Gene Kelly had told me a day or two before that most of what happens in *Singing in the Rain* had already happened for real in Hollywood with the coming of sound. Overnight, diction and dialogue had become vital factors in an industry which until now had been content to trade in thyroid stares and feebly gesticulating limbs. So perhaps there is poetic justice in the fact that most of the songwriters from the good old days appear to be living out their lives like Renaissance princes.

Some impecunious wag had suggested they might hold the Olympic swimming trials in Sammy Cahn's pool, and when I told Berman that one or two of the older composers like Harry Warren did not take kindly to being retired by the industry at the premature age of 83, he replied, "I'm not sorry for those guys; they're all mull-tye millionaires." Later on I reported this to Ira Gershwin, who observed, with a twinkle in his eye, "That's before taxes."

The old silent days are buried deep in a mercifully irrecoverable past, but by the very richest of ironies, it is still possible to savour their bouquet, thanks to the most advanced technology. On the TWA plane taking me home, they were charging a few dollars to watch Charles Bronson hitting people in a charade about New Orleans in the 1930s. I doubt whether the Wright Brothers had this sort of thing in mind when they diced with death at Kittihawk all those years ago, so in deference to their wishes I declined to buy my ticket, and settled back to read Thoreau instead.

But the screen was too big to ignore, and I ended up following the dumb-play with a morbid fascination. When Bronson had finished his virtuso performance, on came *Jaws*, even though nobody had asked for it and nobody had paid for it. As a silent movie it is pretty tame stuff, and at least the experience of watching it in this castrated form gave me a passable line in smalltalk for the next few days. "Have you seen *Jaws*?" "Yes, but I haven't heard it."

A Good Word For The Films
A. P. Herbert

Thuggery is abroad. Banditry is rife. Brigands are about. Or so I judge from the popular Press. Every evening I read of new smashes-and-grabs, motor-highwaymen and Tooting Turpins (so to speak). And we have now, therefore, a grand opportunity to test a favourite theory about a very popular subject—the influence of the cinema.

It is widely assumed and asserted that much of the above unpleasantness is due to the influence of the moving pictures. When a citizen of London, poor and unemployed, sees a Chicago gunman at work on the screen he instantly (according to the theory mentioned) says, "Ha! That's a good idea!" leaves his comfortable fauteuil, walks out into High Street, Surburbia, and robs a bank-messenger or snatches a handful of diamond-necklaces out of the nearest jeweller's window. (How or where in the world he disposes of diamond-necklaces in these hard times I do not know and cannot guess; but that is by the way. Apparently it is still considered by the experts to be worth while to steal diamonds, so the times cannot be quite so bad as one thought. The real crisis will be at hand when diamonds are left about in open boxes outside the shops, like greengages, and nobody bothers to remove them. But this, as I think I said before, in parenthesis.)

The theory is, you see, that works of art and entertainment have a powerful influence on the conduct of the people. A good deal might be said about that theory; but, for Heaven's sake, reader, let us stick to the point! It might be remarked, for example, that if immoral literature is to be blamed for immoral conduct, moral literature might be more often credited with some at least of the good conduct of the people. It very seldom is. The "modern novelist" is often blamed for the excesses of the naughty "modern girl"; but the Victorian novelist is never praised for producing the virtuous Victorian girl. The Victorian novelist is said to be a faithful mirror of the good times in which he lived; and it might be (but is not) said that the modern novelist is only a faithful mirror of the bad times in which he lives. If that be so, it is obviously as foolish to throw stones at him as it would be to throw stones at our own looking-glasses when our faces ceased to satisfy us. But do *please*, reader, let us keep to the point.

That, however, I now perceive, *is* the point, if any, of these observations. If the evil parts of talking-pictures govern our conduct, we must assume that the good parts govern us too. Well, friends, if we don't assume that, it means that the British mind is only open to pernicious influences. And who is going to say that in public? Nobody. Very well, then...

Where was I? Ah! I know. Gunmen. There is threatened a serious outbreak of gunmannery in our country. If it became really serious our gallant police would probably be unable to cope with it; partly because they are not numerous enough and partly because

TRIALS OF THE GENTLEMAN-RIDER.

Unfeeling Friend (to very sensitive amateur rider, who has been badly unseated more than once). "You'll look A 1 in the Music Hall, old chap! There's a cinematograph man at every fence!"

they are largely engaged upon the enforcing of more important laws—the time of selling butterscotch, the hours of backgammon, eating, drinking, dominoes, etc. So the ordinary citizen will have to play his part.

Well, is the ordinary citizen ready? What, in other words, will the ordinary citizen do when he suddenly perceives a "gun" or "gat" emerging from his carburettor or chest-of-drawers? Will he cower or conquer? For my part I have faced the question squarely. That is to say, whenever I creep into my hall, crawl up the stairs or open the larder-door after dark; whenever (which is much less frequent) I take money to the bank I imagine that some thuggish incident is just about to upset me. I look for gunmen under the gas-oven; I expect "gats" in the grocery-cupboard; the police are two or three boroughs away and I must deal with the bandits, etc., unaided. How do I do it? Do I put my hands up and tamely deliver the dough or do I thwart thuggery and deliver it up to justice?

I must confess (brutal though it sounds) that as a rule, in imagination, I take the latter course. The number of thugs, bandits and brigands I have caught (in imagination) under the grand piano or in that nasty dark corner at the bottom of the kitchen-stairs would populate Pentonville for years to come.

How, I say again, do I bring off these feats? And I must record that my chief source of inspiration and strength is the modern novel and the modern film. It must be remembered that even in the most lurid films and fiction the gunman seldom or never comes off best in the end. Sometimes he is bested by the official forces of law and order, but more often by the ordinary citizen, like you and me. And most of us have seen how easily the stupid and cowardly thug can be made to look foolish. When he puts a pistol to our heads we coolly poke a pipe into his stomach, and in the dusk the fellow takes it for a loaded gun. When he hisses, "Hand over the dough!" we reply disdainfully, "Oh yeah...?" When he informs us that we have only five minutes to live, we answer calmly that we left our name and address with three policemen at the corner and that they will search the house if we do not leave it in four minutes. It is bluff, of course, but it always comes off; and how absurdly simple!

If the films do really "put ideas" into our heads which we afterwards employ in practical life, let us all at once study the methods of Mr. C. CHAPLIN. It is quite impossible to imagine Mr. CHAPLIN being overawed by a thug or bandit. Yet (on the screen) he is only a common little fellow like you and me. And what he can do surely we can do.

Let us all practise that disconcerting "Oh, yeah?" (but in private); let us all have our pipes ready; let us all acquire the trip or cow-kick with which Mr. CHAPLIN would so deftly lay low a "smash-and-grabber". And let us all be thankful to the films, which have taught us the wholesome lesson that if we face thugs fearlessly virtue (that is we) must triumph.

I am sleeping alone in the house just now. A suspicious character has been observed in the neighbourhood. Loitering. (Anyone who is not dashing about at sixty miles an hour is a suspicious character in these times.) It is midnight and I hear strange noises below. Some thug is after the goldfish. In the old days I should have thought twice about descending, but now——

"Oh, yeah?" Where is my pipe?

"Do we have a reservation for a Mr. Howard Hughes and party?"

AS HIMSELF

AS DON PABLO

AS THE RAJAH

AS AN AMERICAN

AS A TAXI-DRIVER

AS AN ARTIST

AS AN ACTOR

AS A COWBOY

IN LIGHTER MOOD DISGUISED AS "CHARLIE"

A MASTER OF FILM MAKE-UP
Plus Ça Change, Plus C'est la Même Chose

Alex Atkinson

–A Moving Picture Girl

How many of these there are at present existing in London I have been unable to determine, for there is a continual fluctuation in their number. It seems certain that each day fresh "recruits" arrive, while others sink as it were below the surface, or possibly (although I can trace no proven example of this) rise, by some magical process, to more profitable employment in the industry. The girl whose portrait is subjoined I questioned through the good offices of a prosperous cine-electrician of my acquaintance.

She was a plump, fair-haired child of eighteen, and gave her name as Betty. She explained that she was "the Italian type", although a close scrutiny failed to reveal any marked Mediterranean characteristics. She directed my particular attention to her bosom, which seemed rather too extensive to be comfortable, and was evidently braced by an ingenious device within her corsage to give some appearance of solidity.

Her story was not easy to follow, for she had adenoidal tendencies, and used a provincial accent with which I was unfamiliar. I learned that she had been for two years in London, having told her mother (her father being dead) that she had a place as a saleswoman.

"I come down because my friend Angela was doing all right on the modelling, see. Oh, yes, I have always been dead keen on acting, and used to cut out photos of my favourites and stick them up in my bedroom until Ma stopped me. I had thirty-odd quid when I come down, as my friend Angela reckoned she could put me up for a quid a week on a divan. Oh, I was behind a counter from leaving school, but there's no future. No, I haven't never learned acting, but you don't have to on this job I'm on to-day for instance, as all you got to do is walk up and down and not gawp at the cameras. Oh, yes, *sometimes* you have to act, if you get a 'walk-on'. Like, you might have to be going into a building, or be getting off a bus. Then you have to do what the man tells you, and it's proper hard work."

She told me that she lived at present in a four-roomed apartment with two young men, who were engaged in similar employment. Upon my questioning the morality of such an arrangement she replied that she could "look after herself", and that one of the boys, Harold, had abnormal tendencies anyway. They shared the costs of housekeeping, and enjoyed themselves very much, Harold being of a humorous disposition. She had been home once since coming to London. She was not inclined to go again, as she preferred "a bit of life".

"Most times I'm on the dole. Once I saved up close on sixty quid, but it soon went. You have to register with agents, who take ten per cent, or five if the wage is low. They send as many as ten girls after one job, and in that way you waste a lot of time. Why, the jobs are such as being in a crowd, for which you might get only a few quid for a day's work; or playing a 'walk-on' part, with no words. For that I've had as much as eight quid, being at the studio from eight in the morning to five at night. They do not come up often. Other times you might get three days' work together, if something keeps going wrong, and for that I have had twenty quid in a week, and more. I was once three months without earning a penny. That was in the winter time. Living with two others it is easier, for whoever has money will buy tea, or tinned stuffs, etc., and all will share. Like that, I generally manage to eat something most days and in my job I must watch my figure [this seemed to me a pathetic piece of boasting], so I don't mind going without now and then.

"On this job to-day I'll get seven guineas, for standing by a counter in an advert film. No, I have no other work 'fixed up', but hope for some in a fortnight. Special costumes are supplied, otherwise we use our own clothes. You can easy borrow off of a friend, and must help her out another time.

"I hardly ever see the pictures I'm in. Most times they cut your bit out.

"No, I don't think there's anything else I'd rather do, except when there's no money coming in I often think I might like being a secretary, but I don't expect I ever will. I'm not cut out for it. I'm sure I'll get on in the end."

This appeared to me somewhat of a forlorn hope, as the child showed no signs of ability, or even of interest, in the art of acting. What can be done for such casual workers on the fringes of a mighty industry it is not easy to say. Their trade union can ensure that emoluments are reasonable, but there is no possibility of regular work. Despite these facts, which are widely known, there are always half a dozen applicants even for the most trifling engagement. Unfortunately, too, this way of life presents innumerable temptations, and my information is that they are not invariably resisted.

CHARLIE'S ANGLES

Who's to design Charlie Chaplin's memorial statue?
FFOLKES has been going through some of
the suggestions...

Michelangelo

Man Ray

Arp

Fabergé

Giacometti

Duchamp

Calder

American Primitive

Rodin

No, But I Read The Poem

The film industry's hunger for new plots is currently driving it into adaptations of comic strips, the filming of successful stage plays, and even the purchasing of film rights to novels not yet written. But why have producers never thought of taking poems for their raw material? The English Romantics alone provide hundreds of plot-possibilities, and, before long, reviews like these may be appearing

THE ALBATROSS FILE

Unlike most of my fellow critics I haven't read the Coleridge story on which **The Albatross File** is based, but that didn't prevent my enjoying the film as a piece of entertainment. Nor did the quite unnecessary dubbing of an albatross's cry (by a gannet, of all things). Basically, this is a stirring costume melodrama of the South Seas, spiced with elements of the modern spy/saboteur story. Captain Cook (Marlon Brando) is ordered by the Admiralty to go to discover some more continents; the French, jealous of his achievements, infiltrate his crew with female agents, led by Kim Novak, in the hope of sapping the sailors' morale during the weary months ahead. At the same time they mount a rival expedition. This makes it sound a thoroughly run-of-the-mill picture, and so it would be if the director (John Huston) had not hit on a delightful and thoroughly original expedient: the Mate (Trevor Howard) turns out to be a religious maniac, and from time to time by ingenious camerawork we see suddenly what he thinks he sees. Thus, as he stumbles among the bodies of his shipmates as they litter the decks, exhausted after an orgy (the orgies, incidentally, are no more convincing than most such things, despite all the publicity; I don't see why it was necessary to explain that Miss Novak plays a *renegade* nun) we see them through his eyes, as corpses; he believes, apparently, that he has done something frightful and his punishment is to be the one man left alive. Later, Miss Novak and her lascivious henchwomen are transmuted into an amusing skit of a Victorian group of angelic figures. The whole film begins and ends with him (after Brando has successfully charted the Great Barrier Reef, torn between his duty and a brief, improbable affair with Miss Novak) attempting to foist off his version of events on an impatient reveller. Not a bad film at all.

TREVOR HOWARD as The Mate, KIM NOVAK as Olga, MARLON BRANDO as Captain Cook and A Guest Star in **The Albatross File.**

SMÖRGERFLIDD

It would be difficult to know what possessed Ingmar Bergman to film Keats's *La Belle Dame Sans Mercy,* but whatever it was was no doubt dark and trollish. **Smörgerflidd** (The Mai Harris title-version translates this as *Withered Sedge*) was filmed on a twilit fjord during the rainy season, and ninety per cent of the dialogue is spoken off-screen while we watch mad gulls attempting to find their eggs before nightfall overtakes them. Set during a period of bubonic plague in the thirteenth century, the film explores the delirium of a wretched wight, or *grügg,* as he loiters alone on the edge of the lake wondering why the mad gulls are not singing and whether the time is propitious for him to commit suicide. In a series of flashbacks, the wight attempts to discover the root of his malaise, but, though he wanders from hamlet to hamlet, no one is able to tell him what ails

Still from the controversial gull sequence in **Smörgerflidd.**

him. The lily on his brow causes offence to a group of strolling *fikkers* (dragoons), who cast aspersions on his masculinity, whereupon he tells them about a girl he picked up and attempted to seduce in the meads. (There is, of course, some superb mead photography here, and much is made of the lady's long hair, light feet and so on.) Gunnar Björnstrand is splendidly broody as the wight, and overwhelmingly wretched, but I, for one, found the sweet moaning of Anni Skjörla rather difficult to follow during the second hour of the film. The scene in the elfin grot and the subsequent slumbering on the moss were, unfortunately, cut from the English version, and the motivation of the pale kings and princes in the later ramblings of the wight's mind are consequently difficult to follow, since their warnings now seemed to be directed only at the fact that the wight was mistaken to eat roots given to him by the lady. Bergman gives us no easy solution to the wight's dilemma or his possible course of action, but there is

a deeply moving and highly allegorical sequence near the end of the film, in which the tide comes in, right up to the wight's neck, and a number of mad gulls perch silently on his head and stare at one another. Eventually the tide goes out again, leaving the wight still loitering. It is always possible, of course, that Bergman was merely concerned to point out the difficulties of being a gull during the rainy season.

OZYMANDIAS THE GREAT

Ozymandias The Great is dogged by that most familiar bane of all screen epics, the difficulty of living up to the superb promise of its credit titles. For a full thirty minutes Percy Bysshe Shelley (Ernest Borgnine) writes the credits on the sand of the Libyan desert in a remarkably accurate imitation of the poet's own hand. As he writes the last name a violent sandstorm obliterates everything. When it finally fades, we see two vast and trunkless legs of stone, standing in the desert. Nothing beside remains. The film then crosscuts to the antique land of London's Portobello Road, where a commercial traveller (Robert Morley) is describing to Sophia Loren, Natalie Wood, Samantha Eggar, Brigitte Bardot, Gina Lollobrigida, Virna Lisi and Jayne Mansfield how he plans to bring the legs of Ozymandias back to England for auction. At this point, Miss Mansfield delivers the line (script, incidentally, by Christopher Fry, Harold Pinter, Lawrence Durrell and John le Carré): "Gee, I wonder what the *real* Ozymandias was like..." and we fade-in to the much-publicised naked chariot-race sequence where Charlton Heston as Ozymandias is challenging Ambrosius, Emperor of Malta (played with delicate irony and sophistication by Victor Mature) for the hand of Philomena (Shirley Eaton). The next four hours are a riot of Technicolor splendour, in which the Mighty (a staggering assembly of over eighty thousand genuine Arabs) are invited to look on Ozymandias's works and despair. The authenticity of their subsequent groaning, wailing, and tearing of hair (in magnificent multistereophonic sound) is unquestionable, and many critics in the audience vomited. The rest of the film is concerned with the problem of commissioning the sculpture of the king himself, and the conflict of interests between the High Chancellor (Peter Sellers), the sculptor Enzymo (Peter Sellers), and Sir Harry Bastard (Peter Sellers), the Court Poisoner. The subsequent trial, held by Libyan tradition on the lip of Mount Etna during a thunderstorm, is a tour de force by defence counsel Sean Connery. The symbolic casting of the palace virgins into the erupting crater follows the trial, as a prelude to the execution of Enzymo by the ritual baboon stampede, and just as one feels this superb film to be drawing to a close, at the eleventh hour (literally), the story suddenly shifts to the Bedouin uprising, the sacking of the Imperial Palace, and the assassination of Ozymandias by the slaves. The film closes with the triumphant rebels breaking up the statue, and carrying off the pieces to make pestles.

The Ark built by **Ozymandias the Great** following his misinterpretation of the sacred fir-cones. After an unusually dry summer, the Ark is subsequently dismantled and sold for fencing.

CARRY ON NATURE

Now in colour, mostly daffodil-yellow, **Carry on Nature**, the latest in the Carry On saga relates the misfortunes of a nervous young assistant curator at the Natural History Museum with the improbable name of Blithe Newcomer. (But if you keep a sharp look-out during the credit titles you'll notice that the film is "Based on Ideas by William Wordsworth, Bard of Cockermouth".)

The hapless Newcomer is sent by his boss on an expedition to renew the Museum's wild-flower collection, and sets off on the day when his double, "Mossy" Stone, the mastermind of a bank-raid gang, breaks out of gaol. By a lucky twist of the plot the destination of both men is the same, a spot near Tintern Abbey which harbours a rare specimen of the smaller celandine and also buried loot from Stone's bank raids. The seductive Lucy, waiting there to meet the gangster, meets Newcomer instead...mistakes him for Stone...who accidentally digs up the money just as the police arrive and make the same mistake. Stone, meanwhile, rashly pausing on Westminster Bridge to admire the view, is accosted by Newcomer's boss, who mistakes him for...But I won't spoil it for you. The chase starts early, passing through Yarrow, Stirling Castle and untrodden ways beside the springs of Dove, and includes a very funny street-market scene that briefly holds the gorgeous East End in fee. The familiar complement of policemen, firemen and general pursuit personnel are augmented by a solitary reaper, some nuns invaded in their narrow room, and an idiot boy kept just this side of bad taste by Mr. Kenneth Williams. Mr. Charles Hawtry distinguishes nicely between the tremulous gawpings of Newcomer and the unscrupulous Stone, and John Pertwee and Kenneth Connor squeeze some fun out of Constables Cuckoo and Nightingale. As Lucy, Miss Sheila Sim is a phantom of delight.

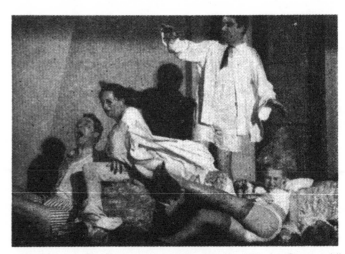

Before the credits Wordsworth (standing) recites *We Are Seven*, while Coleridge, Southey and Dorothy Wordsworth offer group criticism.

"HOLD THAT, JOHN!"

UNCLE SAM. "HELLO, BRITISHER, GOING IN FOR FILM-MAKING? DON'T FORGET OUR OLD SONG, '*WE'VE* GOT THE SUN, WE'VE GOT THE STARS, AN' WE'VE GOT THE MONEY TOO.'"

JOHN BULL (*registering dogged determination*). "NO MATTER; I'M GOING TO HAVE A TRY."

[Teacher's Pet

James Gannon—CLARK GABLE

Cinema Drawings

[Man of a Thousand Faces

Lon Chaney, 1957—JAMES CAGNEY *Lon Chaney, 1930*—LON CHANEY

Joe Chapin—GARY COOPER

[*Ten North Frederick*

[*The Monte Carlo Story*

La Marquise Maria de Crèvecœur—MARLENE DIETRICH

"Saved us a fortune in trick photography."

NO, BUT I SAW THE MOVIE
Alan Coren

Until a very short time ago, no nation on earth enjoyed as splendid a popular Image in the United States as the English; the visiting Briton basked. And no one ever asked him actually to demonstrate those qualities on which his glory was based; he was simply required to Be. Whatever his personal appearance, whatever his character, or behaviour, or background, when he passed through a crowded room, hushes fell, beautiful women gnawed their lower lip, strong men dropped their eyes, and small boys lifted their shining faces, as to the sun. For all knew this man's inheritance. Not, necessarily, the facts of it; but this ignorance was unimportant to them. Across a thousand panoramic screens, they had seen his clouds of glory trailed, and now, encountering the Englishman in the flesh, they recognised the presence of something greater than they knew. And so they roared at jokes they did not understand, because the English Sense Of Humour was a rare and precious thing, they nodded at his truisms, seeing immediately their hoary wisdom, they saw his inarticulacy as noble taciturnity amid the sounding brass; and husbands, noticing their wives' idolatrous looks, dashed in herds to their tailors to order suits made up from old army blankets, specifying the dashing trousers, flared at the knee, the cunningly asymmetrical jacket, the skilfully frayed shirtcuffs.

Americans, in that sweet not-so-long syne, knew where respect was due. Millions of feet of celluloid had taught it them, and they had met nothing to say it was not so. They had seen the Englishmen in War, whistling dirty songs at the Japanese, escaping in guffawing droves from cretinous camp-commandants, knocking back bitter in the mess before going out with a boyish toss of the head to paste Jerry over Kent, while all the world wondered. Americans had gaped at the Miniver set, picking shrapnel out of their tea and fussing over the Young Conservatives' Picnic. In Peace, too, they had seen and doted; England was God's Little Acre, a thatch-dotted paradise of trafficless lanes where blithe spirits in veteran cars chugged from one hunt ball to another, swam in Piper-Heidsieck, watched the dawn come up over Pont Street, and spent their serious hours redecorating mews cottages. Just as Jack Hawkins had been everybody's CO, so now everybody's Daddy was Cecil Parker, and Basil Radford and Naunton Wayne were always running through the drawing-room on the way to Ascot. Between War and Peace, there were Times Of Stress, when the British, played by John Mills disguised as Richard Todd, or vice versa, tightened their belts, stiffened their lips, chased the natives out of the rubber, and went back to their airmail copies of the *Daily Telegraph*. The Common Folk, of course, were a splendid bunch. In War, they died uncomplainingly like flies, sat in the ruins of their homes and told uproarious Cockney stories, and, adrift in a lifeboat with Noël Coward, were never at a loss for a spirited song. When Peace came, they all went back to being chauffeurs, bus-conductors, publicans, comic burglars, bank clerks, and Stanley

Holloway. They were deliriously happy.

When I first went to America, this image hadn't changed much. True, a backward glance from New York towards the horizon might have caught those little fistshaped clouds forming, but it was some time before the first cans of Truth were unloaded on the docks. At first, it was easy to argue my way out of American suspicion. *Look Back In Anger? Room At The Top?* Flashes in the pan, I said. I would laugh nervously. Alarmist minorities, I said. But when the new wave of British film-making broke across this continent and swamped Old Albion in its scummy tide, I knew I was beaten. For, worst of all, it hit at a time when some of the facts of English life were finally filtering through to the average American; word was out that the garlands were showing a tendency to wither on the brow, and the films provided the clincher. America knows. San Francisco cinemas have shown *Saturday Night And Sunday Morning, The Entertainer, A Taste Of Honey, The Long And The Short And The Tall, Sons and Lovers, The Loneliness Of The Long Distance Runner, Term Of Trial,* and *A Kind Of Loving.* In succession; to packed houses; and against the background of *Time*'s articles on the decline of Britain, and Mr. Acheson's penetrating twang.

Now, I'm not complaining. I'm delighted, Lord knows, that English film-men are at last making fine films. I can hold up my head among the cognoscenti. But not among the masses. And this overnight switch of Image is hard to bear. Now those Americans who once looked on me with awe, look with derision, or pity, or revulsion. If they bother to look at all. For they know the Truth. They know that I was born in a narrow street, in a scrofulous terraced hovel, to a withered old mother of twenty-four, her delivery screams drowned by the roar of the machine-shop/pit disaster. As a child, I stumbled wretchedly about in a pall of silicotic filth, unaware of the sun, occasionally catching a dim glimpse of my father, an emaciated creature in long underwear and a cloth cap, as he was dragged home, stewed to the gills on dole-money, from the local thieves' kitchen. I never had much of an education, due to long absences from my hellish school after regular beatings by me mum's fancy-man (Tattersall waistcoat, moustache, Vauxhall), and week-end jaunts to drizzle-swept boarding-houses with the nubile milk-monitor in VA. However, the educational problem was easily solved by sending me: (*a*) to Borstal, where I was thrashed by the staff, humiliated by Etonians, and ostracised by my fellows, or (*b*) to a bicycle factory where I got my kicks from dropping dead rats (with which England is bubonically overrun) into the packed lunches, or (*c*)—if I was a girl—down to the waterfront to watch the boats. A short time later, sex reared the ugliest head outside a Hammer Film; due to the constant presence of drunks in underwear mashing tea all over the hovel, I pursued love's young dream in bus-shelters, grimy cinemas, on canal-banks, behind bill-boards, and so on. My partners in the great awakening were diverse; every American schoolboy knows that I have: (*a*) gone to bed with the foreman's wife and got her pregnant, (*b*) gone to bed with the blonde from the typists' pool and got her pregnant, (*c*) gone to bed with one of the sailors and got myself pregnant. This is the new Time Of Stress and, acting in the new True British Fashion, I faced the problem squarely by: (*a*) nipping off to my auntie, the cheery abortionist, (*b*) marrying the girl and promising her a life of loveless squalor, (*c*) playing house with a young homosexual and waiting for the Day.

But suppose I managed to survive this *jeunesse dorée*; what then? Well, I might have gone into showbiz, and, living the glamorous life of a matinée idol in Bootle summer stock, entered my senior years without (from sheer luck) having got anyone pregnant, and with the comfy recognition that I was merely an alcoholic failure. Alternatively, had I gone into a respectable profession like teaching, I would have got all the plums the other fellows got (penury, frustration, domestic disaster, social rejection) simply by giving private lessons to a little girl to keep myself from the workhouse. Naturally, there was justice in all this—if I hadn't been a dirty pacifist, and had gone off to Burma to whistle with the rest of the lads, I could have landed a job in a public school. Mind you, I mightn't have got a look-in on the whistling routine; the Americans now know that I should have wound up in a grass hut with six typical British chaps, beating the living hell out of a senile Japanese until his mates turned up to square the odds and give us what we deserved.

　　Nevertheless, though I have been passing these last months with all the misery of an ad-man watching the Truth knock the stuffing out of a beloved Image, it wasn't until last night that I actually broke and ran. The cinema that had been responsible for most of the punishment suddenly interrupted its run of English films to show an American low-budget movie, called *David And Lisa*, and since this took as its subject two young inmates of a mental hospital, I went along with glee at the prospect of having the ball in my court

"We'll have to do a re-take of the orgy scene, and this time see to it that they behave themselves."

43

for a rare hour or so. The manager smiled at me in the lobby.

"Hi there!" he said. "Just in time for the short subject. You'll like it. It's an English documentary."

"Splendid!" I said, with a touch of the old panache. After all, I was safe enough. It was probably a Pathé Pictorial, one of those delightfully exportable Technicolor furbelows full of Cotswold centenarians, and Chelsea Pensioners who've made the Brighton Pavilion out of matchsticks. I sat down. The lights dimmed. And on to the screen, in several shades of grey, came Waterloo Station, wrapped up by Edward Anster and John Schlesinger in a package called *Terminus*. Leaden-faced people milled about in the gritty air; a small boy sat on a battered trunk, and howled; queues of people moaned about trains that had left ages before, and failed to arrive. I pulled up my coat-collar. I heard the familiar dark laughter breaking out around me. And when a line of convicts appeared and shuffled into a carriage labelled: "HOME OFFICE PARTY", I stood up slowly, mumbled: "Excuse me" in a deep southern accent, and left. The manager was still in the lobby.

"Where're you going?" he said. "You'll miss *Terminus*."

"You're wrong," I said. "I've been there before. It's where I get off."

He looked at me. "You British and your sense of humour," he said, unsmiling. "Personally, I never went for it. But, by God, I guess you need it, huh?"

"Yes," I said. "I guess we do."

*"Because it's an X-film. **That's** why."*

THE SECRET— OF THE POPULARITY— OF THE PICTURES—

IS THE INFINITE— VARIETY— OF THEIR SUBJECT-MATTER.

La Bête Humaine
Richard Mallett

La Bête Humaine (Director: JEAN RENOIR) is said to be "inspired from" a story by ZOLA; not having read it, I don't know how strongly. It is a very good film, though not exactly cheerful. JEAN GABIN appears as *Jacques Lantier*, an engine-driver who suffers from an intermittent madness that drives him to kill any woman he loves; SIMONE SIMON as *Séverine Robaud*, a girl who tries to get him to murder her husband and is finally murdered herself. (It seems to me typical of the peculiarities of censorship that we are allowed to see almost every move in this unpleasant crime although earlier our ears have been shielded from the assault of the word "*maîtresse*", which has been cut twice, leaving obvious blanks, while the superimposed captions chastely translate it "sweetheart".) The scenes in which we travel on the footplate, as it were, with *Lantier* are brilliant; never has the device of mounting the camera on a moving vehicle been used more success- fully. One almost gets grit in one's eye. It is hardly necessary to say that JEAN GABIN makes a very convincing engine-driver; and SIMONE SIMON, her child-like beauty intensifying the impression made by *Séverine's* cool resolve that her husband must be killed, is much more memorable than Holly- wood every allowed her to be. The whole film, in fact, is memorable as well as absorbing, full of interesting and amusing detail and studded with excellent playing in small parts as well as big: LEDOUX'S, for instance, as the tormented husband, and CARETTE'S as *Lantier's* dryly humorous fireman. Be warned, if you are the kind of person who needs warning when a first-rate film has a gloomy story; but anyhow it will be a pity if you miss this admirable direction, acting and photography.

Christie's Minstrels
Barry Took

When a film runs for two hours and twenty minutes it had better be good. Mercifully **Death On The Nile** which runs that length, is very good indeed and is, of course, based on Dame Agatha Christie's famous whodunit.

The world is divided into two quite separate groups where Dame Agatha's detective stories are concerned, people either regarding them as art or trash, but one thing is for sure and that is that the good lady's work is Big Box Office.

Not that whodunits are easy to transfer to the screen. When the story's about a corpse, some suspects, and a detective who unravels it all, there's not much room to manoeuvre. Remove one thread and the whole garment falls to pieces, and that must be a form of torture to many film makers whose entire *raison d'être* seems to be to mess around with an author's work until it's unrecognisable. Anthony Shaffer, who wrote the screenplay for *Death On The Nile*, had shown admirable restraint and has not only kept the original together but has added unobtrusively to the work, improving it ever so slightly in the process.

Not that the plot had much going for it in the first place, and the film comes out like a lemon meringue pie, a two-layer affair of quite different flavours. The first flavour is the story and is redolent of red herrings. It's also amazingly stilted, unbelievable and old hat.

That a group of people should find themselves on a Nile River Steamer, with someone each has a motive to kill, is fairly far fetched. When you add, as a fellow traveller, a Belgian detective who is not only celebrated but known by reputation to all present you are flying in the face of reason. Try taking a story like that into the offices of EMI and see how far you

get. But, such is the open sesame of the name Agatha Christie that EMI have not only embraced that exact story but have kissed it on both cheeks and invited it to stay for the holidays.

To such people you could sell Westminster Bridge. But, of course, it's not the story but the telling of the story that counts, and here EMI have employed the top people in every capacity and as a result have a winner. The director, John Guillermin, is clearly a shrewd and gifted man. Anthony Shaffer has an international repu- tation, as has the director of photo- graphy, Jack Cardiff. Everywhere that technique can assist the tech- nique is of the finest whether it's continuity, Connie Willis; costumes, Anthony Powell; make- up, Freddie Williamson; or hair- dressing, Betty Glasgow. This is the meringue part of the pie. But no dish however succulent in theory is any good at all unless the ingredients are right, and here it's the actors that give the whole thing its dream topping.

Angela Lansbury as the aging, exotic novelist, Salome Otterbourne, is a walking—or more properly a lurching—marvel. It's a "loud" part and in the wrong hands could have been awful. Miss Lansbury makes it a big perform- ance but at the same time imbues the role with a subtlety that is scarcely believable. A truly delicious piece of acting.

Maggie Smith as Miss Bowers, the acid and tetchy companion of Mrs Van Schuyler (Bette Davis), manages to teeter on the edge of mania whilst giving a performance that crackles with life, vigour and wit. So good is she that Miss Davis, who is herself no slouch at this kind of arch-bitch- iness, has to fight for survival. Jack Warden as the quack Doctor Bessner is also splendid as is I. S. Johar in the only obviously comic part of the boat manager. Mia Farrow, Olivia Hussey, Lois Chiles and Jane Birkin, and indeed every- one in the film, play with strength and rapport, but the ears and the tail go to the film world's latest comedy double act, Peter Ustinov and David Niven as respectively Hercule Poirot and Colonel Race.

There have been other Hercule Poirots and for all I know to the contrary other Colonel Races but Ustinov and Niven are now in the driving seat. Like Basil Rathbone and Nigel Bruce as Holmes and Watson, it'll never be the same without them. They manage to appear solemn but at the same time suggest such mischief as hasn't been seen since George Burns and Gracie Allen illuminated our lives. Niven in the smaller role is as essential to the whole as Wise is to Morecambe. Peter Ustinov is just magnificent as Poirot. His air of dignity tempered by pique, vanity or amused observation as the moment requires is a magnetic study in unforced bravura. That Peter Ustinov is a comic actor of the first rank is not a surprising discovery, it's just that, to be brutal, he hasn't shown much evidence of it lately. With *Death On The Nile* he re-establishes himself as one of the finest film actors in the world.

As if all this was not enough there is a cameo performance from Harry Andrews as a butler. Nothing especially remarkable except that it's hard to remember a British film of recent years in which Harry Andrews has *not* appeared. So much so that when the estimable Mr Andrews isn't in a film I begin to worry in case he's ill.

What other delights are there? Well, the scenery is nice if you like Pyramids, and there's a guest appearance from a cobra which at the preview had the ladies in the audience squeaking and oohing in a most unbecoming lady-like way. They had clearly not read either Sigmund Freud or Jill Tweedie. So, there's a lot to commend *Death On The Nile*. Nat Cohen and EMI are to be congratulated.

French Films and Lily
E. V. Lucas

If the performers in foreign films were to speak English instead of having to depend on captions, competition would be dangerous. And especially so just now with the films that the French are making, in which a captivating naturalness of acting, combined with the strictest economy of method and a

logical use of accessories, makes for an unusual factual illusion. Even when it is largely by captions that, to foreigners, the sense is communicated, this illusion is notable; to the French ear and eye it must be overwhelming.

At the moment we are far from the romantic gaieties of RÉNÉ CLAIR, with the spirit of HENRI MURGER in the background and rippling notes accompanying every movement of the puppets. We have even passed from the splendid inventiveness and insolence of SACHA GUITRY and are experiencing a realistic interlude, with the great RAIMU as the central figure. We saw him the other day at Studio One in *Un Garnet de Bal*; he is here again, at the Curzon, in *Gribouille*.

When the film was called *Gribouille* there was, no doubt, behind it the idea that a modern representation of the proverbial French simpleton would be unfolded; but RAIMU's genius soon made nonense of that, and we have a man of flesh and blood before us all the time, diffusing the very essence of middle-class French phlegm, French humour, French impulse, French fatalism, French materialism, French despair, French resiliency.

The story is simple. A young girl, *Jeanne*, played exquisitely by MICHELE MORGAN, is being tried for the murder of her lover; and *Morestan*, or RAIMU, who keeps a bicycle shop, is summoned to the jury. Believing her innocent, he persuades the other eleven to vote his way and *Jeanne* is acquitted. Later, down and out, she asks *Morestan* for help, and by dint of a little harmless fibbing he introduces her into his house and business, and the trouble, which not only filmgoers

but ordinary observant people would expect, follows: *Madame Morestan* becomes suspicious; *Mlle. Morestan*'s fiancé tends to unfaithfulness; young *Morestan* falls in love with her and becomes a thief; *Morestan* himself, although his heart loses no single auriferous grain, has to lie really hard and loses his good temper.

The end is inconclusive, but never the acting, which is superb throughout. How I wish that the caption device could be superseded so that such films as these might have general circulation.

Mildred Pierce
Richard Mallett

Mildred Pierce (Director: MICHAEL CURTIZ), like *Double Indemnity* (also a James M. Cain story, by the way), is very much helped by smart, slick, wise-cracking dialogue put over with dazzling competence and perfect timing. But this is helped proportionately more, I think, because although it has many of the attributes of a ''whodunnit'' it is basically the kind of tale that might be and usually is told in a very heavy and emotionally strained fashion. It is, of course, what is called a ''woman's picture'', a ''vehicle'' for JOAN CRAWFORD, and therefore it is emotionally strained as often as this can be managed; but the acid, astringent and sometimes funny line of dialogue that will cut through the hot-house atmosphere is never very far away, and (unless you prefer to steam without interruption) very welcome it is. This is a story of intense and passionate mother-love, of a woman willing to sacrifice everything for the happiness of her selfish, snobbish, egotistical daughter, and perhaps the public that likes this kind of theme ''straight'' would prefer to have rather more of Miss CRAWFORD'S very well managed emotional scenes and rather less of the entertaining conversation of JACK CARSON and EVE ARDEN. Possibly these (as I think, misguided) people would even prefer to have less time spent on those other small things, details and ingenuities of technique, that brighten a film for those who value them: such as for instance here, the echoes and the unidentified whistler of ''Drink To Me Only'' in the police-station, or the signing-off of a scene by the camera's turn aside to show on a wall the shadow of the players. But for me these make the best moments of the film.

Short Story

SUICIDE AT MALIBU
Elizabeth Troop

Benito Pastmaster was going grey. His mistress, Esme Pastmaster, exclaimed about this frequently. They were very close. It may be asked why Benito and mistress shared the same name—Pastmaster. But only by those who do not know that in fact Benito Pastmaster, in spite of the Italianate gigolo-sounding name, was a large, ageing black poodle. They were a familiar couple on the beach at Malibu, a stone's throw from Hollywood. (Of course, how far a stone could be thrown was ceasing to have any meaning for Benito, or indeed Esme. They were neither of them as young as they had been.)

As they toddled along, they dreamed. Esme dreamed of the days in Mittel-Europa and Shaftesbury Avenue, between the Wars, when she had been a musical comedy star, all the rage. Before Benito, before Malibu, she'd been, among other things, a Princess. Polish, of course, but a Princess, no less. Her creamy breasts and thighs had been lusted after by every eligible male in his prime in those Lehar and Strauss years. Rich admirers offered rubies and diamonds. They were accepted.

Benito's thought-processes were more olfactory. Smells in the studios where he waited, when Esme had transferred her talents (unsuccessfully) to the Silver Screen—the odd couplings with other pampered pets around the azure swimming pools, when he was a gay young dog.

Affectionate and tender, innocent *and* lucrative, thought Esme, looking back. All the blonde years, the milk and honey years.

It was hard even to lift one's leg at his age, thought Benito, who always seemed to have sand up his nose.

A blonde, but not always, not from the start. That first bottle of peroxide was bought daringly from the local chemist's shop when I was twelve, recalled Esme. In Burnley.

Burnley, hated Burnley, with its cobbled streets and clog-shod workers, clattering their early-morning way to the mills.

She would never be one of those, she swore. Was damned if she'd go into a mill with her voice.

That voice, which had been picked out in church choirs and infant classes and which pierced the neighbourhood as she practised, and drowned the wail of sirens calling the multitudes to work; that voice was going to pull her out of the mire, she was sure.

Her mother didn't go to the mill, preferring domestic service at the biggest house in the area. Oliver Clegg was the last in the line of a once powerful family; a bachelor of middle years. He was fond of young Esme. She found she could entice warm lozenges from his waistcoat pocket if she sat in

his lap. (The family fortune had been founded on throat and chest lozenges, in this land of the bronchitic.)

Esme would sing with him, when he was in the mood to strike chords on the piano: "Where e'er you walk, cool gales shall fan the gla-ade . . . trees where you sit, shall crowd into a shade." Esme's mother soon put a stop to that. When she said Mr Clegg had offered to pay for singing lessons she was forbidden to go there again.

"I'll never forget yon house," she warned her ma. "And I'll have one like it one day."

Asked by a school chum how she would get one, she said

men would give it to her. A man like Mr Clegg. Men paid ladies with beauty and talent. Like what? said her friend. Most people are afraid to know that, said Esme, but I'm not. Nutty as a fruit-cake, barmy, they called her, screwing their fingers into their temples and raising their eyes to heaven, to show how daft she was. It didn't do to get above yourself around there. The women had a quick flowering. Married young while the bloom was on them. However dark the houses each one emerged, virginally satin-sheathed, for her one bright day. Then came rounded bellies, soiled aprons and down-at-heel slipppers. Part-time at the mill, kids running bare-bottomed in the alleys. Varicose veins and pulled-down mouths. "But not for me," sang Esme.

Esme bought sepia postcards of stage beauties,

conned her mother into paying for elocution lessons, ninepence a week. She was no longer understood in the neighbourhood. Draped herself in the net curtains, crimped her hair, refused to eat chips and pease pudding and tried to enlarge her button breasts.

Esme, sixteen, ran off with a traveller in ladies' shoes. He was Manchester-based. Sampling one city, she desired another and took the train to London.

Her aunt, married to a baker in Kennington, put her up for a while, with the rest of her brood. Until she became the sequinned assistant of a magician at the local music hall—then she had to go. Her aunt washed her large, bony

hands of her, saying she would come to no good.

Having had a long line of moral disapprovers already, Esme had only to think of them to return to the primrose path of non-virtue. She had never understood what was so bad about donating your body for pleasure, and so good about donating it for hard work. Crazy logic, she thought, shrugging her plump shoulders at her latest conquest. Women like her aunt, her mother—conformity took their youth and gave nothing back. Their men turned sour, beat or hated them—hers courted, cajoled and enjoyed her. So the sneerers acted like compost on Esme, activating her gardens of delights. To Esme, joy was the only moral responsibility. Playing the dumb blonde was not so dumb. Making a virtue of necessity must be rewarded. Esme got hers.

During the Second World War Esme left for Hollywood with a small-part German actor with a toothbrush moustache. He had an uncanny resemblance to Hitler; without the latter's histrionic ability. In Hollywood he was restricted to valet parts, or third-rate gangsters. An expert in discomfiture (it was, in fact, real) he allowed, because of despair, any humiliation. As he cared little about class distinctions (being an aristocrat) he lost, for Esme, and for most people, any he might have had. She after all, only slept with gentlemen, not gentlemen's gentlemen. One of her principles.

With Jock she had to resign those principles. By this time, Benito, who at the time of her birth wasn't even a twinkle in his great great great grandfather's eye, was with her—had been with her, through all the green years and the lean years—her last male admirer.

Jock, she supposed, had saved her from despair. She could never really forgive him for that.

The studios had tried to make her over into various stars, a pseudo-Jeanette MacDonald—an ersatz Dietrich. They failed, reported cattily by the harridans of the gossip columns in *Movie Weekly* and *Star Secrets*. All she read, those days, having moved from her mock-Tudor Beverly Hills mansion to a shack on the beach at Malibu. She downed liquor, first from a glass, then from the bottle. Benito hated her to drink, hated following her zig-zag footsteps along the deserted strand. Also he got glass in his paws from the broken bottles.

Jock met Esme after his abortive job with a hearty star who was not quite so virile as his parts suggested. Benito arranged this seemingly accidental event. He'd never seen himself as a canine cupid, but still, he told himself doggedly, something had to be done.

Jock McTavish had reached the Pacific coast after his disillusionment with his own depressed land. But the California Technicolor proved almost worse than the Scottish sepia. He had fled to the hearty star from the attentions of a voracious Hollywood hag-on-the-decline. Bed and board. Bed and bored. Bedded and boarded. He escaped, bumming his way around the Los Angeles area: waiter, soda jerk, barman,

"In the play he said '_____!' and in the book he said '*****!!!' "

bar-fly.

This was until the wiles of Benito Pastmaster, poodle extraordinary, changed his life.

Jock was washing dishes at a beachside hamburger joint used by the college surfing trade. Because Benito found food at the shack in short supply (Esme took liquid lunch, and dinner too) he frequented the back door of the joint, accepting scraps with a dignity suited to his advanced years. He was tolerated when the place was half-empty, when the evening disco crowds came he was ejected. He usually lurked in the environs of the garbage cans.

Jock, though disliking most animals, took to Benito because of his weary persistence. It reminded Jock of his own behaviour. Stubbornness was his major quality, too. Benito had by chance the one virtue that appealed to Jock.

Jock disliked the sycophantic attitude of most dogs, was delighted to find one who disproved the rule. They regarded each other with great respect. Benito didn't even give as much as a wag of the tail for scraps received. Neither did Jock.

Fellow survivors in the game of chance. We're still in there—Jock said to the mutt as he handed him hamburgers that had been toyed with and left by the over-fed youngsters.

Then came the time when Jock had to put his loyalty where his mouth was, so to speak. Benito was banned on grounds of hygiene. Jock suggested that with kitchens like theirs, they must be jesting. They fired him on the spot.

The end is unimportant, he said to Benito, as they huddled in a doorway in the unaccustomed rain. Persistence is all, friendship is all. He patted Benito's old head, which smelled of wet wool. Whereupon Benito led him home.

It was as if the dog had been working towards this all summer. He pushed open the door of the shack with his nose. After noting that Jock had followed him in, he curled up on a threadbare rug, turning three times in a sort of superstitious way. He seemed to expect no welcome.

Esme was sprawled on a day bed, covered in movie magazines and astrological charts. Jock, leaning over for a better view, heard Benito growl. He recognised her; had seen her at the beach café sometimes, a blowsy blonde, usually the worse for wear. He had never connected her with Benito.

So Jock discovered his mission in life. Without suspecting it, he had swallowed Benito's bait.

Esme stirred, smiled and went back into her stupor again. Jock picked up a Mexican poncho from the floor, wrapped it around himself and did likewise. Whenever the cold dampness and the sea noises woke him he saw Benito's eyes on him, like two red coals in the dark.

Jock and Benito went to the restaurant at dawn next day and stole a French loaf from the doorstep and some oranges from the store room at the back. Jock had a key and he took what he regarded as his severance pay from the petty cash. They bought coffee and dog biscuits from Pepe's Cut-Rate Super Store on the way back. Benito, who hadn't seen a dog biscuit in years, was ecstatic. So this was the way it was going to be . . .

Back at the hut Jock scoured out a rusty kettle and put on water for coffee. Esme opened one eye to tell him the water was usable, in spite of what the notice above the faucet said. Then she slept again. By the time he had created a life-giving resurrection breakfast of orange juice, coffee and bread she was wide awake, showing few of the ravages of what must have been a heavy evening's drinking. He had stumbled on endless bottles under the sink as he searched for the kettle.

She rose. Fifty, sixty? He couldn't tell. Battered, but salvageable. He asked if he could move in with such quiet authority that, mollified by the breakfast, she agreed. First she asked Benito, who thumped his flea-infested tail on the floor.

They talked for hours, decided that what each of them wanted was to return to the Old Country. Benito pricked up his ears at that. They drank a toast to that.

Jock suggested carefully that sex should not have a major part in their relationship. Benito saw that although he had been

quite careful in the way he phrased this, Esme's child-like face trembled as Jock skated over the thin ice of her vulnerability.

They had a good fall that year. Jock dried her out, he had made her admit it wasn't spirits but spirit she needed. He had to admit, Great Romantic though he was not, that she had lived a Life. In spite of himself he was thrilled that she had known Ivor and Noel, Counts and Princes, Ziegfeld and Billy Rose. Finally—the Hollywood saga. Then she sobbed. She had flopped—hitting it as she did at the coke-vitality, Grable and Faye time.

Off the bottle, slimmed-down, a new agent later, she took on bit parts. She got Jock a job in her old studio, Wardrobe Department. Nightly he brought home

clothes for their new life. For himself two chauffeur's uniforms and a dress suit. For her, Ingrid Bergman-type gear, sporty but elegant, and a couple of evening dresses that had graced Grace Moore.

In this way, eating at the studio commissary, clothing themselves from Wardrobe, they stacked up dollars for the return home. Benito guarded that hat-box where the dollar bills nestled under ostrich feather-trimmed picture hats. A silver grey Rolls to match the chauffeur's uniforms was dreamed of, evenings, sitting on the beach, watching the tangerine sun go down.

Esme blossomed. Sought out old admirers who could be touched for a small role. She got quite a reputation as a character

DIGNITY AND IMPUDENCE;
Or, The Rival Commissionaires.

actress; soon Jock was wearing the chauffeur's gear for real, driving her to the studio in a second-hand Ford.

They never forgot their aim: London. It was something they both rather dreaded, having, it seemed, hit a winning streak at last. But they had an ideal: old age pensions, crumpets by the fire on blustery evenings. Nostalgia spurred them on.

Benito had been left to his own devices since they had been working so hard. Now, suffering from depression, it was suggested (in whispers) that he might visit one of the many dog-psychiatrists abounding in the area. Jock finally said no to this, it would cut into their savings too much. Benito punished them by failing to greet them when he heard the car draw up. After all, he had brought them together. He could only assume they would stick by him. They did seem touchingly concerned. His hearing was bad, but he thought he heard them discussing his adoption by someone kind—apparently he was too old to go into quarantine in the Old Country. Then he heard Esme say who in his right mind would want a fourteen-year-old poodle with chronic fleas, almost blind in one eye, with the disposition of a crotchety old man? It would be difficult, agreed Jock. Benito was mad at that, and pissed on their new rug.

One evening, they fed him royally, on steak, cut up into chewable pieces by Esme's red-tipped loving hands. Jock then measured him, saying it was for a new coat. But Benito had seen the baroque von Stroheim type coffin they had smuggled in from the studio. It had been used for a pet chimp's funeral.

Benito gave Esme's pearly toenail a farewell lick, for old time's sake.

While they were dining à deux, dressed in their costumes, Benito toddled off to the ocean, the blue Pacific.

He was written up as the only known dog suicide in Malibu. Or indeed, anywhere else.

Having nothing to detain them, they now set sail from New York.

Donald Sutherland
talks to David Taylor

Interrogatory pause follows fathomless, reflective interlude after narrative lulls and revelatory interpunction as we begin to wrestle with meaty prose, this sweaty Chelsea afternoon, to sum up meanings and perspectives all over the place and to pile up an impasto of this assuredly complex, mettlesome person, human being, actor. Five minutes in and there is no mistaking that there is to be no kind of bullshit, no quickie biographical listings or hasty assumptions which predetermine, don't they, and fog; and so don't let's anybody come across cute or anticipatory, OK? This here's a serious zone, this is a big house and an even bigger world outside of it and so settle down, pull up a malty Scotch but not for Donald, thanks, who's off it, plus no ice because the fridge is busted, same as so many things, and we'll start out with Fellini, touch on poker, Henrik Ibsen, parmesan, the Ferrari GTB-275, Las Vegas, Hollywood, Maxwell House and stuff like that. Outdoors, the heat is stifling.

Not really a star, Donald Sutherland itemises, he's a very successful character actor, "better suited maybe to doing less but doing more because that's the way the roles come'', which is currently thick and fast, despite some sonofabitch once dubbing him the poor man's Steve McQueen. Fellini's *Casanova* is now being canned, steaminess included, to follow such as *Novecento, Day of the Locust, Don't Look Now, Klute, Kelly's Heroes, M*A*S*H, The Dirty Dozen* and *Billion Dollar Brain*, aside from TV work in from *Hamlet* to *Flight Into Danger, Lee Harvey Oswald, The Avengers, The Saint.* He's busy. He never has yet directed, though ambitions are there already; actors do not, or should not, determine any film's direction, they collaborate only, which is one big change from the days when the studios sewed up everything. Certainly Sutherland comes across cool but not at all acquisitive, does not own a home, nor even an apartment, stays fluid, as he can. A man such as Fellini, whom he enormously admires, is reluctant ever to part with the whole of his vision for any film, any idea; will disclose just so much as you may need to know for immediate purposes. He has control, does Fellini.

Control is a skill which plainly fascinates Donald Sutherland. He is a man with no obvious vices this afternoon, who used to get through a bottle of Scotch a day, then quit: period. He quit smoking at the same time. The first was so dreadful that he hardly noticed the second, he says. Scotch tastes good, it smells good, same as this cheese, which he eats with pears. But you have a choice of will at all times; there to be exercised, professionally and during social mufti. A certain amount in life will go its own way, that's understood. A talent fades, a talent resumes. Man like Ibsen started out like a house on fire then in twelve years wrote next to zilch until in one year he tapped out a half dozen winners and people asked what the deleted came over Henrik? And nobody knew. It's a gamble.

One day, one night last week Donald says he was playing poker, seven through seven, and there's no way he could be made to *work* those kind of hours. He lost. His father, who's 84, still loses, is still playing the tables in Las Vegas only he bets small. There never was a time, back in St John, New Brunswick, where Donald was raised, when the family was poor or deprived, though pop was, from time to time, broke. It comes, it goes. Best Donald ever won was a Ferrari at a long-drawn-out game between shooting for a movie. It went, boy it went, finally went altogether. But then, de Sica lost *millions*. Different people exercise different levels of control, that's all. Donald does go carefully, he's a professional and, he admits, an honest man, straight at all times with the IRS. Eschew goods and chattels, you can imagine, it becomes straightforward. What the hell, he eats; eats well. He has a just terrific Australian cook travels with him, at least as a rule, only right now he's down with hepatitis. He makes his own coffee, out of a jar.

Gradually, the broodiness disperses. Two hours in and we're being invited back, any time, for a hand of cards. ffolkes, archetypal of cinema buffs, achieves an empathy, that's for certain. Toddlers toddle in from the garden, talking French, the malt flows, stories are swopped, Oscar Wilde quoted, hypothetical odds calculated, expletives reinstated, beards grow. Sutherland wanted to be a sculptor, once. He does not, he says, ever set out to be argumentative, recherché; just that sometimes talk can turn out a whole lot more diverting that way, better than PR-oriented yerch, any day. In films, as in anything, you can approach with dull, objectivity. Or you can immerse, and then relate, and hope to emerge with some touch of understanding, either from what you have known, or from what you have dreamt. Without that, what the expletive? Better to play cards.

"We've seen the queue for 'Star Wars' three times, now we're going to see the queue for 'Close Encounters of The Third Kind'."

KISSES OF DEATH
Fenella Fielding

Romance—that delicious, driven state, all divine imaginings, giddy, balloony, powdered further and further by delays, separations and other assorted difficulties—is so very agreeable. It never goes out of style, everyone keeps doing it, everyone keeps laughing about it and reading about it, but most enjoyable of all is seeing movies about it. A really good romantic movie has the entire audience identifying like mad—"Oh, it's just like us," or "Oh, if only we were like that."

If there were an absolutely new good romantic film on now, I would rush off to see it at once, but until one happens, I don't mind a bit going back to see *Les Enfants du Paradis*, which I did a week or so ago.

It is so stunning.

It is stuffed with enormous talent. It has the great Arletty, Jean-Louis Barrault, Maria Casarès going wonders with one of those awful parts where she loves him and he doesn't love her but he marries her just the same and thinks all the time about the one he did love and didn't do anything about, Pierre Brasseur going it a bit, Robert Dhéry playing a small part (must have been very small, I couldn't spot him for certain) and a great many other marvellous actors whose names I was too slow to identify. It's set in a never-never land of 1830-ish theatre and thievery that helps it to be romantic in that you aren't distracted by mental comparisons of the social code of then and now and can be swept away by the people and the plot and the plots and the sub-plots, and their own absorption in their artistic activities. Although Jean-Louis Barrault looks more like Kenneth Williams than he did the last time I saw the film—no disrespect intended to either party—I still wouldn't mind being able to mime "While this beautiful lady was watching my performance, the watch of the gentleman standing next to her was stolen by a rogue who then disappeared into the crowd. Unhand her immediately, she is innocent," as splendidly as he does, with his good, floaty arms, and drooping so beautifully in his white satin. (I actually can do "This lake was made from my mother's tears," but it's never come in useful.) And I can't imagine any female creature not wanting to be Arletty, I can't imagine any man not wanting to be initiated by her. "Love is so simple, Baptiste," she says, her girl's voice coming out of her woman's face, and she manages to make this sound like a revelation, an ancient truth, the answer. You agree at once, against all the odds; yes—*yes*, of course it is, you hadn't realised it before, but you definitely do *now*. Well. To blague you with stuff like that takes more than talent—it is stupendous—it is R-romance!

Incidentally, nobody dies in *Les Infants*, except for the Duke, who deserves it for marrying Arletty who is far too good for him, and for making philistine remarks about *Othello*. Anyway, death would be sheer ostentation for this couple, they have quite enough to put up with as it is. Still, death, while not to be used indiscriminately, can be crucial to romance; the definite obstacle, you might say; the great sealer. Marguerite *has* to die at the end of *Camille*, otherwise how on earth could it possibly finish? If she were just to go on and on being extremely ill for a long time, Armand would get fed up with her, or might even get T.B. himself, which might be more real, but infinitely less romantic. No, *she* has to die, and *he* has to live, forever will he love and she be fair, and that's that.

And Jeanne Moreau has to die in *Jules et Jim*, because Truffaut says so. And whatever he says goes, as far as I'm concerned, because I adored this movie. And I don't want to know what's wrong with it. As a matter of fact, there's nothing wrong with it, please don't say another word.

Punishable pride prevented me from seeing *Love Story*, in which Ali McGraw's celebrated death-scene made nations crumple with sobs. I suppose I just hated the idea of being programmed to cry in advance, and, too, maybe unfairly, I did have the feeling that it would be like having a hosepipe put down my throat and being force-fed with Miss Dior. Pity really. Both of them so young, and so lovely, with oh so much to live for, and to be struck down so cruelly just when everything was going to be all right. Why, I believe I'm crying *now*. I must go and see it immediately.

Or I could make amends in a different way. I never see films about lions, either; no special reason, my loss I have no doubt, I expect I just prefer people. But a romantic movie about lions ought to get everybody, and the story shouldn't be too difficult. You see, there are these two young lions, university students, he rich and fond of sport, she poor and keen on music, yet just the same they fall in love in spite of these vast disparities. It isn't easy for them, either. The boy lion's father disapproves of the girl lion, but just the same they bravely set up home in a tiny flat, and there are lots of charming little scenes while they are adjusting to each other. She, the girl lion, has this sweet maddening way of playing Beethoven's Ninth on the stereo with the sound up too loud, which makes him nick himself while he's shaving—you know the sort of thing. Rows, reconciliations. They go skating together. Then they discover that she has leukaemia (careful, here, Wild Life Preservation might have a word or two to say about this), and they are so brave about it. In her death-scene, I am going to insist that she wears very little make-up, but looks so very beautiful just the same, and when she finally dies he says, "A lioness is a man who cries", or something of that sort. Oh, Lord, I'm crying again.

MARX, Groucho
PUBLIC ENEMY

The U.S. Secret Service has a list of 38,000 potential assassins. Among them, apparently, is Groucho Marx, because he once remarked jokingly that Nixon should be shot. His reference number is CP2307000925

Priority Mauve / Off-record / Xerograph Negative / File 'n' Destruct.

Chief,

You requested I make Class "B" Slash Five assessment Suspect CP2307000925. This has been difficult assignment, on account of Suspect has so many aliases—F. Datsun Fleischmarkt, Ecology Freak; Memphis Q. Tennessee, Convention Plumber; J. Wilkes Booth VIII, Presidential Contractor; and Eldorado Morgue, Licensed to sell, Mary-Ann; to name but a hatful.

I report the bugging of one of his offices and enclose certified verbatim transcript of tape, containing two-shot dialogue between Suspect and Mrs Elvira Porterhouse, Female Caucasian, five-ten, two hundred pounds, Schmautzer-income-rated Plus 70, no record, husband employed at residence as full-time houseperson.

(*Transcript commences*)

Mrs. P: I understand, Mr Fleischmarkt, that you are keenly interested in preserving the environment?

Suspect: This is Tuesday, baby, so the name's Booth and anyway, if it's *your* environment you want preserving we'll need a beer-barrel. Come to think of it, we'll need a beer-barrel in any case. Let's you and me get stoned, Elvira, the night is young and I wish I could say the same for you.

Mrs. P.: I would have you know, Mr. Booth, that I signed the pledge as a young girl!

Suspect: So you can write, eh! Sign here, my fees are nominal, it's the expenses that'll hit you between the eyes. And by the way, where *did* you get those big brown eyes? Take 'em back, they're not a pair.

Mrs. P: That is enough, Mr. Booth! I came here to discuss the environment, not to . . . what *is* your profession, pray?

Suspect: I thought you'd never ask. Good afternoon, my name is J. Wilkes Booth VIII and I slay Presidents! You get the style, Elvira? I picked it up at a teens-matinée of *Bonnie and Clyde*, together with a lapful of jelly-sandwiches and a bad attack of second-degree eczema!

Mrs. P: I have never been so outraged in my life!

Suspect: I have, sweetheart, but then I've been around longer than you. On the other hand, if there's anyone longer around than you, Ripley held out on me! Kiss me, you gorgeous creature, either I'm burning with desire or there's a cigar smouldering in my vest-pocket!

Mrs. P: As you have no interest in the environment, Mr. Booth, I shall leave at once!

Suspect: Elvira! Mrs. Porterhouse! Don't say it's all over between us! Marry me and let us go down Life's Subway together and perhaps, one day, the patter of tiny feet? Say, have you ever had the feeling you're foaling?

Mrs. P: How dare you!

Suspect: What d'you say to rubbing out the President?

Mrs. P: This is disgraceful!

Suspect: OK . . . Rockefeller?

Mrs. P: That is the most disgusting thing I have ever heard!

Suspect: It is? Remind me to tell you the one about Teddy Roosevelt and his horse.

Mrs. P: I am leaving now, Mr. Booth, and I warn you that I shall speak to the first patrolman I encounter!

Suspect: Oh, so you're not choosy, eh! It's women like you who've got this city a bad name . . . Los Angeles! You're a disgrace to the fair sex, and that goes double for redheads!

Mrs. P: *Good*-bye Mr. Booth!

Suspect: My final offer . . . Jimmy Carter!

(*Sound of slammed door and broken glass*)

Suspect: Crazy broad! I'd have done it for . . . ah, so you figured I was going to say peanuts, eh! You're darned right I was!

(*Transcript ends*)

My assessment is we have grounds for search-warrant and according to camera-squad we ought to find plenty. Already they report observation of live seal, Keystone Cops automobile-horn, dog-catcher's equipment, bar-room piano and one harp.

I think this thing is bigger than we suspected and also dangerous because, going by the way this guy walks, he's carrying knee-cap holsters.

Bernie.

As They Might Have Been

Marilyn Monroe

Medea, or Camille – in such a part
You glimpse Monroe's superb dramatic art,
When simply-falling drapery divulges
No inkling of her celebrated bulges.

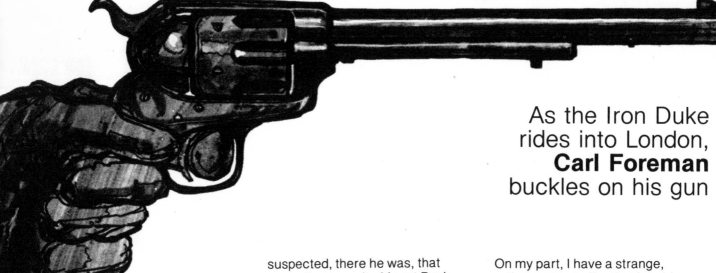

As the Iron Duke rides into London, **Carl Foreman** buckles on his gun

Western movies being disaster at the box office these days, "Big John" Wayne—as the British press fondly calls him, or old Duke as his friends know him—has shifted over to cop movies and is making one in England now, a veritable milestone in the history of the British cinema. And a week or so ago, I was in the counting house, fondling the paltry residue of all that good old Moscow gold we used to get so regularly from Comrade Beria, back in those marvellous subversive Hollywood days (it would come in bullion, wrapped in back issues of the *Daily Worker*), and ruminating on the vulgar iniquities of a wealth tax, when the children rushed in screaming hysterically, "Daddy, Daddy, come quick! John Wayne is on the telly, and he's saying ever such nice things about you!"

Going by past performance, I took this shrill piece of reportage with what turned out to be justified scepticism, but, nevertheless, I followed the brats back into the culture room to see for myself. As I

suspected, there he was, that marvellous granite Mount Rushmore face going delicately puce with the effort of control, sparks coming out of his ears and scaring hell out of poor Mike Parkinson, and gravelling, "What about Carl Foreman? I'll tell you what about Carl Foreman and his rotten old *High Noon*!"

It had been remarks of this nature that nitwit babes had taken for compliments, which may or may not be a lesson to makers of political broadcasts and TV commercials. But for me, adrift in a dizzily changing world, with all our tried and tested values being shot to hell, it was nice to see old Duke still standing tall and fighting the good fight against the devil and all his minions. I brushed aside *Private Eye*, *Morning Star*, *The Thoughts Of The Chairman*, *Stalin's Report To The 18th Congress*, Murphy's *Street Fighting And Urban Terror* and Weintraub's *Advanced Agitprop In Cinema And TV*, and sat gratefully down to watch old Duke expose me and *High Noon*, once again.

I think it incumbent upon me to explain at this point that old Duke and I have an odd but enduring relationship, dating back to the days when Dick Nixon was Duke's favourite California congressman and obviously destined to bring America back to the Americans, that is to say, the real Americans.

On my part, I have a strange, rather corrupt affection for old Duke, despite everything, and that covers a slice of territory large enough to contain the corpses of more than three hundred careers. I have always liked him on the big screen, and I have always been grateful for his leadership during the darkest days of World War II.

In those days, remember, we amateur civilian-soldiers were led by relatively untried generals like MacArthur and Eisenhower, whose most serious exposure to enemy forces had been mainly against the unemployed veterans and Bonus Marchers of World War I. Imagine, therefore, the inspiration and courage and selfless devotion to the fatherland old Duke gave us with films like *The Flying Tigers*, *Back to Bataan*, *Flying Leathernecks*, *The Fighting Seabees*, and all those other great war films that made him the undisputed Box-Office Champion Of All Time, and very rich in the process. As Raoul Walsh, who discovered him, says, Duke is not only a great actor but a Great American, and so say all of us.

But on his part, old Duke suffers from the Foreman-*High Noon* syndrome, a nervous disease causing anger, truculence and visible discomfort. For the benefit of younger readers, *High Noon* is a movie I once wrote when I had nothing better to do, and to

58

mention it to old Duke is like complimenting Mr. Nixon on his clever appointment of Mr. Jaworski. I will not say that he froths at the mouth, but my eight-year-old, gazing raptly at the box, thought he'd been eating soap.

Anyway, there I sat enthralled, as old Duke once again exposed all the hidden subversive bits I had tucked into that apparently simple home-made American celluloid pie.

"Here's this church," Duke growled, "supposed to be an American church, and all the women are sitting on one side of the aisle, and all the men on the other. What kind of an American church is that? And all the women are telling the men to get out there and fight those killers, and all the men are afraid, what kind of a Western town is that? And then at the end, there's this sheriff, he takes off his badge and he steps on it and grinds it into the ground, what kind of a sheriff is that?"

What kind, indeed? Horrid doubts assailed me. I remembered no such incidents in the film, but over the years old Duke has developed such an impressive persona of rock-like sincerity that I was more that half convinced. Had I in fact, under the influence of the Protocols of Zion, written in a synagogue instead of a church? Was my sheriff (marshal, actually) one of those bitchy foot-stampers? Wiping tears of shame and self-contempt from my glasses, I hurriedly screened my copy of the film, and realised, with ineffable relief, that old Duke had either never seen it, or was talking about some other movie, or had seen it and had, as we used to say in the real old West, disremembered it.

Well, they say that when a man starts growing old, the first

faculty to go, or is it the second (I forget which), is the memory, and there is little doubt in my mind that old Duke's remember-machine ain't what it used to be. For example, *International Who's Who* says that he was born on th 24th of June, 1924, but in the *International Motion Picture Almanac*, a publication that has a very long memory indeed, the date given is May 26, 1907, a fair discrepancy by any standards. But, anyone can forget when he was born or overlook a mere seventeen years. What is more curious, considering old Duke's present holy war against *High Noon*, is what he said about the flick on television to all the world the night Gary Cooper won his Academy Award for his performance as the (sic) sheriff.

"Why can't I find me a scriptwriter to write me a part like the one that got you this?" old Duke demanded as he handed Cooper his Oscar. "Good sportsmanship is okay as far as it goes, but when I leave here I'm going to get hold of my agent and damn well make him find me a writer who can write me a picture like *High Noon...*" Alas, *autres temps, autres pensées,* but that night those words from old Duke's manly lips had a certain bittersweet charm, I can tell you, considering that he could have got me very easily, except that I was black-listed in Hollywood, and looking for work in England.

Well, John Wayne's memories of old films are exquisitely unimportant to practically everyone. But his lapses of memory, about Hollywood during what is now called the McCarthy period, and the real-life role he played in those unhappy days, are a mustang of a different colour. Very vague, he is these days. Ask him if there was ever a political blacklist in Hollywood, and he will look you in the eye and say, oh, dear me, no, never. Or, if there actually was one, unbeknownst to old Duke, it was probably the commies who were trying to black-list the real Americans, who naturally defended themselves and saved Hollywood, if not, for that matter, the nation, itself. But no one was really blacklisted, ever.

Ask him if he was a leading member of that scurvy gang of character assassins calling themselves The Motion Picture Alliance For The Preservation Of American Ideals, which together with the House Un-American Activities Committee and a gaggle of frightened studio bosses, persecuted and hounded hundreds of innocent people out of the American film industry, and he will tell you that to the best of his memory it was a fine group of patriotic Americans devoted to celebrating national holidays, making flags for school-children, and honouring the nation's war-dead.

Ask him what he thinks of Joe McCarthy, and he will tell you that, as near as he can remember, the Senator was a much vilified, much misunderstood, great, great, American.

Ask him if it wasn't indecent, if not to say vicious, to break Larry Parks, live, on television, and then destroy him forever in films, and he will reply cynically (and untruthfully) that Parks, then at the height of his career, wasn't working much, anyway. Or at least, not as much as old Duke. Ask him if it isn't true that for quite a time you couldn't work in Hollywood unless old Duke, Hedda Hopper, Ward Bond and a cheap-jack union boss named Roy Brewer passed on your "Americanism", and he won't remember any such thing. Or other things such as suicides and broken homes and heart attacks and people dying long before their time, like John Garfield and Joe Bromberg and Robert Rossen, and others. No, old Duke just doesn't remember the days when he rode the Hollywood range, keeping the country pure at any price.

But I remember. I remember the meeting I once had with old Duke some twenty years ago in Hollywood. I was already on the List and out of work, but still hanging around in the quixotic hope of breaking the ugly thing. The meeting was ostensibly arranged so that I could plead with old Duke on behalf of a press agent who had made the mistake of speaking to me in public, and who was to be punished by losing all his clients.

This historic confrontation at the Beverly Hills corral took place on a Saturday morning in the offices of the investment manager for the richest and most patriotic movie stars in Hollywood, of whom old Duke was both. We were alone, equally uncomfortable, like two teenagers in a whorehouse, and the meeting began with old-world courtesy and tact. For openers, old Duke magnanimously agreed to let my errant friend off the hook. Then he got down to the real reason for our get-together, which turned out to be little old silly me, past president of the Fabian Society And Wine And Cheese Club. Silly old me took several minutes to realise that good old Duke had given up his Saturday morning solely to help me hit the sawdust trail to political salvation. All that was required were a few public confessions, complete with breast-beating, and a reasonable amount of informing on old friends, passing acquaintances or absolute strangers, for that matter. Just a little co-operation, that was all, and I'd be working again.

As I said, it was several minutes before old Duke's siren song came through loud and clear, and I think that the reason for the delay was that old Duke must have been indulging one of his better-known habits before his arrival. For a while there, the aroma across the desk gave me one of the best highs I have ever enjoyed. But eventually my head cleared, and I said no. Old Duke then told me that if that was my final decision I would never

work in films again, or probably in anything else. It was a pity, he said, because obviously I wasn't a commie bastard, really, just a dupe.

I asked why they were blacklisting people, and he replied that fire had to be fought with fire, and that the ends justified the means. I remarked that the communists believed that, too. He ruminated for a while, and then dismissed the point as irrelevant. I said there were other places where films were being made, and I could always try my luck abroad. Good old Duke averred that the blacklist would follow me overseas, and that in any event my passport, if I had one, would be made invalid, and he then reeled off the names of a dozen others who would soon be unable to leave the home of the brave and the land of the free. And, you know, it all came true. Old Duke may not be able nor care to remember some things these days, but he sure had a lot of inside information then.

Well, all that was a long time ago. If I were old Duke, I would wash my hands very often, but foolish old liberal that I am, I can't help feeling a ridiculous sympathy for the old mastodon, because I love my country as much as he does. But it's all turned sour for him. Everything he has believed in is falling away, like the flesh on a rotting corpse. He stands alone, like a wounded bull in an arena full of jibbering drug addicts, most of them traitors, draft-card burners and deserters, and nobody cares.

His old friends are long gone. John Ford, a cinematic genius but a political illiterate, and Ward "The Hangman" Bond, who could smell a Jew-commie a mile away, and poor old Hedda, are all dead. Ronnie Reagan, who never came near being Box-Office Champion any time ever, is Governor of California and could even become President one day. Chuck Connors goes to Moscow and kisses and hugs commie commissars all over

"I must say I'm enjoying my metamorphosis from dirty old man to avant garde eroticist!"

the place. Frank Sinatra and Sammy Davis, of all people, have become old Duke's political bedfellows. Spiro Agnew has been exposed as a petty crook, and John Connally has been charged with accepting bribes. Earl Warren betrayed every decent American who believed in law and order. And Dick Nixon has taken a hell of a long time to die in public, long enough, perhaps, even for old Duke to realise that he has been riding the wrong horse all this time, and that in trying to save America he has in fact collaborated with its real corrupters, seducers and traitors. And all that money he made during the war years and afterwards is worth a lot less with every fleeting inflationary day, and his taxes and mine have both gone to support, mostly, governments of fascists and thieves throughout the world, and that is why people don't love America the way they should, by rights. There's a payoff for you.

And now, fellow Americans, a final small irony. Old Duke has often told the world how much he reveres Sir Winston Churchill, and I share his admiration for the great man. But perhaps old Duke ought to know that when Sir Winston and I were discussing the film about his early life, I felt he ought to know how it happened that I had come to live and work in Britain, and that upright folks like Big John Wayne were agin me. W.S.C. laughed, and said, "Oh, I know all about you. But we don't like political blacklists in England. And speaking for myself, I don't care what a man believes in, or believed in when he was a boy. My concern is whether or not he can do the job."

In a way, I feel badly about informing on the old gentleman, because it may shatter the last of old Duke's illusions. He may get to thinking that Winston was more Limey than he was American, or that he had feet of clay, or, and this may well be the horrible truth, that he was despite all appearances, a crypto-commie. Old Duke knows all about those varmints, and he just might up and organise a branch of The Motion Picture Alliance For The Preservation Of American Ideals right here in London.

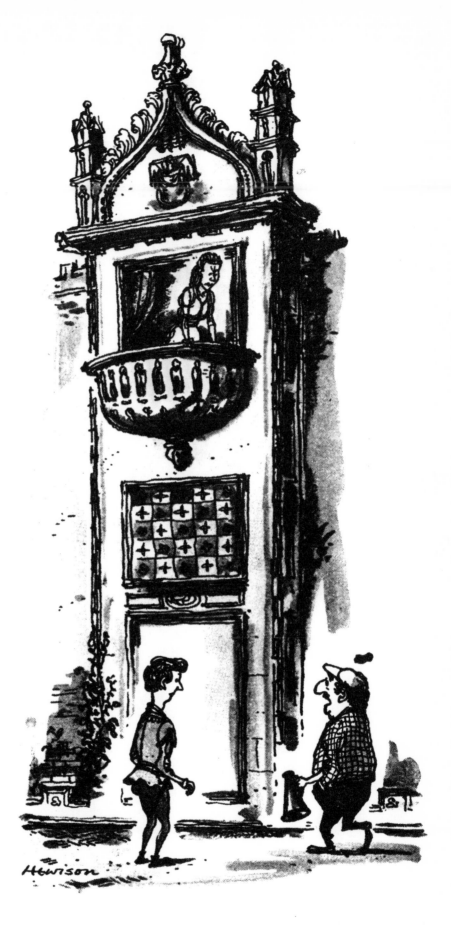

"Wait a minute – what's this going to be like on the wide screen?"

What Happens at Saturday Morning Cinema

Peter Buckman is one of the few adults ever to have been and come back again. This is his incredible story.

When you'd rather climb Everest than take them to the zoo again, when another minute of "children's television" will make you join the Angry Brigade, when there are absolutely no films in which you can honestly and decently answer the inevitable "What are they doing, mum?"—then perhaps you ought to consider the blessings of Saturday Cinema. At about 9.30, every week, some 350,000 kids riot in the stalls of our local cinemas. No adults are allowed, except supervisory staff. I was granted special dispensation to bring you this report, and I can honestly say that, for me, the cinema will never be the same again.

I remember once being allowed to go as a kid, and thinking what a noisy clubby place it was, with everyone shouting for the characters they knew and I'd never seen in the flesh, such as Batman—still going—much more baggy and saggy than the seamlessly tunicked figure of the comic strip. Well, the noisy clubby bit hasn't changed at all nor, at least where I live, the fact that the audience is predominantly working-class, in fine contrast to the well-modulated tones of the characters on screen.

In our local ABC, where I crept first, the manager was opening the proceedings with a bonhomie that did him credit so early in the day, and which the kids totally ignored.

"What're you all here for?" he bellowed jovially through a microphone.

"**** off!" the kids replied, without malice.

"Are you happy?"

"NO!"

"Glad to be back at school?"

"BOO-OOO-OOO!"

"Now if anyone's got all the badges you can buy at the kiosk, I want him to come up here and he'll get a prize." Two kids fell over themselves to mount the stage, as bemedalled as generals. The manager spelled out the first one's display—it read "ABC Minors"—and gave him a box of chocolates. The other boy received a clip round the ear. Then the screen lit up with the words of the ABC Minor's song: the kids sang lustily, though not, as far as I could tell, the words on the sheet. The manager retired to loud cheering, which continued as the first film began.

"HOPE SPRINGS ETERNAL."

Archie. "THIS IS THE LIMIT; I'M GOING."   *Reggie.* "WAIT HALF A JIFF; HE MAY BURN HIMSELF."

All eager, I leaned forward to catch the credits and the opening dialogue. I was apparently alone in my interest. No one went shush, or looked around indignantly, or muttered things under their breath. The kids nearest me—and they weren't very near, as if I had a contagious disease—had their feet on the seats in front and were unwrapping sweets with no attempt at decent mufflement. I considered composing my features into a stare that would both chill and silence, but there was no point in starting a fight in the first five minutes.

The cartoon, which I alone received with respectful attention, was an all-American one concerning a firefly whose light dimmed, who had it mended, and who then saved an aeroplane single-handed. It was followed by "A Deb in Sicily", featuring little Deborah taking a Sicilian holiday all by herself. There were only two moments when the kids gave this any sort of notice: the first when a bikini-clad model appeared on the beach, bringing whistles and cries of "Cor—lovely!" from boys who at full height would scarcely have grazed her navel, and the second when a jolly fisherman prepared a sea anemone for eating, at which the entire cinema echoed to the sounds of retching.

The third film brought resounding cheers: the week's instalment of "Panther Girl of the Kongo", a black-and-white American number made, I should judge, when Bundles for Britain were still a necessity. Though I thought she had nice legs, Panther

63

Girl herself was so completely asexual neither the boys in the audience nor those on screen were at all aroused by her. When, in fact, she was attacked by a crocodile, the cheers were stupendous.

This film ended in mid-flight, and immediately the lights came full on—none of the subtlety reserved for us weary grown-ups—and instantly the tart usherettes and the rheumy-eyes caretaker were wagging fingers at the kids in an attempt to control them. What went on in the interval, apart from the consumption of an incredible amount of confectionery, appeared to be a series of mobile fights for territory. The older kids looked after the young in their care, making sure they got to the loo and sweet-tray, and that they weren't attacked too often. Gangs of small girls incited similar gangs of boys to attack them. Black fought with white in a sexual war. As far as I could tell there was no necking in the back.

The lights went down and a film from the Children's Film Foundation was announced, to prolonged booing. Now I had been told that the CFF is immensely popular, that, financed as it is by the British Film Industry itself ("no Goverment sponsorship whatsoever"), it was the principal and most trusted provider of material for these shows. Certainly its morality would cheer any parent: no violence, plenty of action, "a constructive production policy aimed at increasing international understanding". But whether four hundred kids, on their own in the dark, appreciated such uplifting sentiments was not clear to me.

The film was "Tim Driscoll's Donkey", and the kids' noise did not cease throughout its length—at one point becoming so noticeable that the usherettes came shining their wrathful torches amongst the aisles. It made no difference. The hero of the film was an Irish lad much attached to his donkey, which he allowed to be taken away through the knavery of a jealous contemporary. For this, the audience jeered him, in terms such as "Bloody stupid idiot". While any extended piece of dialogue only increased the noise in the auditorium, they proved they were following the action by screaming at the screen when they didn't want something to happen, and working themselves up into an orgy of participation over a chase sequence. When all ended happily, to prolonged cheering, many

kids dashed on to the stage and dived under the curtain. They were chased off by the caretaker with a broom. Were they, I asked, looking for the incarnation of their fantasies? "Not bloody likely" I was told. "Just making trouble."

My visit to the Odeon the following Saturday was more eventful. Things seemed quieter during the first half—sometimes they began with sing-songs ("when there was the staff available" the manager somewhat mystifyingly explained), but they had abolished the Odeon equivalent of the "ABC Minors" song, because some critics told Lord Rank it was indoctrination. The opening film was the last episode of "Jungle Girl" (indistinguishable from "Panther Girl" in age and tone), and this was rapidly followed by the first episode of a CFF serial, "Treasure in Malta". Though the heroes of this seemed to me to be insufferably public-school, and the characters so stereotyped as to be laughable to any kid who watched television, it was received in relative calm. It was during the interval that the kids showed what they truly thought.

As soon as the lights came on full, they were running up and down winning easy victories over the chasing staff. Anyone who was caught was threatened with the bogey of the manager—"If you don't watch it, he'll have you out. WALK, don't run." And as soon as the kid was released, he ws off again. It was a permanent game of "Relievo" in adult territory.

Absorbed, I was approached by a diminutive and dirty kid who jumped on the back of the seat in front of me. "Hello," he said, and I thought how kind it was of him to befriend me, considering I stood out as a pipe-cleaner amongst matches. "Can you," he continued, "give me sixpence?" I fished in my pockets embarrassed by my wealth, trying to decimalise, and found two new pence, which I gave him with a warm adult smile, and asked if that was enough. "No," he said. But he vanished towards the sweet-tray, returning some minutes later. "There's nothing I can get with it," he said. "Oh," I returned. "But I haven't got any more"—a black lie to this innocent, but what was I to do, give him the money I was saving to buy comics with? He vanished without further comment.

During the second half, as I was getting absorbed (again I was the only one) in an American comedy, "The Incredible Mr. Limpet", about a brow-beaten man who turns into a fish and then leads the US Navy to destroy the entire U-Boat fleet, I felt a tug at my sleeve. "Here, mister," said a voice, "I've lost my tooth."

Automatically I became the concerned adult and began looking for the missing object. I was not yet on my knees when it struck me that teeth are not easy to find in the dark. I straightened, and addressed my friend soberly. "You should get sixpence for it," I said. "Yes," he said and held out his hand.

They may not enjoy the films, but they certainly know what's going on.

Explosions of cheering greeted the victory of the American fleet, and after a splendid cartoon, again American, the kids were chased out of the cinema. The fact that they go every week regardless of what's on must mean that the atmosphere is what matters, that they care about being with their friends, in the dark, with no adults yet on adult turf, and that they can shout and show off as much as they like. Maybe there are undercurrents of sinister gang warfare, maybe the strong bully the weak, maybe the poor rob the rich, but parents may rest assured, none of *that* kind of thing gets on the screen.

As I was leaving, the manager pointed to the last kid to go, my tiny toothless friend. "You want to watch that one," he told me. "He doesn't look like much, but he's a real terror."

PINEWOOD TOURS LTD

Summer Timetable

YES, IT'S TRUE! You too can now join one of the first ever behind-the-scenes tours of a British film studio! For a mere £19.99 plus VAT and exciting bring-your-own packed lunch we will take you by coach into the heart of the Buckinghamshire countryside where, in the grounds of a stately home much admired by those who've never seen Woburn Abbey, half-empty studios stretch as far as the eye can see. You too can be a part of this excitement!

WITNESS before your very eyes the collapse of the British film industry!

THRILL to the sight and sound of films being halted in mid-production as tension-packed union disputes are fought out in detail.

REMEMBER the golden era of *Stop Press Girl, Carry On Cruising, The Black Knight, There Was A Crooked Man* and other celluloid classics all filmed at Pinewood and some not much later than 1956.

INSPECT Roger Moore's shoes, a wig once worn by Alexander Knox, and the mother-in-law of two girls who had small parts in *Carry On Up The Khyber.*

RECALL the magic of *The Mackintosh Man, Legend of the Werewolf, Deadlier Than The Male* and other unforgettable screen greats.

Fully costumed "extras" of the type tourists will be allowed to meet at Pinewood

GAZE at a near-personally signed still of Roger Moore, one of a limited edition of five and a half million and available for you, yes you, to take home for a mere £17.45 plus VAT and frame extra.

ASK YOURSELF whatever happened to the British film industry, whether Phyllis Calvert ever married Nigel Patrick, where is Mandy now, why there isn't a God and whether Alexander Korda ever paid any of it back.

CONSIDER whether we weren't better off in the days when Alistair Sim was a child star and John Mills still not promoted above the rank of Able Seaman.

WONDER whether or not to buy a rare photograph of Richard Attenborough not looking nervous.

NOTE that these studios were built in the 1930s by the late and great millionaire Charles Boot, and ask yourself what would have happened had he found something more sensible to do with his money. Would there have been an Anna Neagle? Could Dulcie Gray ever have met Michael Denison? Would the world have been a fit place for Bryan Forbes to grow up in?

FORGET the fact that two-thirds of the films that were made at Pinewood are not shown nowadays even by Grampian television at eleven-thirty on a Saturday night in August. Forget the fact that the only stars to be seen having lunch in the studio canteen these days are grown men with wives and mortgages to worry about trying to stuff ham sandwiches through the apertures in their Womble masks.

LAMENT the passing of Finlay Currie and the fact that half the character actors in the land, men and women who fifteen years ago wouldn't have been caught dead taking orders from John Gregson, are now doomed to guest appearances in *Within These Walls.*

EXPLORE the famed Pinewood Museum, where one of Raymond Huntley's used moustaches, several of Bill Travers' sandals and an eyebrow pencil once the property of Margaret Lockwood are handsomely exhibited in neon-lit glass cases.

AMAZE your friends with an instant photograph of yourself in a plastic replica of a car of a type once nearly driven by somebody in a James Bond film.

TOUCH the stiff upper lip once worn by either Donald Sinden or Kenneth More in films with very long titles usually involving metaphysical concepts allied to a Wordsworthian appreciation of nature, eg *The Cruel Sea, Above Us The Waves, Beneath Us Our Feet* etc.

DEBATE among yourselves whether Richard Wattis was fundamentally more or less of a gentleman than Reginald Beckwith, and whether you'd have allowed any daughter of yours to have married Ian Carmichael.

PONDER, as you leave the studio gates with the theme tune from *Carve Her Name With Pride* still ringing in your ears, whether there was any film ever made at Pinewood that would not have been vastly improved by the casting of Alan Ladd and/or Dolores del Rio.

THE CRESTED MUFFIN

LANTERN
LECTURE
PROF. CORNCRAKE
ON
LITTLE KNOWN
BIRDS OTHER
CURE

Save The Tiger
Benny Green

There are several effective ways of sending a man off his head and the most effective of these, as the laboratory behaviourists discovered a long time ago, is to destroy his environment, spiritual as well as physical, artistic as well as moral. Even though the personality disintegration which follows is a common enough malaise in times of social cataclysm (like war, revolution, famine, pestilence, the twentieth century) nobody has ever found a cure. In the old days disaster brought the vulture, today the psychoanalyst, whose job it is to decide on the behaviour of his patient (at least in theory; in practice he never decides anything), the point at which nostalgia congeals into neurosis, disillusion into delusion, melancholia into megalomania. The predicament is commonplace and so is its exposition in the arts.

What makes **Save The Tiger** something out of the ordinary is that its makers have an inkling that there is one generation in particular—my own, as it happens—for whom the threat of emotional dispossession, of environmental disinheritance, is different in kind from that which faced previous generations.

The film's title may serve as a convenient allegory to illustrate this. The tiger is threatened with extinction, an unthinkable proposition which Man, in the course of befouling his own planet, has ingeniously made possible. But for whom, apart from the tiger, will the tragedy be most shocking? Not for the Past, which has gone to its grave aware of tigers; nor for the Future, which will inherit a world reconciled to their being absent; but for the generation which bridges the last thirty years, a period in which almost all the sacred cows of the capitalist west have been measured up for the abattoir. When a man grows up with the reassurance that certain tenets are constant, only to discover at fifty that they weren't constant at all, that the young have not so much rejected them as never even heard of them, then it is reasonable to expect him to let off a few howls of anguish. *Save The Tiger* is one long howl of anguish and not seriously flawed, as it might so easily have been, by the scars of self-pity.

Jack Lemmon gives one of his finest performances, a painfully honest and sensitive portrait of one Harry Stoner, a Los Angeles clothing manufacturer who computes one morning that what with mortgages and taxes and school fees and silk suits it is costing him $200 to get out of bed each morning. He and his business partner are on the brink of bankruptcy, and are realistic enough to admit it. Where they differ is in what to do about it. Harry wants to burn one of their factories and collect the fire insurance, but his partner baulks at so criminal an act. Cooking the books or procuring for out-of-town buyers, that is one thing, but arson is quite another. It is this clash between the old morality and the new which defines the predicaments of Stoner's generation. Stoner, explaining the intensity of his own patriotism, says that when he was a kid, he would stand for the national anthem even when alone in a room. "Now," he says, "They're making jock-straps out of the Stars and Stripes. Maybe it's healthy. I don't know." But whether or not it is healthy is not the point for Stoner. What matters is that times are changing at such an alarming rate that he has lost his bearings.

At key moments in his day of crisis, Stoner reverts to the classic tactic of the man unable to cope with today, a retreat into yesterday. The first hint comes when at the start of the day, he lies in bed, presses a switch that sets in motion a programmed tape machine and we hear Benny Goodman's *Stomping at the Savoy*—the sophistication of the technology making a bizarre contrast with the innocence of the music. A beatific smile lights Lemmon's face, and it is worth noting that the only moments when peace and gentleness show in his expression are those when the past obtrudes. When his wife asks him why he no longer watches baseball, he spits out the same contempt for the contemporary game that I often do myself when people talk of Boycott in the same breath as Denis Compton. "Today," sneers Stoner, "they play on plastic grass", and later h is found gazing out of the window dreamily reciting the line-up of the old Brooklyn Dodgers.

Up to a point, Stoner's tragedy is the usual one of a man obliged, like the rest of us, to conduct his terrestrial affairs while travelling forward along the railway track of Time, even though it is perfectly normal sometimes for the imagination to move backwards along that track. So the body decays while recollection endures and the resulting tension is one that every human being has to learn to live with. But what makes Stoner's tragedy different—and this is a factor which will cause posterity one day to feel infinite compassion for him—is that for the first time in modern history the scenery that lies ahead on the track is utterly different from the scenery that lies behind. It is not possible for Stoner to reconcile what is coming with what has been. A young girl propositions him within two minutes of their meeting; there is something wrong with the new music; Mars is being photographed; day-to-day friendliness between strangers has gone; when he asks the girl what her three wishes are, she replies, "Peace, Harmony, and to make it with Mick Jagger."

The film's climactic moment comes when in a beautifully played scene where Stoner spends a night with the girl, and they invent a game in which each partner throws off a famous name. Stoner's list is bizarre, and we know from its very first item, that he is a man in deep trouble. The name he utters is Moe Purtill; later his list reflects the days of his youth when he was a dance-band drummer. Jack Teagarden jostles La Guardia, Fats Waller follows Jackie Robinson. And as he throws any of a discredited ritual, talis-ans of a past so utterly dead that e girl has never heard of them. ho were Mel Powell and Helen Connell, she wonders.

The trouble with Stoner is at nobody warned him that he will one day have to cope with the Bomb, Vietnam, moon-landings, pollution, over-population—or saving the tiger. He is a man conditioned to the assumption of the world's infinity who suddenly finds himself in a finite madhouse. Is there any salvation for him? The film offers two hints. His oldest employee reveals the secret of his contentment, joy in the crafts-manship of his work, joy in the loving kindness of his wife. And in the final scene, Stoner, having wandered into the park to watch kids playing baseball, re-enacts the shadow-play of an old movie half glimpsed on TV, by finding the ball at his feet, picking it up and winding up for what we know will be the last symbolic baseball pitch of his life. As the image freezes, Stoner leans over the fence watching the game, and we hear the romantic naivety of his lost youth expressed in the open-hearted candour of Bunny Berigan's title I Can't Get Started. Joy in work, joy in wife, joy in youth, Candide all over again, a panacea whose platitudinous nature is probably explained by the fact that it is the only one which ever seems to work. As for Moe Purtill, those who don't know who he was had better see Save The Tiger and find out. For not until they do understand who he was and his vast symbolic significance will they ever appreciate the tragedy of poor Harry Stoner.

Air Force
Dilys Powell

Any movie called Airport involves the threat of disaster; Wings means heroism, Airport means the bottom fals out of the plane. The question is: what does the addition of the word Concorde contribute? You can také **Airport '80: the Concorde** in two ways. You could say, after following the liable to attack by jet fighters and inclined to get in the way of military missiles. On the other hand you could say—that if, taking evasive action, it can outwit a missile which has been directed to choose it as target, can bring down a jet fighter, and cross the Alps with a large hole in its belly, Concorde is the safest aircraft in the world. I should like to add that it is also the most beautiful: a living arrow, a bird, an eagle among farmyard geese.

Having decided that, for the purposes of the film, disaster is threatened by agents other than a blizzard or a bomb, the author of the screen story has to fit up the place with suitable accessories. We have had a blocked runway, a stowaway, a pregnant stewardess and a would-be suicide planning to leave the insurance money for his wife (this in the first Airport). We have had a mid-air collision, a film star—Gloria Swanson, in fact—and a rescue pilot dangling from a helicopter Airport 1975).

This time we have a girl carrying documents implicating her lover in illegal arms sales: a deaf-and-dumb child; and a mother accompanying a live heart for transplant to her dying son (it won't keep, you know); the lot strung together by Jennings Lang, who was executive producer of Airport 1975. There are, you will observe, certain constant factors in these air-disaster fantasies. All the films derive from Arthur Hailey's best-selling novel Airport. They all have George Kennedy in the cast—he has been maintenance manager, runway clearer, airline executive and now a pilot who, with Alain Delon beside him at the controls, manages some pretty fancy stuff, bringing down a jet fighter in flames by firing his revolver out of the window, looping the loop and thus throwing the hand-baggage about the place and standing the passengers on their heads. The newcomers are a black jazz musician, a lady (Hiya, Martha Raye!) who prefers to spend the entire trip in the lavatory, and a young pair who, as the aircraft, by now out of control, heads for the Alps, pronounce themselves man and wife and receive a blessing from a fellow-passenger.

All, in fact, that is needed to complete the fun is the release from the baggage-compartment of a giant tarantula.

Nothing Fresh
Richard Mallett

It is at first a little surprising that JAMES CAGNEY should have chosen for his first independent production a good old "warm-hearted" sentimental story that might just as well have been chosen for him by any one of the big producing companies. Second thoughts suggest that he may be meaning to play safe with the box office the first time so as to strengthen his position for experi-menting later; but second thoughts also bring to mind the acknowledged truth that the equivalent aim in literature ("I'll make a name with popular stuff and then write good stuff") has defeated everybody that was ever tempted by it.

Meanwhile, Johnny Vagabond (Director: WILLIAM K. HOWARD), though not particularly inspired, is quite worth seeing if you like Mr. CAGNEY. The fable is one of those affairs about a passer-by—in this instance, a tramp—who stays just long enough to put everything right, and then ambles on again talking (or singing) about the delights of the open road and no responsibilities— the frame-work of so many hundreds of popular picaresque novels. The place is the little town of Plattsville, the time 1906, the trouble political graft and blackmail, the victim the old lady who owns and runs a local newspaper, the rescuer a tramp (Mr. CAGNEY) who used to be a newspaperman himself. You can work out the details for yourself from that; hardly any of them are fresh. The part of the old lady "introduces to the screen" a stage actress, GRACE GEORGE, who seems a little worried by the lights and has a tendency to load with infinite soft-eyed charm and wisdom even such a remark as "You'll find some old razors on the shelf in the closet"; but then it is, after all, that sort of part, and many will delight in it.

"Barely two weeks after Israeli commandos rescued the Air France hostage
About ten international film companies have approached the Israeli Governmer
production only; the supplicants have been given unt

53 MINUTES AT HOLLYWOOD

At 1.33 AM on Thursday, July 29, Sam Hofmeister, stocky, balding, rubicund, 59-year-old President of the Hofmeister Iron, Steel, Blouses, Real Estate & Soft Fruit Corporation of Pittsburgh, picked up the green onyx telephone that always stood beside his bidet at 10896 Alopecia Drive, Palm Springs, and dialled a nine-digit number.

2,896 miles away, in the art deco midtown Manhattan apartment of lithe, freckled company accountant Jason Gunnaf, 38, the phone rang. Gunnaf picked it up.

"Yes?" he said.

"Tell me," said Sam Hofmeister, "either I'm going mad, or didn't we buy a movie business some time last week? I seem to remember where we sold off a lot of old galleons to Borneo."

"I have it right here, Mr President sir," said Jason Gunnaf, rolling out from beneath small, liberated Puerto Rican soubrette Maria Sona y Lumiero, 22, and reaching for his bedside snaplock briefcase. "Also, we sold off six hundred horses to the Fassbinder Hamburger Corporation of New Jersey, plus seventy-six World War Two Brewster Buffalo fighters to the Free Malawi Front. It was a very nice deal, sir, we currently stand in at three million, four . . ."

"Never mind that!" snapped Hofmeister. "What I want to know is, do we still hold the bulk of the hardware, cameras, lights, all that crap?"

"As of this moment in time, sir," said Gunnaf, frantically thumbing the buff foolscap manila folder. "I am in a high-expectation situation vis-à-vis the potential . . ."

"That's okay," said Hofmeister, "hang on! Don't sell!"

"Don't *sell*?"

"Right!" said Hofmeister. He bit the end off a $1.95 Ramon Allones corona and spat it into the dog's shower cubicle. "We are gonna make a movie, Jason!"

It was 4.38, Eastern Standard Time.

___

IN TEL AVIV, it was 11.38 am. In the Defence Ministry, Shimon Peres looked across his walnut Peres Bros. (estab. 1963) desk at Chief of Staff Mordechai Gur. He was holding a telegram.

"It's Paramount," said the Minister of Defence, "they say they've got Paul Newman."

Gur stood up.

"Give me ten men," he said, "plus expenses. I'll have him out by six pm. Or for you, five-thirty!"

"You don't understand," said Peres. "They got him under contract. They want him to play you. They're asking me for the complete dossier on the Entebbe caper. What do I do?"

"Tell them they should go drop dead," snapped Gur. "I have already stated publicly that I shall be played by Warren Beatty or nobody. This Paul Newman is 51 years old."

"They say that unless they have the dossier within twenty-four hours, they will turn the whole thing into a musical starring Barbra Streisand as you," said Shimon Peres.

"Blackmail yet!" cried Gur. "Give in to it, Shimi, where will it end? Next thing you know, Warner Brothers'll make it a wacky comedy. I could come out Tatum O'Neal."

"I was just getting around to that," said Shimon Peres.

It was 11.51 am.

___

AT 6.30 AM, Californian time, Sam Hofmeister was in his Palm Springs office. His six-man board sat ranged in a semi-circle around him on identical avocado fauteuils. Standing before Hofmeister's desk was his coloured liftman, Claude. Hofmeister stared past him at the board.

"Paramount have Newman," he barked, "Warners have Bronson, Fellini has an octogenarian whore with a tin leg! We must strike while the iron is hot, gentlemen! A second to lose there ain't."

"How do you know all this, SH?" enquired an executive Vice-President.

"Intelligence reports," said Hofmeister. "My doctor has a doctor whose brother is one of Yizhak Rabin's doctor's doctors." He glanced up at the cleaner. "Claude, we go into production this afternoon. I want you should play Idi Amin."

"Betray my African brothers to line the pockets of the international capitalist Zionist nexus?" cried Claude. "Is there a percentage of the gross?"

"Plus residuals," replied Hofmeister, "also you get first crack at the wardrobe mistress. I understand she is a dead ringer for the young June Havoc."

"Who plays Mordechai Gur?" enquired a director.

"My son," said Hofmeister. "Who else?"

"Can he leave the practice?" said the director.

It was 6.44 am.

___

AT 2.15 PM, Californian time, three Hercules transports taxied down a runway carved out of the Death Valley sand, past a cardboard mock-up of Entebbe control tower swarming with extras. Above them hovered a Bell e-57 helicopter, full of Warner Brothers lawyers.

"Just say the word," wept the producer, "that's all I ask!"

The lawyers shook their heads

"You are currently," they said, "infringing eighty-seven different copyright laws. As co-signatories to the Berne Convention, the United States has a . . ."

"But it's *history*!" shrieked the director. "It is public domain!"

The lawyers glared at him bitterly.

"Public domain, public domain!" they mocked. "Do you have any inkling whereof you speak, schmuck? There are at least eighteen books currently on the

peration Entebbe is well on its way to becoming an epic of the wide screen.
r assistance. Israel's reply has been that it will offer help for one major
e end of this month to make their pitch."—*The Guardian*

Palm Springs, dawn, July 30. The numbers indicate the heroic stands taken by agents, immediately prior to negotiation.

entire action."

The lawyers sighed.

"We need time," they muttered.

"TIME! TIME! *You're* telling *me* about time?" screamed the Studio Chief. "Precious seconds are ticking away while we're spit-balling here! Do you realise Universal has already shot the Giscard d'Estaing nude sequence?"

The senior lawyer smiled.

"Relax," he said. "Their production came to a halt an hour ago. The French threatened to withdraw their Ambassador unless the scene was cut. Also, the West Germans took exception to the militaristic score that plays under the Bonn sequence; they say that if the past is continually harped on by Hollywood NATO is just an empty pretence and they might as well pull out and use the money to invade Poland."

"How do you know this?" gasped the Studio Head.

"My doctor," murmured the senior lawyer.

It was midnight in Kyoto.

Time was running out.

In Elstree, grown-up people were sobbing into their ermine hems.

stocks and about to be on the book-stands. Use two connected words from any of these—such as 'Good morning'—and you are staring down the wrong end of a multi-million dollar lawsuit! International law must be respected. Are we brigands?"

"Is there no way round this?" cried the producer. "Can we not negotiate with someone? Can we not do a deal?"

The lawyers shrugged, calculating their fees on small bright Sony pocket computers.

"I could have a quiet word with my wife's doctor," said one. "I think he knows someone."

It was 2.38 pm.

AT THE SAME MOMENT, not a hundred miles from that very spot, Columbia Pictures were having a not entirely dissimilar problem. The only difference was that *their* Hercules transports were taxi-ing past a cardboard mock-up of Nairobi control tower. Also, their lawyers were international lawyers.

"Election year," said the senior lawyer to the Studio Head. "That's your problem right there. When word gets out that Brando is to black up as Jomo Kenyatta, I do not see how the State Department can fail to intervene. I do not need to remind you of the overtones of Stepin Fetchit, nor of our present diplomatic interface with the Third World. Also, there is the question of oil prices: unless the Entebbe raid is shown as a complete failure, central heating as we know it will cease to exist."

"We have Omar Sharif," said the Studio Head, "as Moshe Dayan. Surely that goes some way to pre-empting Arab demands?"

"It's a vignette," said another lawyer, "a guest appearance. Also, its effect is worse than nullified by having Woody Allen as the British Prime Minister."

"There has to be comic relief," said the Studio Head. "The scene where he goes to see the Queen and is busting to tell her his troubles only she insists he eats the chicken soup first is central to the

AT 5.45 AM, Californian time, on Friday, July 30, three old Dakotas with "HERCULES" painted on the side in rough lettering landed at a tatty airstrip twenty miles outside Palm Springs, Cal. From these, some forty men sprang, many with the stethoscopes still swinging from their necks, and raced into the tin shed which served the airport as an administration building.

The controller woke up.

"It's ten bucks, including five minutes over Disneyland and souvenir tee-shirt inscribed I HAVE FLEW WITH JACK'S RED ARROWS. No cheques."

"Take it easy," barked Dr Nathan Hofmeister, pulling an airgun from beneath his operating gown, "this is a movie! Just relax and nobody will get, you know, hurt!"

They started shooting at 5.58. By 6.51 it was all over. In 53 minutes, while the major companies were still asleep, or locked in small legal print, or desperately raising funds and contacts and mutual doctors, or otherwise hamstrung by regulations, sensitivities, difficulties, fears, threats and assorted involvements, Hofmeister Iron, Steel, Blouses, Real Estate, Soft Fruit & Movies Inc. had the whole thing in the can, including strip sequences, dance routines, four hit songs, two explicit copulations, three conscious echoes of the Great Thirties, and a brief intermezzo in which a Kung Fu sheriff chopped down a thing from outer space.

After which the three Dakotas took off again, and disappeared into the dawn.

———————

AT 8.15 AM, Sam Hofmeister received the rapturous applause of his board.

"Incredible, SH!" they cried. "A coup! A master-stroke! A story to thrill the world for all eternity! A blow for freedom! A rebuff to all those who said heroism was dead! A..."

Sam Hofmeister held up his hand, and lowered his eyes modestly.

"A man's gotta do what a man's gotta do," he said.

"Can't you get him to smile a bit more, this is a musical after all."

My Short Life As An Assistant Cinema Manager
Andrew Barrow

Mr Webster, the Manager
"Have you been in cinemas before?"
Herbert, the Commissionaire
"D'take sugar in tea?"
Mr Webster
"Once you get used to the hours it's alright."
The Queen, on a newsreel
"I welcome you all here and feel sure we shall see some fine football."
Herbert
"Must be getting near sales time, Linda."
Jack Hawkins, in "League of Gentlemen"
"So relax, get a good night's sleep, and good luck!"
Linda, after the sales intermission
"Sold five tubs."
Nigel Patrick, in "League of Gentlemen"
"The lease is up, old darling. What now?"
Mr Webster
"What time will you have your lunch?"
Alice, counting money in ticket office
"Five and five's ten."
Lydia Sherwood in "League of Gentlemen"
"It's only because I love you so much."
One of Mr Webster's complaints about his job
"There's no social life."
Extract from letter from patron
"Why, oh why, must we have those terrible cartoon films? They are an insult to the intelligence of an adult audience."
Mr Webster on telephone to area manager who is about to go on holiday
"Going anywhere nice?"
Linda
"May I go for my lunch now?"
Mr Webster
"Monday and Tuesday I have off but then all my friends are at work."
Roger Livesey, in "League of Gentlemen"
"Let me see your menu cards for the week."
Memo from head office
"Any event which you consider may have publicity value should be notified to me immediately."
Nigel Patrick
"You know I suddenly feel rather sad."

A note left on Mr Webster's desk on his day off
''Please give these chocolates to Mrs Winmill, morning cleaner.''
Mr Morris, Relief Manager
''What are you *doing* in this business?''
Jack Hawkins
''Don't worry. I know old Bunny's capacity to the last ounce. By tomorrow morning this'll just be part of a monumental hangover.''
Mr Morris, listening to World Cup on his transistor
''By golly, they've equalized. It's going to be some game.''
Nigel Patrick
''Give them their money's worth at the trial, then flog your memoirs to the Sunday papers. There's always an angle.''
Mr Webster
''D'you still not want to be a manager?''
Bud Abbott, to Lou Costello
''Lay out my noo bloo suit.''
My statement
''There's no question of me wanting to be a manager. This is just a temporary job.''
A Trailer
''How d'you do. I am Alfred Hitchcock and I want to tell you about my latest motion picture, *Marnie*.''
Mr Webster
''Why, what's wrong with being a manager?''
The Queen
''I welcome you all here and feel sure we shall see some fine football.''
Herbert
''I owned two chip shops before the war in Warrington.''
Jack Hawkins
''So relax, get a good night's sleep, and good luck!''
Label on film can
''Inflammable film—Worthless if damaged.''
Alice, to patron who has just said "What?"
''I don't know what you've been taught but I've been taught 'Pardon' or 'I beg your pardon'.''
Nigel Patrick
''The lease is up, old darling. What now?''
Mr Webster's lunch
''I had a steak pudding. Once you got through the suet 'twasn't bad.''
Lydia Sherwood
''It's only because I love you so much.''
Mr Webster
''The trip over to Leicester Square makes a bit of an outing. I'm here from 9.30.''
Roger Livesey
''Let me see your menu cards for the week.''
Mr Webster, on telephone to manager of another cinema
''It's a bit risky, isn't it? If you get any more you have to have them kicking around the office floor and that's where the trouble starts.''
Nigel Patrick
''You know I suddenly feel rather sad.''
Mr Webster
''No, I wouldn't mind hot soup in the winter. That's a good gag. Get Herbert with a big ladle.''
Linda
''Oh no! I just go upstairs to the staff room and have my sandwiches.''

"No, I'm his elder brother!"

Jack Hawkins
"Don't worry. I know old Bunny's capacity to the last ounce. By tomorrow morning this'll just be part of a monumental hangover."

Mr Webster, on telephone to home of ex-usherette
"Oh, I see. Mmmm. No. Well, will you ask her to return the overall? Is she coming back at all? Will you ask her to return the overall anyhow?"

Nigel Patrick
"Give them their money's worth at the trial, then flog your memoirs to the Sunday papers. There's always an angle."

Delivery man
"Are you going to sign this, chief, or the bloke downstairs?"

Mr Morris, relief manager
"I sometimes wonder if there is such a thing as an interesting job."

Alice
"Mr Webster's just been on the phone. He said 'What sort of day have we had, Alice?' "

Bud Abbott, to Lou Costello
"Lay out my noo bloo suit."

Mr Webster's description of his two days off
"Yes, very nice, thank you. Quite nice indeed."

Herbert, having somehow upset Linda
"Listen, Linda. I said nothing!"

Mr Webster
"I was on the train at 8.20 this morning. Sunbury."

The Trailer
"How d'you do. I am Alfred Hitchcock and I would like to tell you about my latest motion picture, *Marnie*."

Mr Webster
"Count the ice lollies that are left. Tip them out and count them."

The Queen
"I welcome you all here and feel sure we shall see some fine football."

Mr Webster, commenting on Herbert's absence
"He often does that. He'll turn up again in four or five days' time."

The lonely projectionist
"That music? It's the start of the big feature."

Mr Webster
"I've just had head office on the phone. They say they don't want your services any longer."

The Last Australian Hero

The filming of "The Adventures of Barry McKenzie" by **Barry Humphries**

Commissionaire (to old lady who has been examining all the placards). "STEP INSIDE, LADY, AND SEE THE MOST MARVELLOUS——"

Old Lady. "OH, ARE THERE MORE INSIDE? WELL, WELL, I THINK THESE ARE QUITE MOVING ENOUGH FOR *ME*, YOU KNOW."

Mucky Pup ("*It's Hilarious!! Watch your friends' faces!!!*") is a curious substance sold in novelty emporia and Tottenham Court Road joke shops. Manufactured in Tokyo, it is a convincingly glistening dollopy scroll of bright brown plastic which people with an irrepressible sense of humour place mischievously on their friends' drawing room Axminsters. If there is a dog or a kiddie around you can imagine what a load of fun is in store for the Mucky Pup purchaser.

On a sunny January morning in Earl's Court a group of Australian film makers could be found scattering about twenty pounds' worth of factory fresh Mucky Pup on the immaculate pavements of kangaroo valley. A street scene in *The Adventures of Barry McKenzie* was about to be shot and our chosen location just didn't look authentically English. To make matters worse it wasn't even raining, and an adjacent phone booth was conspicuously operable. In fact, it must have been the last unvandalised public telephone in London. Clearly the person whose job it had been to discover film locations which typified English squalor and desuetude had blundered badly, and the Australian designer and his assistants were frantically sprinkling fish bones on the footpath and piling overflowing garbage cans in people's doorways.

In the back of a van our graphics designer was hastily writing a sign which said

"Remember, Leprosy Inoculations are Compulsory" while highly paid extras attired themselves as bowler-hatted beggars and starving stockbrokers. Disguised as a Cypriot crone, an actress waited patiently at the upper window of a derelict dwelling we had requisitioned and suitably defaced, for the cameras to roll. When Barry McKenzie stumbled out of his taxi (which had taken him from Heathrow to Earl's Court via Stonehenge) it was this lady's task to eject the brimming contents of a chamber pot into the street below whilst another extra, picturesquely disguised as a beefeater, rummaged hungrily in a faked-up dustbin. But still it hadn't rained. The weather was positively bloody Australian, in fact.

The enormous cost of making the real England look really English was borne by the Australian tax payer. Long before, when it was first proposed that a major motion picture be made of Barry McKenzie's scabrous comic strip adventures the problem had been who was going to foot the bill. One of us knew the ageing whizz-kid who wrote the then Prime Minister's speeches, and a daring ruse was hit upon. Affairs of State in Canberra being what they are, it was rightly assumed that the PM rarely had time to check his copy before holding forth to the House, and so it was that one fine morning he overheard himself pledging a quarter of a million dollars of the taxpayer's money to finance a courageous new film venture which would spearhead the fledgling local cinema industry and put Australia in the centre of the cultural map where it belonged. The money duly changed hands with a murmur of incredulity in the Press and a rancorous howl of protest from Australian film critics who all had the grubby and time-worn screenplays of their own cinema epics stuffed in the bottom drawers of their copy desks and naturally resented two hundred and fifty thousand of the green folding stuff finding its way into rival pockets.

The Art of the Film is a serious business, even in Australia, and public monies should properly be spent on cinema dramatisations of aboriginal folklore, or "relevant" and "viable" social documents about the agony and the ecstasy of "real" Australians in settings of kangaroo-infested bushland or gleaming Sydney skyscrapers. Fantasy, humour and downright ribaldry were the enemies of antipodean culture. Barry McKenzie might achieve a cheap and contemptible success at the box office, but in doing so it would demolish our international reputation as a race of suave sophisticates. People might even think we were *all* common.

Hardly believing our luck, we leapt aboard the first plane out of Sydney to spend the money so generously entrusted to us, but not before a little man from the Ministry of the Environment, Aborigines and the Arts (a cinderella portfolio customarily assigned to the Party dunce) had rushed across the tarmac and uttered the amazing line: "I hope you won't be using any Australian *colloquialisms* in this movie of yours!" We assured him that our artistic intentions were impeccable, not to say ponderous, and that no one viewing the finished product would thereafter suspect Australians of vernacular usage. We said something like that anyway, and privately wondered if any of those chastely spoken experts on the environment or the abbos had ever glanced at our script.

The yarn we were about to spin on celluloid concerned the vicissitudes of a foul-mouthed Australian virgin (or latent heterosexual) marooned in London and prey to a horde of perverted rapacious Poms. The hero, of course, bore the name of Barry, antecedent of Monty Python's Bruce and the popular forename of most likeable and intelligent Australians. According to an encyclopaedia of Christian names, Barry is Old Welsh for "a spear". Time and long usage have rusted and blunted its meaning, however.

In photographing Barry McKenzie's misadventures it was necessary for our expatriate film company to acquire a London office and a vehicle. Thus, within a week of arriving in London, we bought a second-hand van which irretrievably packed up outside Harrods and might still be there, and we rented a flat in Soho which enjoyed the propinquity of Wardour Street without the advantages of hot water or electric light. Although the landlord was a Greek and the car salesman a fellow Australian, we were already experiencing at first hand the commonplace discomforts of English life. In a grisly fashion, life was beginning to imitate art, and Barry McKenzie's fictitious persecutors beleaguered his biographers. The pinguid landlord's name was, astoundingly enough, Mr. Damocles (which is old Greek for Barry) and the coin-operated telephone in our jerry-built high rise apartment jangled constantly with plaintive calls from previous Pakistani tenants demanding refundment of their £200 deposit.

One of the film's most important props was an elaborate meter which was to adorn Barry McKenzie's hotel room. Since it was supposed only to accept pound notes and emit flashing lights the machine had to be specially constructed and a quiet and ingenious little Englishman was given a very large sum of the Australian taxpayers' money to build it. We never saw him again, though in all probability he went into the accommodation business in Earl's Court, profitably equipped.

It still hadn't rained. London had rarely looked lovelier in January. Short of shooting the film in our own flat we were at our wits' end to convey the ghastliness of English life, when Miss Undine Voide turned up at the Savoy. Miss Voide worked for the Dept of the Environment in Sydney and had been assigned the onerous task of flying over and checking up on how we were spending the cash. The heart-breaking pleas from the Pakistanis were now interspersed with telephone calls from this suspicious hireling of the Australian Government who was demanding to see our accounts and, worst of all, our rushes. Luckily we had a fair bit "in the can" as they say in Hollywood, but try as we might, a few proscribed colloquialisms had somehow crept into Barry McKenzie's dialogue.

The next fortnight was spent hiding the film from Miss Voide and simultaneously granting her access to *some* of our impeccable bookkeeping. Luckily she was more interested in staying at the Savoy and shopping at Fortnums on her expense account then sabotaging our work of art, so that she was somehow sent back to Sydney with glowing accounts of our progress and integrity without once meeting a single member of the production company.

Meanwhile there were ominous rumblings from a famous airline which has certain Australian associations. We proposed to film part of Barry's trip in one of their planes and they were deeply distressed by a line of dialogue in which the hero, in response to the hostess's "Is there anything I can do for you sir?", bluntly proposes a spot of dalliance in the airborne toilet. A celebrated Melbourne brewery was likewise apprehensive lest their distinguished product become linked in the public's mind with such a coarse and undesirable consumer as Barry McKenzie.

However, in the face of injunctions, boycotts, threats, and outraged protests a film was made. It opened in Australia a year ago to a scream of abuse from the critics. In eight weeks, thanks to our colonial customers, the government got all its money back and they have now made so much profit that the Department has been able generously to subsidise other film makers; our talented critics amongst them. *The Adventures of Barry McKenzie* is now unleased upon an unsuspecting Pom public. Columbia Warner thought it might be a good idea to add subtitles: e.g.

BARRY (to irritating Englishman): "I hope all your chooks turn to emus and kick your dunnee down."

SUBTITLE:

"*I hope your poultry transmute into ostriches and demolish your outdoor earth closet.*"

We tried it but there wasn't enough room left on the screen for the picture. Alas, as for the Mucky Pup, it ended up on the cutting room floor.

Rod Steiger
talks to David Taylor

He's glad to see the sun's out at last, he's Rod Steiger and he's hungry for something nourishing and Chinese, as far as we can make out above the din of aeroplanes over Twickenham studios. Useful courtesies to piece together in the droning confusion since the man who strides purposefully off the set is unrecognisable with his head shaved nearly bald and a trim, triangular beard gummed to his chin, like a face from a Wanted poster with extras crayonned in. We pile hurriedly into the welcome hush of a chauffeured motor, burble backwards into the gatepost, and set off at the second attempt for Richmond where there's a spot does an excellent Peking duck with all the pancakey trim and, as he goes on, that's far better than any canteen, today especially when they have a hundred or so extras in to do the House of Lords scene, first fine day this week by the way, isn't it? Certainly, we say, and hello.

You have to concentrate talking to Rod Steiger who, apart from having the shivers if described as burly (though it's not unfit and is, as he acknowledges "better than fat") talks readily, wittily, animatedly and haphazardly, impatient of showbiz glitter, anxious to allow the conversation to wander where it will. Off duty, he does not put on any act, please understand that. I forget how we got on to guns but he now demonstrates the principles of marksmanship, does an impression of Wyatt Earp's draw and swinging aim, using a picked spare rib; and then attaches that to a brief résumé on Van Gogh and his underrated brother, Theo Van Gogh; blending it imperceptibly into the ins and outs of a mortgage and the odd way people are seated across the floor of the Upper House. Sweetheart: that's another word people always attribute to him. Sweetheart this and now hear that, sweetheart, they say. Like Steiger was for real the gumchewing tough-guy sheriff from *In The Heat Of The Night*. Either that or they've seen *The Pawnbroker* and imagine he must be Jewish. That's his own favourite of his films, incidentally. Challenging, because the man didn't want to be alive. First thing Steiger did was cut one third of all his scripted dialogue because he argued that if a man wanted simply to exist without being noticed, he wouldn't do much talking.

The thing is to work yourself up to the pitch where you sympathise wholly with the character; if it's not convincing, it's nothing. A really good film should have some kind of social comment inherent in it, Steiger believes, but its main business must remain at entertainment. If audiences want a lecture they should go to college. Hero or villain, it's the exploration of character that counts. He's no time for any actor who is more interested in his own narcissistic image than in exploring a plausible character. And that's not to say that he, Steiger, despite an awesome list of character-acting triumphs, has not made some instantly-forgettable duds. He'd appreciate it, too, if they would stop re-running some of them on TV, sweetheart. Sorry, couldn't resist it. How's the duck?

Listen, acting is a job and you have to work at it like any other. You don't sit about mooning over the techniques of so-called method-acting. Personally, he's not able to idle about for more than a couple of months at a stretch without getting itchy for more work. Earning the money you're mister, resting you're a schmuck, you hear them say that. Another thing, you hear people in an elevator talking over why they don't plan on seeing the movie you're in; and it's terrible. Of course he minds critics, nobody's really that insensitive they don't. Fine, so long as the criticism stays professional, just don't get personal, that's all.

Anyhow. So the new film is about a man who just wants to live quietly with his family but the whole thing blows up in his face when his wife and child are accidentally shot dead by a British soldier in Belfast. Hell-bent on revenge, he plots to blow up Parliament and himself during the State Opening ceremonies. Yes it's a delicate area, but yes it is also deeply fascinating for an actor to explore the man's obsession. Instinct leads you to suppose that an actor of Rod Steiger's obvious intelligence will not allow the film to be reduced to a tasteless exploitation of the Irish mess. He most certainly does not believe that films should make use of human sickness without constructive purpose.

Nor does he believe in rushing his lunch. Having established to his satisfaction that the vibrations were right, he'd talked expansively into overtime. We shot back into the car, steered cleanly into the studios again and watched him adjust his wing-collar, throw the hidden switch and perform, unrecognisable again.

"I'll bet Peter Fonda eats his greens."

THIS MEANS WAR MOVIES!

Stanley Reynolds surrenders to the latest advances in the cinema

"In private life he's a major."

Any sweet innocents who thought they were seeing at least the hint of a gleam of a dawn of reason and non-violence when the news came that Cowboy and Indian films were no longer box office and no one was making Gunsmoke and Injun films for the telly any more, well, they better not read any further. The big news from the cinema world is war movies.

This will come as a surprise to anyone who has been seated in front of a television set man and boy these past twenty years. My own children are convinced the Second World War is still going on and who can blame them? It is going on in just about every other film they see on the box. Some time ago one of them, just having mastered reading but slow still on history, came racing in to me with tears of cynical laughter pouring down his chubby cheeks. He thrust a full page advert at me.

"Look at this!" he said. "Can you imagine anyone stupid enough to go on this?"

It was an advert for the Japanese airlines. Some sort of all-in holiday. He thought it was yet another Jap trick, like that sneak attack on Pearl Harbor. When I told him the war was over, had indeed been over since 1945, he looked at me in disbelief. And why not? Only the evening before he had been watching some Hollywood Marine chew the pin off a hand-grenade, shout, "Eat death, yellow dwarfs!" and hurl it at a Nip machine-gun nest. Someone was telling him lies.

The most surprising bit about all the new war movies is that someone actually feels we need any new ones. Any television viewer would think we had rather too many of them as it is. And yet the biggest budget films now in the making or about to be released are about the war or wars. There is Sir Richard Attenborough re-creating the battle at Arnhem in *A Bridge Too Far*. Jack Higgins's best-selling novel about a Nazi commando squad attempting to kidnap Sir Winston Churchill, *The Eagle Has Landed*, has just been filmed. Gregory Peck has signed a contract to play General Douglas

MacArthur in a film biography. Peter Bogdanovich, the infant prodigy of Hollywood, is now collecting stars and money to produce a film called *Big Red One*, the story of the US Army's First Infantry Division in World War Two. Ernest Hemingway's rather scatty novel about hunting Nazi U-boats in the Caribbean during the late hostilities, *Islands in the Stream* is being filmed with George C. Scott in the starring role. Francis Ford Coppola is doing a surrealistic war film on Vietnam called *Apocalypse Now*. *Dog Soldiers*, another Vietnam movie, is being made. Charlton Heston stars in a newly released film about the air war in the Pacific called *Midway*. The list could go on.

In some cases the movie world's new love affair with realism is costing mind-spinning sums. The battle of Arnhem in *A Bridge Too Far* is going for 25 million dollars, which is probably more than the real fight cost. Added to this the poor extras who were hired to play the British commandos had to go through commando training so they would look right. The production costs of Sam Peckinpah's retreat of the Wehrmacht across Russia after the battle of Stalingrad, a just-finished film called *Cross of Iron*, have not been released, but Panzer tanks don't come cheap these days. Adolf is perhaps squatting on the coals right now, tearing his hair, chewing the carpet and complaining to Himmler that if he only had Peckinpah's budget . . .

Old soldiers may want to pause here and wonder at the pay some of the Hollywood soldiers are getting for fighting around Arnhem. Robert Redford is being paid 2.3 million dollars and James Caan is getting one million. Think of the nylons and the chewing gum a G.I. could have bought with that sort of loot.

The craziest situation, however, is the filming of *Apocalypse Now*. Because Vietnam itself is now under new management Francis Ford Coppola, the director, has had to go to the jungles of the Luzon peninsula in the Philippines. The Luzon, of course, will ring a bell with all veterans of old WWII war movies. It was here that a host of Hollywood GIs held off the Nips with the ammo running short. Indeed, Francis Ford Coppola better get out of the jungle soon be-

cause no doubt Gregory Peck will be renting it next for his Douglas MacArthur movie. But the weirdness of filming *Apocalypse Now* in the Luzon comes because the Filipino army is actually fighting a real war there. It is not a big war, a low budget job in fact with an unknown director and no stars, but it is a war with real bullets.

I am never too sure about real wars these days, but it seems the Muslim extremists have taken to the jungles in the Philippines and here is Francis Ford Coppola making this film and trying to borrow helicopters from the Filipino army and the Filipino army actually rather wants to use these helicopters to get these Muslim extremists; if, that is, it is indeed the Muslim extremists they are fighting; it wouldn't be the Muslim moderates would it? You never can tell these days.

Which, of course, brings us to the reason they are making all these war movies. *Apocalypse Now* is the odd man out because it is about Vietnam. *Dog Soldier* is not actually about the war in Vietnam but about a soldier returning from that war. *Apocalypse Now*, the first major Vietnam war film since John Wayne's abortive *Green Berets*, is also only sort of about Vietnam. Students of literature will perhaps be amazed when they learn that it is based on Joseph Conrad's *The Heart of Darkness* and is about a soldier sent to assassinate Marlon Brando who plays an army officer who has gone mad and is fighting everyone in sight.

The reason for bringing back 1939–45 in a big budget way is that you can actually kill Nazis in them in a very violent manner and no one will mind. The Red Indians are no good any more as baddies. Even the Japs, once such a good source for war movies, smiling sinisterly, all teeth and spectacles, are no longer acceptable because they are not white and racism might creep into it. *Midway* is a film about the air war and so it will be more or less machines getting shot down. That's a bit cleaner than bayoneting the Nips like in the old films. And I'll bet the Nips don't smile when they machine-gun a fellow parachuting from his aircraft in *Midway* like they did in *Wake Island*, that great 1940s US Marine *v*. Tojo's Hordes, which had Brian Donlevy, as the Marine commander, saying, "Send us more Japs," when he was asked by his superiors if he needed anything.

Even the Germans, who you might think must feel a bit sensitive about the way the war never seems to end, are not overly troubled about World War Two flicks. This is because the baddies are not really Germans, they are Nazis. If you were a science fiction writer and you were hunting about for a nice name for a race of really bad guys you could not do any better than Nazis. It is only an abbreviation for National Socialists but it has a marvellously evil ring about it. Hitler himself, who was by all accounts not too clever about these things—he had his boys dress in black, didn't he?—did not like the name Nazi. But there they are, dressed in black with death skulls on their caps, and Robert Redford can pocket 2.3 million dollars and shoot them until the 25 million dollar budget runs out and no one will be offended.

If Hitler hadn't invented them Hollywood would have had to do it. Hitler, it should be said, had better taste in films. *It Happened One Night*, that merry comedy of the 1930s starring Clark Gable, was his favourite film, which he used to keep re-running up there at the Eagle's Nest. It must have been pretty boring for his house guests but it rather destroys theories about cinema violence breeding violence in the streets. World War Three isn't going to be started by anyone who spends his time watching World War Two in a cinema.

83

After Star Wars, what?
Barry Took

Even before it opened in Britain, **Star Wars** had been hailed as a breakthrough in cinema entertainment, the biggest money-spinner of all time and fun for the whole family. As there is nothing left to say about it, I am inaugurating the Took patent do-it-yourself film reviewing kit. All you do is tick the appropriate box, and lo and behold you're a critic.

I liked *Star Wars* because it's
- [ ] wonderful
- [ ] marvellous
- [ ] Miss Annabelle Lee

I will go again because
- [ ] I loved it
- [ ] I couldn't take it all in at one viewing
- [ ] I fell asleep

My family thought it was better than
- [ ] *2001 A Space Odyssey*
- [ ] Handel's *Messiah*
- [ ] A visit to a Belgian horse butchers

Those robots were so cute they reminded me of
- [ ] Sir Keith Joseph and Margaret Thatcher
- [ ] *The Two Ronnies*
- [ ] Two robots

It'll be surprising if *Star Wars* isn't the picture of the year, but what else is there in store?

Well, I don't know but here's my Preview '78—or—Films I Have A Horrible Suspicion We're Going To Be Seeing In The Year To Come.

...RM

...Story of Wally, a rogue whale
...impregnates Barbra Streisand
...out her noticing) and, unable
...ce the competition of her
...ving stardom, leaps out of his
...at the San Diego Zoo and
...rns to the Pacific where he's
...d by pollution.

...N CAMP

...Russell's story of how Hitler's
...osexual love affair with
...mel loses him the war.
...mel is played by Rudolph
...eyev, and Montgomery by
...r Pears.

...R WARS II

...Minelli and Robert de Niro
...shooting a sequel to *New*
...*, New York,* but there's a dis-
...ement about billing.

...CIVILISATION FAMILY

...n, Pop, two kids and a dog
...e their log cabin in the Rockies
...set up home in Los Angeles.
...e they find it's not as idyllic as
...thought and have to fight
...g, muggers, junkies, the
...son family, child porn-
...phers, movie producers, and
...r endemic hazards of city life
...re they at last come to terms
...the Great Indoors and lock
...nselves in the wardrobe.

**...HOULDN'T HAPPEN TO A
...GE**

...ky goings on when Venice
...DRY (!) just before the tourist
...son starts. The Doge (Peter
...nov) is at his wit's end (Roy
...ear). How are they going to fill
...Grand Canal with water? Well,
...ocal council (Irene Handl,
...e Milligan) are sitting at a café
...king Chianti when suddenly the
...n crier, Luigi (Terry Thomas)
...this novel idea . . .

**...LAST REMAKE OF BEAU
...JMMEL**

...ky, swivel-eyed funster, Marty
...lman is Beau Brummel's twin
...her, Hümmel Brummel, and

has to save the day when Beau
appears at Court in baggy britches.
With Peter Ustinov as the Prince
Regent, Irene Handl as Mrs Fitz-
herbert, Roy Kinnear as Mr Fitz-
herbert and Terry Thomas as the
Duke of Wellington. Narrated by
the wacky Huw Wheldon.

UP YOUR PIPE

If you laughed at *The Confessions
Of A Plumber*, you'll scream at this
laugh-an-epoch spin off from the
people who kept the British film
industry alive until all the money
had gone and the cleaners had
stolen the carpet. (N.B. This is a
silent film. It doesn't have pictures
either.)

THE LOWERING INFERNO

Someone at a preview lights a
cigarette while sitting next to
Alexander Walker.

PORN COCKTAIL

After the dirty versions of *Alice In
Wonderland, Cinderella* and *The
Wizard of Oz*, there are bound to
be more porno films based on

children's stories coming our way,
such as *The Old Woman Who
Lived In A Shoe*, which helps us to
understand more about foot
fetishists. (See also *Puss In Boots*.)
Midshipman Easy, a new slant on
Captain Marryat's yarn. *Snow
White*—a bad batch of LSD turns
normal men into gibbering dwarfs.
Dick Whittington—a boy's love for
his cat takes a tumble on the outskirts of London when he hears the
fateful words—turn again Whittington. He does and things start to
happen in a *big* way. And finally,
what will undoubtedly be the *biggie*
of 1978—

ANY DAY NOW

The story of a shy, young film critic
mocked by the older and wiser
reviewers for his gaucheness but
who, in spite of their jibes and
vulgar horseplay, wins through in
the end and actually gets to sit next
to Alan Brien at a preview. In the
end, his eyesight and reason gone,
he sits alone in a deserted cinema
mumbling phrases like "psychological insight", "Bertolucci",
"landscape of the mind", and
"tits".

The Petrified Forest
E. V. Lucas

Except for those who liked the play and want to see the same emotions screened, I should say that *The Petrified Forest* is a very poor title; for the first suggestion it brings to the mind is scientific rather than human. ''Hullo!'' we say, ''fossiliferous stuff'', and look for a less instructive or even less forbidding programme. But we should be wrong.
The Petrified Forest has nothing really to do with wood that has become stone, except that symbolism is drawn from it; it has to do with the adventures and visions of that wandering fantast (a little like the central character of *Eyeless in Gaza*), *Alan Squier*, played by LESLIE HOWARD, and the franknesses and ambitions of *Gabrielle Maple*, played by BETTE DAVIS, and their plight when the killer, *Duke Mantee*, played by HUMPHREY BOGART, comes along and changes philosophical conjecture into reality. We may not believe in quite such coolness as the lovers display under the threat of death; or that the rain of bullets, when the firing does at last set in, would be so ineffective; but the hero starts far more hares than films are accustomed to, and that is much to the good. Also LESLIE HOWARD has a persuasive way with him and BETTE DAVIS has exactly caught the matter-of-fact eagerness of the Arizona innkeeper's daughter with French blood in her (and radiance added), while the expression of expectation and delight on the face of her grandfather (CHARLEY GRAPEWIN), when he is assured that some real

''killin''' is bound to set in, is something to rejoice in and remember. But I think it highly improbable (*a*) that *Alan Squier* did not have any money, and (*b*) that he would order a meal without saying so and offering to do work in return; and I shall always regret that he and *Gabrielle's* lover did not participate in a fight for the girl, in which blows were exchanged and *Alan* won. But we cannot have everything, and *The Petrified Forest*, as it stands, is an excellent film.

Hemingway and Lermonton
Richard Mallett

Readers of ERNEST HEMINGWAY'S novel will not recognize very much of it in *To Have and Have Not* (Director: HOWARD HAWKS). There is the sea-fishing episode, and the juxtaposition of the tough competent man of action and the uneasy blowhard (a situation noticeable in very many Hemingway stories); and there is a great deal of more or less self-conscious Hemingwayese in the dialogue, so that sometimes one feels as if one is listening to a parody. But the pre-war story has been shifted to Martinique in 1940, and we get Vichy and counter-Vichy, fat Gestapo and lean Resistance, and the end is one of those last-minute escapes... However, as you know, the main excuse for the film, the peg for all the publicity, the reason for most of the queues, is LAUREN BACALL, of the hoarse voice (artificially acquired), the ''down under'' look (conscious and cultivated), and a certain natural piquancy of expression. She stands up under her reputation pretty well. I don't maintain that she justifies all the posters say; nobody could be so ''sultry'', so ''sensational'' as all that with so comparatively little to go on; but

No Offence
Richard Mallett

For good emotional acting see BETTE DAVIS in *Now, Voyager* (Director: IRVING RAPPER). Here is the transformation (with the help psychiatry) of a fat, gloomy, dow spinster with a nervous breakdov into a spectacularly smart, slim, cheerful young lady of irresistibl charm. Miss DAVIS takes the obvious chances well in the early part of the picture, achieving a n able intensity of hysteria; but she also excellent in the more delica portrayal of the transitional stag when the ''fledgling'' (as the psychiatrist calls her) is timidly testing her social powers and discovering with astonishment t she is taken at her face value, admired, liked and even loved.
The story of all this is ma unexpectedly absorbing by goo performances from all the playe concerned: PAUL HENREID as th married man with whom the ''fledgling'' spends a week-end Rio, GLADYS COOPER as her domineering mother, CLAUDE R as the psychiatrist, and many ir smaller parts.

she does all right what the story demands, which is mostly to throv off brief, tough cynicisms with enormous casualness, preferably from a lounging position, at the same time performing business with cigarettes, matches or drinks. For that matter much of HUMPHREY BOGART'S performance can be accounted for under this head, though he does get quite a bit of action too. Then there is the Martinique background (slatted screens, sliding striped shadows), and—for me the most interesting thing in the picture—the legendary composer of ''Stardust'' in person, HOAGY CARMICHAEL, excellent and in good swing form as a café pianist.
The film is in the line of *Casablanca* and *Passage to Marseille*: one can recognize that similar tested ingredients have been carefully mixed, in the hope of repeating a success. But it is the new ingredient, Miss BACALL (with her trailing clouds of publicity), that will really be responsible for the success of this one.

Disney Heights
E. V. Lucas

I had the privilege of visiting the WALT DISNEY studio and meeting the magician in person. The creator of the most influential animal in the world I found to be a smiling easy-going young man in shirt-sleeves and a light-blue jersey, who, as he sat back in his chair with his long legs on the desk and smoked a cigarette, gave no sign of being concerned with his constant and far-reaching activities. But with the actual drawing of his pictures he personally has long ceased to be concerned. The assistants of the Old Masters in the studios of Florence, Venice and Rome took the brush only for certain parts of the work; but WALT DISNEY'S huge staff of young men in this pleasant sunny mountainous corner of Hollywood draw every line, of which there are many thousands. Not, however, until the Master has passed the scenario.

Anyone who says that the production of these animated cartoons and Silly Symphonies is done by machinery is ill-instructed; they are all "done by hand". I saw the draughtsmen at work, all in shirt-sleeves and blue jerseys, all smoking cigarettes, and in spite of the monotony of their task, all jolly; and that it is monotonous will be appreciated when I say that hours and hours of diligence on the part of one artist with ten underlings are able, in a week, to account for only half a minute of screen time. A laborious beginning for so much liveliness!

I forgot to ask these young men if, as they add line to line, they ever give a thought to the resultant laughter as far away as Labrador, Valparaiso, Cape Town, London, Adelaide and Buenos Aires.

The multiplication of drawings is, however, simple; what seemed to me more intricate was the wedding of every moment to a musical note, a mystery explained to me with great patience but not, I fear, to much purpose. Simpler was the exhibition given by the gentleman—I think his name was SHAW—who talks the baby-talk and whose voice is with me yet. I remember him also as offering at last an opportunity to vary the standard American courtesy. "Pleased to have heard you," I said as we parted.

English readers will be surprised to learn that *Mickey Mouse* as a money-maker is more powerful off the screen than on. It is the various toys and nursery accessories bearing his effigy that produce, I was told, the real revenue. No self-respecting American child, for instance, would be without a *Mickey Mouse* watch, even though it sets his parents back a smacker and a half.

Brief Encounter
Richard Mallett

I highly recommend the new NOEL COWARD production *Brief Encounter* (Director: DAVID LEAN), which I think is perfectly admirable in almost every way. It has the rare and outstanding quality of being adult throughout, adult in theme as well as in treatment; and it has a most exquisitely sensitive and moving performance by CELIA JOHNSON as a provincial wife contentedly married until she casually meets a man, also contentedly married, with whom she falls passionately in love. She "didn't think such violent things could happen to ordinary people"; she has a sense of guilt at feeling so intensely, away from her husband (who is a good, considerate, pleasant man); and at the end, agreeing that "the furtiveness and lying outweigh the happiness we might have together", she allows the dangerous connection to be broken, hoping her misery will pass. The sad little story is beautifully done, with only a fraction too much emphasis on the "comic relief" (STANLEY HOLLOWAY, JOYCE CAREY) and much quite first-rate detail. Try not to miss *Brief Encounter*.

The Browning Version
Richard Mallett

That *The Browning Version* (Director: Anthony Asquith) consists essentially of an excellent acting performance by Michael Redgrave is hardly to be contested, but it offers a great deal besides. Terence Rattigan has expanded his short play into a film of average feature length, and the additional scope is well used. There are classroom scenes in the school that are reminiscent, with the natural difference of emphasis, of those in the Swedish film *Frenzy*; and also reminiscent of *Frenzy* is the opening, which introduces us to the school by following the headlong progress of a boy late for morning prayers. But that difference of emphasis is all-important, for of course our sympathies here are engaged less on the side of the wincing pupils than on that of the embittered master. It is the profoundly disappointed, humourless Andrew Crocker-Harris of the stifled emotions and the precise finicking enunciation who is the dominatingly pathetic figure in this story, and Mr Redgrave's portrait of him is first-rate. The climax, when a kindly-disposed boy gives him as a parting present "the Browning version" of the *Agamemnon* of Aeschylus (of which Crocker-Harris had himself started a translation in his brilliant, hopeful youth) is genuinely moving. I'm not quite happy about the later scene at the speech day, where we are asked to believe that sympathetically loud and even enthusiastic applause follows the retiring master's—let's face it—thoroughly uncharacteristic public confession of all-round failure; even if this were convincing, it would be wrong, I think, because it provides another *kind* of climax. But the picture as a whole is a distinguished and entertaining one, giving good acting opportunities to other people in smaller parts and successfully capturing the atmosphere and "feel" of an enclosed community.

THE PROBLEM OF CROCKER-HARRIS
R. G. G. Price

These notes on Mr. Terence Rattigan's new film, *The Browning Version,* are intended to suggest solutions to only a few of the difficulties raised by this puzzling work. They can pretend neither to completeness nor to finality; but if I have succeeded in clearing some of the ground for other workers I am content. It is by the pooling of ideas that scholarship progresses.

After eighteen years Crocker-Harris is forced by ill-health to retire from teaching Classics to the Lower Fifth. Judging by the style of the women's dresses, the film has a contemporary setting, and if we place his retirement in 1950, we must place his appointment in 1932. As he joined the staff direct from Oxford he would have been a contemporary there of Mr. Auden, Mr. Spender and Mr. Betjeman. It is true that he looks more than forty; but what we see of his wife makes it probable that he aged young. Pedantic, chill and terrifying, he is known as the "Himmler of the Lower Fifth". His scholarly little jokes, his fanatical emphasis on accuracy and his sarcasm belong to a past age. I suggest that this is because, while at Oxford, he may have been influenced by the Victorianism of Mr. Betjeman, and feels for the great Victorian schoolmasters an enthusiasm that Mr. Betjeman's other disciples feel for encaustic tiles and stained-glass windows.

As a young man, Crocker-Harris had begun a translation of the Agamemnon in couplets. The film contains no quotation from this and we can only guess what it was like. It might have been contemporary in inspiration, that is to say, Audenesque, yet it seems more likely that his Victorian pose would have extended to choice of verse-forms, and it is significant that when we first see him in action he is inciting his Form to turn the first three verses of 'The Lady of Shalott'' into Latin verse; we are probably intended to see in him an amateur of popular Victorian poetry.

This explanation does, I think, cover the archaism of Crocker-Harris's teaching methods. A much more difficult problem is the disparity between his attainments and his educational status. He had gained every possible prize and scholarship at Oxford and is described by the Headmaster as the most brilliant scholar on the staff. Normally he would have got a Fellowship, or at least a Sixth Form, yet he takes only the Lower Fifth. More curious still, his successor, who has precisely similar qualifications, expresses delighted surprise at being given so high a Form. Here the clue is given by the repeated references to the Upper Fifth's studying science. Crocker-Harris has a private pupil who longs to take up science but cannot do so until he has obtained his promotion, and this he can only do by mastering Aeschylus. No Aeschylus, no Chemistry. Aeschylus is, in any case, not a beginner's writer, and the only satisfactory explanation is that the Lower Fifth was the top form on the Classical Side—in this school Sides being not parallel as elsewhere but successive. The Upper Fifth would be the beginning of the Science Side. Hence, to be appointed to the Lower Fifth was to be appointed to the senior Classical post.

The School organisation has other peculiarities which render this theory less unlikely. Crocker-Harris is bitter that he is granted no pension after eighteen years' service, though he would have become entitled to one in a short time. "A short time" cannot surely be more than two or three years, so it seems that the School pensions off its staff in their early forties. There are other indications of the exceptionally high regard in which the staff are held. We see them entertained to a luxurious meal followed by billiards and fireworks. They are allowed to mingle with parents in the tea-tent at a cricket match and eat the same food. On leaving, they make farewell speeches to the School, an opportunity which those who were well acquainted with school staffs would hesitate to offer.

The Chairman of the Governors is a general and a peer, which suggests a public school. The buildings are old; but there is no evidence that the school itself shares their antiquity. I diffidently suggest that the school is a very new Foundation, perhaps occupying a disused almshouse. It may well have been established in a hurried attempt to help deal with the increased school population of the 'twenties. Plunging into this new field, eager to fill a want, the Chairman, who may have had no clear recollection of his own school days, can be excused for his curious choice of a Headmaster, whom we first see giving out notices in chapel. The man noticeably lacks the pursed lips, the bulging eyes, the calm assumption of authority of the professional Head. His manner more resembles that of the harassed secretary of a golf club urging members to be good chaps and replace divots. Perhaps the general was also chairman of a golf club and got the applications mixed. It is no wonder that this hastily improvised Foundation should show only intermittent resemblance to an ordinary school.

There are, no doubt, many other problems for later generations of scholars to investigate. I can only claim the indulgence so often generously accorded to the pioneer.

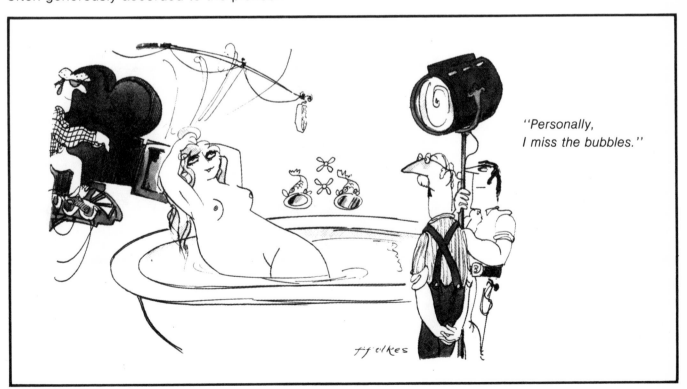

"Personally,
I miss the bubbles."

[*Funny Face*

Jo Stockton—AUDREY HEPBURN   *Dick Avery*—FRED ASTAIRE

Cinema Drawings
SHERRIFF?

[*Moby Dick*

Captain Ahab—GREGORY PECK

[*The Curse of Frankenstein*

The Creature—CHRISTOPHER LEE

[*The King and I*

The King of Siam, 1862—YUL BRYNNER

Alex Atkinson

-Sellers of Ice-cream, Nuts, Soft Drinks

Drinking and eating as frequently as possible between meals must be counted among the principal pleasures indulged in by poor people of all descriptions, whether clerks, policemen, civil servants, schoolmasters, novelists or pensioners. It was therefore inevitable that there should spring up, in London as in all great cities, a brisk trade in soothing tit-bits; and these are now to be had in considerable variety, at all hours. The methods of sale vary. With regard to the street sellers, their number has fallen during the last twenty years. From one of the few remaining independent purveyors of ice-cream I had the following explanation:

"It's hardly worth the flipping candle nowadays, guv'nor, whether you're flogging [selling] ice-cream or roast chestnuts; for the public can get their ice-cream in any sweet-shop or café, and in the winter time there's few will fancy nipping out to buy chestnuts once they've turned the telly on. Oh, it's the telly as is killing the chestnuts, you mark my words. As for the ice-cream, the big firms is squeezing out the like of me, by perviding it at every hand's turn, all wrapped up, so the housewife will get it with her groceries, even, and store it in her fridge, which all the poor have fridges nowadays. All you can flog now on the street is beads and bangles, and it goes against the grain with me, being as I was brought up in the ice-cream, and so was my dad."

Among other methods of sale, apart from shops, the chief are "slot-machines", and large emporiums called "cinemas", where dainties of all kinds may be indulged in by as many as a thousand people at a time, often in surroundings of oriental luxury.

One such establishment, which I observed at first hand, was flanked at one side by a commodious open space, where customers were encouraged to leave their motor vehicles while feasting within. The exterior of the building was decorated with representations of noticeably plump women yielding to embraces of the most abandoned nature; presumably these scenes were intended to show that a woman will be the more likely to enjoy all the advantages of society if she is well fed.

An entrance-fee was charged, varying in accordance with the part of the building chosen for the "picnic". Thus, for a couple of shillings customers were accommodated at ground level in cramped surroundings which rendered the full enjoyment of a meal rather hazardous; while for sums ranging up to half a guinea more comfortable seats were provided, in the upper parts. Here the advantages were, that the floor sloped steeply enough to facilitate the disposal of rubbish; that a metal container was allotted to each customer, attached to the seat in front, for smaller items of litter, such as toffee-papers (in the cheaper seats such containers were usually *shared*); and that the service was, on the whole, more personal, with less emphasis on queueing.

For those who could not wait, packages of chocolate and sweets were on sale in the entrance-hall itself, as well as copies of a magazine in case the time should pass heavily during the actual junketing. Inside the "auditorium" (as the banquet halls are named) I found, upon my arrival, complete darkness, and the sound of shrill music combined with the intermittent boom of some monstrously over-life-sized conversation. These latter noises, which accompanied the flashing of

moving-pictures upon a screen, were provided by the management, presumably to drown the continual champing, sucking, blubbering, rustling, chewing, splashing, snorting, snuffling, gurgling, crackling, slobbering sounds inevitably attendant upon the stimultaneous consumption, by upwards of five hundred close-pressed people of cold drinks and sticky snacks. I later learned that the profits from the sale of these sugary provisions were large enough to pay for the hire of the moving-pictures; and, as the manager explained, the customers had now come to accept these picture-plays as an integral part of the beanfeast.

Certainly the picture-plays were not shown to the best advantage. For one thing, the management, conscious of the danger that the "films" might one day start to come between the clients and their food, and thus reduce profits, had arranged that the public might pass in and out at any time; with the result that the screen was almost continually obscured by those arriving or departing. For another thing, the customers, arriving as they commonly do in the midst of some complicated story, have neither the chance nor the inclination to pick up the threads, being more concerned to open up such packets of food as they have bought at the entrance.

For their convenience, uniformed ladies are encouraged to roam the darkened aisles, equipped with torch-lights which form a never-ending source of excitement, appearing now here, now there, like Will-o'-the-wisp. These sprites bear trays of cold drinks, peanuts, mixed nuts, ice-cream, chocolates, chewing-gum, and such delicacies as may be fashionable. (I learned of one establishment where, in the after-noon, the lights having been turned up, a matronly lady will parade the aisles offering for sale cups of tea, which she will pour from a large pot, while conversation becomes general. I could find no evidence of the sale of hot meals.)

I was informed that, ice-cream being the most profitable line, managements will often arrange to have the furnaces stoked to capacity, so that the atmosphere becomes unbearably tropical. Later, when ice-cream has sent the customers half mad with thirst, tempting advertise-ments for soft drinks are flashed upon the screen, and the tortured souls besiege the uniformed ladies, pitifully clamouring for fruit juices to ease their parched throats.

In the seat next to mine an elderly man mumbled as he ate cheese sandwiches from a brown-paper parcel. He then brushed the fragments into my lap, and fell to snoring. Since his head rested on my shoulder, and I could not find it in my heart to curtail his brief escape from the tedium of his existence, I remained until all had eaten and drunk their fill, when the playing of the National Anthem signalled the end of the beano. In the entrance-hall the manager bowed good night to his patrons. He was clad as a head waiter.

"This is the big scene where Sir Francis is rounding the Horn and discovers you in the sail locker."

Liv Ullman
talks to David Taylor

During the filming of *Lost Horizon*, a shallow and by all accounts dismal sort of musical in which she was lumbered with the beguiling part of a sweet, yet sexy, Shangri-La school-ma'am being serenaded up the Himalayas by a snow-blown Peter Finch, Liv Ullman grew accustomed to the gushy style of Hollywood's treat-ment of wide-eyed Scandinavian blondes with great potential—to the roses, the limousines, several acres of plush accommodation with swimming-pool, that sort of thing. Then she left directly for Faro, the Baltic hidy-hole of Ingmar Bergman, to make a TV series on marriages busting up, and perhaps to recall in the situation of log-lined, stoic discomfort and outside toilets, the occasion when her own marriage to an Oslo psychiatrist did just that. The bust-up led to a steamy relationship with Bergman which produced very worth-while films, lasting traumas and one illegitimate daughter. Now she has returned to London to begin filming the life of Queen Christina of Sweden, a secretive neurotic whom no one loved, who then abdicated, fled to Rome, and drank. One way and another, Liv Ullman says disarmingly, her work has given her a rare perspective.

Refreshingly, it has not given her self-indulgent airs. Plonking on to a sofa in the Dorchester, she was quick to tell us that she's frightened stiff of being turned into a "typical" actress. If people

choose to dig, they can cite some pretty awful upheavals in Liv
Ullman's childhood and conclude she was the lonesome, Nordic
misfit in search of a role, they can instance her romance with
Bergman (who, incidentally, has an astonishing capacity to make
films with former bedmates, sometimes three or four at a time) and
assume that Liv Ullman is a dedicated art-house creator; or they can
come up with the fact that she reads an awful lot and is therefore
plainly unhinged. Such is the stuff of a good story, Liv Ullman
recognises, and adds whimsically that she has done her best to
indulge the journalist's needs. As far as she's concerned, acting is a
job. She does not pretend ever to have been so absorbed by any
particular part to lose sight of her (glib word) identity. If you moon
about acting a part the whole time, she maintains, you lose the
capacity to observe in others what may one day turn out to be
useful. You fall victim to so much histrionic guff. Just about the only
distinction amongst actors that she is prepared to acknowledge is
that some are more suited to Shakespeare and his ilk, others to
naturalistic, modern parts.

According to the popular image, the sort of part which would
suit Liv Ullman is one demanding rarified glamour, perceived in
depth. Recently she was splashed across the cover of *Time* as
"Hollywood's New Nordic Star" and summarised thus: "Liv: the
name rhymes with believe, achieve—or grieve. Also Eve. In
Norwegian, it means 'life'. It fits the face—the glints of crystalline
fjords and upland meadows in the eyes and hair, the shadowy
secrets around the wide, sensual mouth. It carries the aura of
innocence, of candour, of mischief." All of which went up the spout,
giggles an acutely embarrassed Liv, with *Lost Horizon* for which,
she admits, there can be no excuse. "It was fun at the time, so put it
down to experience. I am ashamed to sit through it, never mind, on
to the next."

Liv Ullman abhors pretentiousness, she says. She happens
to believe that films often do work out better if she is emotionally
involved with the director, but that does not mean she plans to go to
bed with every one (particularly, as ffolkes cynically pointed out,
when she has yet to work with Hitchcock) and while she happens to
enjoy reading very much (she also likes to write an everyday journal)
that does not mean she can waft about quoting chapter and verse of
quintessential Proust or glum Nordic sagas. On the one hand she
reads for entertainment (Agatha Christie on the set, between takes)
and on the other hand precisely because she is aware of the
dangers of a surfeit of pap entertainment, which bothers her. In the
same way that films like *The Sound of Music* and *Lost Horizon* give
her the willies about the future of the cinema, so the fact that nine
people out of ten never reach beyond the pulp paperback unnerves
her. People can and do stretch their tastes, given the chance, she
maintains. Witness that Bergman TV series on marriage's up and
downs (very arty of its kind) which successfully cleared the streets
of Copenhagen when it was shown there.

At which point a gent arrived with a parcel, come to teach Liv
Ullman how to play the lute (another thing which Queen Christina
did). In the space of twenty minutes or so, we seemed to have
summarised a lot. With Liv Ullman, it's not so unusual. Just about
every day, people stop her in the street and remark that she's the
spitting image of Liv Ullman, though younger, of course. "Do you
think so?" she is accustomed to answer back, "That's what everyone says. What do you think about Liv Ullman, by the way?" And on
the basis of those answers, she's now got a pretty shrewd idea of
what makes her, and the profession of acting, tick.

He Came Out of Nowhere!
He Was a Composer!
He Was the First!   And the Best!

LEE MARVIN is

MONTE VERDI

THE MOST HEART-
WARMING MOVIE
EVER MADE!

YOU'LL WEEP!   YOU'LL LAUGH!   YOU'LL LOVE!

PAINT
YOUR
WAGNER

He Drove A Myth Across A Continent!
He Gave Men Dreams To Dream!

Hear Howard Keel Sing
"Just A Gott At Twilight"
"Nibble A Happy Lung"
"I'm Singing In The Ring"
and many, many more!

ALSO STARRING
Jon Voight as
King Ludwig II,
Woody Allen as Schopenhauer,
and Raquel Welch as Nietzsche

"If it comes to that, after our movies you're something of an anti-climax."

A Night at the Movies
Benny Green

Whenever confronted by the pitiable spectacle of a professional film critic, the layman invariably reacts with a compromise between gawping awe and pulsating compassion. Pity the poor fish who has to sit there in the dark at half past ten in the morning trying to focus his scrambled wits on the endless succession of twilight melodramas which constitute his day's work. All true, but there is another side to the medal. Because press shows cater exclusively for the non-paying customer, cinema managements dispense with the hard-sell accoutrements of the normal visit to the pictures, thus sparing the reviewer exposure to some of the most fiendish devices ever conceived by the mind of man for boring a person to death. However, it is no bad thing for the professional reviewer to step down into the crowd from time to time, if only to get some idea of why the paying customer is gradually ceasing to be one ...

I am sitting in a London cinema in the expectation of seeing a new movie which my fellow-critics have hardly deigned to notice, and who can blame them? It is one of those movies with the demented look about it of having been manufactured specifically for what Wardour St. calls the holiday trade. That is to say, it has been put on with an eye to the thousands of schoolchildren who annually intimidate well-trained parents into taking them somewhere. The odd thing is that although the movie has received no critical acclaim, and indeed almost no critical attention of any kind, a strange process of social osmosis has been operating, for although it is midweek and early evening, there is a queue outside the cinema. A small queue, but in crisis days, cinema queues are like garlic; there is no such thing as a little.

Soon I am sitting in my seat looking for my holiday film. But instead there looms up in the dark a cinematic brontosaurus I thought was extinct aeons ago. I am gazing once more on that visual-aural bromide, the News bulletin. Stupefied, I sit there witnessing in black-and-white what the entire country watched in colour last week on TV. More amazing still, the commentary proceeds just as though this is 1935 and Stanley Baldwin is still sleeping in Ramsay Macdonald's hammock. I learn that our Queen is still "monarch of nearly a quarter of the earth's population", although what this proves, or implies, or symbolises, we are not told. Then we see a new sound stage being opened at Bray Film Studios, and are told that this heralds a new golden age in British movie-making. J. Arthur Rank, are you sleeping there below?

The News then ends and the cinema curtain comes down. Then, almost immediately it goes up again, and a new super-production called Pearl and Dean begins to wend its relentless way into our pocketbooks. Girls sip alcoholic beverages, tubes of toothpaste explode in the faces of Russian wolves of both the two- and four-legged kind; motor cars gleam with lascivious intent. The commentary is subtly different from the News bulletin. It hectors less, nudges more. It is less naive, more devious, and if anything, marginally more ridiculous. But the Pearl and Dean saga finally ends, and down comes the curtain again. Then it goes up again and we settle down to a series of trailers which cleverly make everything look like a cross between Portnoy and Decameron Nights.

The trailer for *The Hireling*, for instance, cross-cuts scenes and dialogue in a way that never occurs in the actual film, somehow achieving an altogether randier effect than the film itself, which is really a most chaste and decorous affair. Then a Japanese gentleman appears, whose only accomplishment in life, apart from saying imbecilic things with somebody else's mouth (the dubbing is atrocious), appears to be kicking people in the face and grunting. There then follows a trailer for *The Discreet Charm of the Bourgeoisie*, which once again manages to make the movie promise unmentionable erotic diversions, so much so that I make a mental note to see the film just to check up on the trailer.

Then the curtain comes down; then the curtain goes up again, inspiring metaphors of April umbrellas. Now we get a succession of shorts. The first two feature Donald Duck, the third Little Hiawatha, the fourth Mickey Mouse. These four cartoons have been run in reverse chronological order, as though with the specific intention of proving to us, as if we needed any, that over the years the Disney aesthetic has been steadily coarsening in almost precise proportion to the degree of its commercial success. After the Mickey Mouse saga, the curtain comes down again and the house lights come up. I glance around at the decor and get the uncanny feeling that I am sitting in a stage drawing-room magnified several times. A girl appears with a tray of what are laughingly described as refreshments. There is a buffalo charge towards her by customers with an uncontrollable craving for ice-cream at inflationary prices.

The girl finally beats an orderly retreat, the sucking stops, and the lights go out. Up goes the curtain and on comes the main feature.

It is now just over one hour since I took my seat, and my condition is so grave that even were D. W. Griffith to appear and box six rounds with John Huston, I would probably give it a bad write-up. My sensibilities have been numbed, anaesthetised, battered into a pulp. I no longer care what the main feature is about, or even if there is no main feature at all. Why not go back to the News bulletin? Perhaps by now the fact that our Queen is still monarch of nearly a quarter of the earth's population will stir me. Perhaps now I am ready for it. But the main feature does appear at last. It is called *The World's Greatest Athlete* and is by Tarzan out of *The Jungle Book*. A lad called Nanu, not connected in any way with Zola's courtesan of almost the same name, wins every event at an athletics meeting. The juveniles around me laugh fairly regularly, but then there is no

accounting for taste. The cinema is Studio One, so it is no hardship to crawl next door and catch up with *The Discreet Charm of the Bourgeoisie* at Studio Two. Surprisingly enough, although this is Luis Bunuel and pretty heavy intellectual stuff, exactly the same thing goes on. Before the main feature, we get an excruciating United States Air Force propaganda short, which uses the excuse of aerobatics to assure us that the American eagle is ever on the alert to forestall the attacks of hostile powers. I come out into the street and the newspaper headlines tell me that the American Air Force in Cambodia has just bombed itself. I make a note to write to the cinema owners advising them that to put on to the screen in 1973 a short made about the American Air Force in 1960 is a trifle rash. I stagger home to bed, slightly incredulous at my own conclusion, which is that the best art I have seen all day is the cartoon about Mickey Mouse at the Circus.

"Er . . . Whoop! Yip! Yip! Yolo! Yolo! Yolo! Yeeeeaaah! Whoop! Yipeee! Yip-Yip-Yip! Hah!"

SOCIALLY SIGNIFICANT STRIPS

Salaud was furious...

Bryan Forbes reviews

Bryan Forbes has produced, directed, written and acted in many new films. This is the first time that he has written all the reviews of a new film

DAILY MIRROR

A frank and daring look at sex in a reformatory for teenage girls, *I Am Inexplicably Orange*, is the perfect straitjacket for a wet afternoon. This off-beat Danish offering, which arrives at the New Limits this week (Cert X) after winning five major Festival prizes, will have Lord Longford and the R.S.P.C.A. joining forces. Not my cup of tea, but keep a look out for magnificent Mary Magda Lane, who plays the drug-crazed wardress to the manner born. Since her debut in this film, MML has been snapped up by Ned Sherrin for his zany comedy *The Notebooks of Marcel Proust* (which Wardour Street wags are already calling *Down The Elstree Way*).

VARIETY

THE PORN IS GREEN
Danish megger Kottbullar lenses offbeat skin pic that is topless and topdrawer, with added Freudian schleps. New hero should hold his own in most situations and wow matrons.

Mary Magda Lane as the drug-crazed prison wardress in
I AM INEXPLICABLY ORANGE (New Limits cinema, from April 7)

EVENING STANDARD

One is grateful for small mercies. In a full week which included the new Ken Russell offering, a musical version of *Thus Spake Zarathustra* with Richard Crossman in the name role, I turned my other cheek with some relief towards *I am Inexplicably Orange*...

CATHOLIC HERALD

I Am Inexplicably Orange
(*New Limits, Cert X*)***
Not Recommended.

MORNING STAR

Absorbing study of penal conditions which must draw comparisons with Long Kesh.

THE NEW YORKER

I Am Inexplicably Orange is a long, long way from Janet Gaynor. Grindingly boring, it has something going for it, our amazement that we're actually in the cinema, fully clothed, and watching it. But, awful as the probability is to contemplate, it may be boffo at the B.O. There's almost nothing to say about the leading actor, except that, on the evidence, he needs to consult a dermatologist. Trying to review this film is like attempting to commit suicide out of a basement window.

THE OBSERVER

I Am Inexplicably Orange *I found explicitly boring. The synopsis states that the hero, played by Jan* Tunberger, once earned his living as a circus regurgitator, and I am amazed that he did not fetch up the script before it was too late. The leading lady generates about as much sex appeal as a sackful of dead voles.

TIME

I Am Inexplicably Orange *is a rat-infested comedy that pulls out the laughs the way a catheter drains urine. The latest offering from true Danish Blue director Mansson (Douche-Moi) Kottbullar throws more than a few Schlagobers in the spectator's kisser. With all the delicacy of a Chicago slaughterer, Kottbullar sets out to prove that there are more ways than one to sever the jugular, and labours in*

"I AM INEXPLICABLY ORANGE"

vein. His leading actor, Jan Tunberger, should give celluloid a rest and ply his talents on Fifth Avenue where mugging is a fine art. The rest of the cast consists of reformatory teeny-boppers celling-out love for lustiness. If you liked The Singing Nun, Orange will peel you off.

NEWS OF THE WORLD
Mary Magda Lane brings her ample talents into full view in I Am Inexplicably Orange. Just the job, and as you can see from Magda's photograph, her prison uniform has no room for remission.

THE GUARDIAN
Ever since I reviewed Kottbullar's concoction at last year's Cannes Festival, most of my most boring friends (that is to say most of my friends) have been screaming "But where can I see it?" At long last I can give them the answer. They only have to take a number 14 bus to the trendy end of Fulham Road and search out the New Limits cinema. In its original version I thought I Am Inexplicably Orange something that Richard Roud should have gone monstrously overboard for, because I considered it the definitive vibrator movie. On a second viewing, with its sexual nuances dubbed into E. Nesbit English, I'm not so sure. The visuals are still stunning, of course, but the leading lady now looks as though she should bath more often. But perhaps that's a fault in the print.

SIGHT AND SOUND
Kaernemaelkskoldskaal (English title I am Inexplicably Orange, Cert X) is at once too remote and yet not remote enough, and clearly demands our respect if not our complete understanding. Kottbullar has regurgitated

Peckinpah in the same way that his ex-circus hero rejects the rats, and yet here; in his fifth film, he explores the religious syncretism inherent in the subject matter in a way that brilliantly illuminates Eric Pollen's thesis on The Life and Death of the Non-Film Film. Pollen argued that "to understand Kottbullar's post-Brechtian techniques, you have to accept the fact that the director is primarily talking to himself." This over-simplifies, perhaps, the cathartic quality of Kottbullar's images, and ignores the stated aim of despising theoretical cinema in favour of critical polemical cinema. Kaernemaelkskoldskaal is, in essence, a series of primitive improvisations and is capable of being viewed on two planes. Some audiences will merely see it as sex-spectacular camp, but to me the triumph of the film is in the translation of the amalgam of violence and perversion into a social parable. Crudeness and the occasional lapse of taste are still there, but the modulated tonality of the whole, counterpointed against the remarkable electronic music of Arne Ravut, is never tricksy. There is a wistful, restrained perform-ance from Jan Tunberger.

HARPERS & QUEEN
The film is urbane, chic, with flashes of wit, and more openly daring than Ma Jour Chez Madame de La Pin du Tour. Civilised enter-tainment of a different kind, this piece of surface froth is almost consistently amusing. (See fashion pages for variations on Romand's stunning prison costumes.)

PLAYBOY
A three hour bloodbath into oblivion, I Am Inexplicably Orange separates the Polanskis from the boys. A new Danish star named Jan Tunberger, who looks like a

cross between Vanessa Redgrave in drag and George C. Scott, plays the hero, one of those zip-bulging studs for whom women of all ages are willing to get liberally liberated (see our exclusive uncoverage in PLAYBOY, October 1943). Jan is a one-time circus regurgitator who lands himself the job as gardener at a reformatory for teenage girls. Immediately seeded No. 1 by the Chief Wardress (shapely Mary Magda Lane, who locked herself into our centrefold as Miss February), Jane deftly keeps his jockstrap in place despite five rapes, a garroting, two murders and a benefit performance of his one-time occupation. In a never-to-be-forgotten scene which may make Fellini retire, our hero does for rats what Cagney did for the grapefruit. All things, it seems, come back to those who only stand.

Hearts of Darkness
Dilys Powell

About a third of the way through **Apocalypse Now** I said to myself in a flash of recognition: Mistah Kurtz, he dead! It is the epitaph, casually pronounced by a servant, on the maniac (or the genius) who is at the dark heart of *Heart of Darkness*; I had read that the film was based on Joseph Conrad's story, but I had forgotten.

Based? It draws its life and its moral intensity from Conrad. The expedition up some fearful jungle river with Kurtz at the end of it, the man disintegrating, the obedient tribes—everything is Conrad except that Francis Coppola, director and co-author of the script, has clothed the tale in the bloody tatters of war. The plan to exterminate the powerful figure who has cut himself off from the war is the counterpart of the scheme in Conrad—only now the ferocity of the military machine replaces the savage meanness which Conrad saw in the exploitation of a primitive country.

For this is a war film: Vietnam war. The military emissary has been a CIA man; he knows about assassination. But before he sets off he sees an exercise in war. An American Lieutenant-Colonel, played with superb confidence by Robert Duvall, plans a raid. The victims, schoolchildren and farmers, look harmless enough; it is disingenuous of Mr Coppola to insist that he is not taking sides about war, merely presenting the violence. Anyway the air is loud with helicopters. They belt out the Ride of the Valkyries: it scares the hell out of Charley, says the good Lieutenant-Colonel. On the ground figures scatter and run, buildings dissolve, bridges crash; white planes sow a furrow of flames.

Is this what Kurtz means (yes, it is Marlon Brando) when he mutters "The horror! the horror!"? And horror it is; Coppola has given a tangible shame to react against. But then, like Conrad's Kurtz, he has created his own kingdom of terror in his isolated base up river. I think Coppola, like Conrad, intends his words as a comment on some baseness in the human condition—something more than a precise application to images of destruction and despair.

Publicity, I fancy, has done *Apocalypse Now* more harm than good; audiences expect a revelation and find only a terrible obscurity, critics are driven into hostility. Yet it really is an extraordinary film. Finely played, yes; but somehow the normal terms of reviewing seem out of place. It is as a huge shadow of the merciless and the horrible that it asks to be judged; it has the size for that.

Its images are sobering; they diminish one's self-importance. That brings me back to my beginning. Coppola and his co-scriptwriter, John Milius, have set the film in the world of now, but it is still Conrad's *Heart of Darkness*; everybody concerned, it seems, has read the story. A list of credits is supplied to those interested. And everybody is mentioned from T.S. Eliot, who is quoted in the script, to the production accountant (whom, since *Apocalypse Now* cost thirty million dollars, may heaven preserve). I counted three hundred and thirty names in the list. But one I couldn't find. I couldn't find the name of Joseph Conrad.

Successes
Richard Mallett

One of the very few novels lately filmed that I happen to have read, *The Lost Week-End* (Director: BILLY WILDER), is a remarkable and astonishing success. Astonishing, because there might appear to be little enough in the theme—a dipsomaniac's week-end, completely shadowed by his efforts to get whisky—to diversify even a short novel, let alone a film

completely absorbing and withou[t] a blank moment from beginning t[o] end. It is perhaps inevitable that parts of the story should have bee[n] simplified and made more obviou[s] for the sake of the film audience: there had to be a trick first-meetin[g] episode for the man and the girl with some business over a cloak-room ticket, the near-suicide poin[t] had to be made with some business about a gun, the hints o[f] perversion had to go, and so on. But these additions and omission[s] have been made in such a way a[s] not to do violence to the tone of [the] narrative or falsify the atmosphe[re] of the original.

The only real trouble is w[ith] the audience. It is a conditioned reflex among filmgoers to regar[d a] drunk as automatically a comedian, to laugh at almost an[y] reference to drinking; dipsoman[ia] as a disease, as the cause of utt[er] physical and mental collapse, is far outside their experience tha[t] they are apt to regard RAY MILLAND'S powerful and express[ive] demonstration of the wreck it c[an] bring about as rather exaggera[ted] and feel uneasy at the sight of i[t] if they were being asked to remember that incurable defor[mity] and death may result from a sli[p on] a banana-skin. Thus there is a certain amount of the usual unthinking laughter from the people who always begin to co[me] when the dialogue needs any listening to, but that is not a sc[ore] on which one can criticize the [film.] It has in fact been made grippi[ng] enough to hold even these sim[ple] minds; and they can, in a way, [be] envied, for they will take th[e] softened ending seriously a[nd] believe that the hero is cure[d] like that. Nobody who has r[eally] grasped the implications of [most] of the film or read the book, [can] believe it.

Does all this give yo[u a] gloomy impression? I hope y[ou will] be convinced that intelligent writing, first-rate acting—M[r] MILLAND has the part of his li[fe,] some of the subsidiary peop[le] brilliant—and sustained men[acing] direction and the use of the camera make the "facts" of [the] story completely irrelevant. I [feel] that no one capable of notici[ng] even a little more than "what happened then" will fail to ge[t] real satisfaction from *The Los[t] Week-End*.

First in to Bat
Dilys Powell

They take the supernatural seriously in the German cinema, and Werner Herzog has written and directed a **Nosferatu, the Vampyre** which has unusual intensity. Once or twice a title has the ring of absurdity. "Is it possible," asks Lucy, as the rats swarm and the square is congested with coffins, "that we have all gone mad?" Quite possible; but one scarcely laughs. For the image dominates, and the spectator is frozen by the image.

People who have never seen Murnau's *Nosferatu,* made in 1922, may still have some idea what its blood-sucking Count looked like; the shaven head, the bat-ears, the long curved nails have been celebrated in handbook photographs. Herzog, skipping the Dracula portraits drawn by Bela Lugosi and our own Christopher Lee, has followed the physical characteristics assumed by Max Schreck in Murnau's film. But he has gone farther back than to Murnau, farther back even than to Bram Stoker, who in 1897 wrote *Dracula,* the novel which started Draculamania. What he has done is to go back to the mood and the manner of the gothic literature of the late eighteenth century.

As long as the mood is sustained by the visual images, the film works. The soulful face, a sad pale oval, of Isabelle Adjani as the heroic Lucy is perfect for her romantic self-sacrificing role. The landscape is the country of eighteenth-century melancholy: the fast-flowing streams, the dark gloomy mountains where the clouds drift and gather, the tunnel of the cliff where the traveller looks back apprehensively as he enters. Especially the Count himself (Klaus Kinski) stirs an authentic horror—the chalk-white face, the loose twisted mouth with the two teeth always noticeable but never exaggerated, never, in the fashion of British vampires, Hammered. One does not laugh even when, attaching his mouth to some innocent neck, he emits faint sucking noises.

It is when the visual image fails to dominate that the exercise in film-making falters. I am thinking of the passage when the doctor, a scientific man, is summoned to attend a patient. Which one? he asks. The one who bit the cow, says his assistant; and the invalid, an apprentice vampire, as we discover, is found insanely cackling.

Overplayed, the performance underlines the nature of belief in horror films. In context one will believe in vampires, werewolves, and characters who spend the daylight hours tucked up? in coffins. Far more difficult to accept some trivial social improbability. Early in *Nosferatu* Lucia's husband (Bruno Ganz) is summoned by his employer, who is already overcome by maniac giggles and entrusted with a mission. He is to travel through the forests to the distant castle of Count Dracula, who wants to buy a house. Civilly the young man enquires what the job entails. And his employer, by now cunvulsed with mirth, replies that it will cost time, sweat "and perhaps a little blood". The question is whether in the circumstances the most loyal and willing employee would at once set off, as Lucy's husband sets off, without asking a few more questions.

Unless, of course, he was taken by the Churchillian ring of the recommendation.

Manhattan
Dilys Powell

Restraining, as the screen explodes with the sound of *Rhapsody in Blue*, a mad desire to rush out into the aisle and dance—after all one must consider one's neighbours in the cinema—I settle down to watch Woody Allen's **Manhattan**; it can't, I say, it simply can't merit this splendid Gershwin. But it can, it can; the music and the film deserve one another. Woody Allen has used Gershwin all through; and music and narrative are so perfectly linked in mood that when a tune ends short on a change of scene the visual screen carries you along. You feel none of the usual exasperation at the cutting of music in the cinema.

The film, shot in deeply satisfying black and white, has the nervous tension and the romantic excitement of a beloved city. The characters belong to a well-to-do, restless, intellectually pretentious society; they throw up their jobs, throw up their wives, write books about their partners in marriage, divorce and again divorce. A wife makes off with another woman whom, she insists, her husband then tries to run over with his car. Couples exchange partners and change back again. They talk solemn nonsense about art, about life; a complex of metal in a modern art gallery has "a marvellous negative capability . . ." And a girl who hasn't been exactly lonely in bed (she is played by the ravishing Diane Keaton) is heard irritably remarking—one knows what she means—that she is at once "attracted and repelled by the male organ".

A hopeless lot, these figures, portrayed with so accurate a brilliance by Michael Murphy, Meryl Streep, Anne Byrne and of course Miss Keaton. One ought to find them undeserving of serious attention. But one doesn't, not in Woody Allen's incomparable satire one doesn't. One likes them, listens to their talk of sexual frustration, sympathises with their inability to decide on anything. And they are held together as a human group by the wit and charm of the figure presented by Mr Allen himself.

Charm? Yes, charm. Mr Allen has moved in the past from knockabout burlesque to farce, from farce to satire, to comedy, at last to the Bergmanesque psychological enquiries of *Interiors*. I didn't care for *Interiors*: not because I wanted Mr Allen to go on being funny (I had never found him particularly funny) but because I was not emotionally held by the situations. But I go overboard for *Manhattan*. Mr Allen has long been using the screen to work out his own problems. This time, with the introduction of an innocent, generous girl, very young, very vulnerable (she is beautifully played by Mariel Hemingway) the problem finds a stabilising element: love. It is an element which relaxes Mr Allen's fast frenzied style. And now I do laugh—laugh at the comedy which I think is natural to Woody Allen: dialogue-comedy, scattering literary references and impudent questions and retorts; ironically he felicitates himself; one might almost say he betrays himself. It is a dazzlingly funny performance in a film dazzlingly funny, true. touching And hours after I have seen it I am still humming Gershwin and wondering why on earth I have ever listened to The Who.

The Gospel According To
Alan Coren

1 The book of the generation of Jesus Christ Superstar, the creation of Norman Jewison, the associate of Robert Stigwood.

2 Now the birth of Jesus Christ Superstar was on this wise: When as Norman Jewison was associated with Robert Stigwood, before they came together, he was found to possess the film rights to the production.

3 Then Robert his associate, being a shrewd man and not willing to end up with a turkey on his hands, was minded to forget the whole deal and start from scratch with an adult western based on Gammer Gurton's Needle.

4 But while he thought on these things, behold, the angels of the Broadway production appeared unto him saying, Robert, thou associate of Norman, fear not to take unto thee the co-production: for that which is conceived has already grossed two million bucks, and the movie version shall be good for ten times ten of that.

5 Then Robert did as the angels of the Broadway production had bidden him, and took unto him Norman Jewison.

6 And he knew him not till he had brought forth his first draft: and he called its title JESUS CHRIST SUPERSTAR. And lo! it went into

production.

Now when Jesus Christ Superstar was born in Judea in the days of Golda Meir, behold, there came three wise men from back east to Jerusalem.

2 Saying, where is he that is born Norman Jewison? For we have all been stars back east, and are come to audition for him.

3 Now when Golda Meir heard these things, she was troubled, and all Jerusalem with her.

4 And when she had gathered all the chief scribes together, she demanded of them where Jesus Christ Superstar should be born.

5 And they said unto her, In Bethlehem of Judea: for thus it is written in the screenplay.

6 And Golda Meir said unto them, What is in it for me? For is not Bethlehem in the Occupied Territories, and liable to saddle me with international complications on account of this being an American production and we had enough trouble getting the Phantoms without a whole new headache about US expansionism.

7 And the scribes grew exceeding wrath, and said unto her, Look, it makes no difference to us, for two pins we'll shoot the whole megillah in Spain.

8 And the three wise men spake, saying, Listen, we turned down three very meaty character parts in Hawaii Five-O to come over here and where the hell is the goddam casting director?

9 And Golda Meir said to the chief scribes: All I ask is you should just take a look at my daughter's eldest boy, a natural, not only does he act, but a voice he's got on him like Caruso, also dances, you'd think it was Ned Kelly himself.

10 And Norman Jewison waxed fearful, for the scribes were exceeding powerful, having already tied up ten per cent of the gross: And he took the scribes aside, saying, Look fellahs, let us write a small part in for the kid, maybe Simon Peter, or something, not that I would want to interfere with your artistic integrity or your business managers.

11 And so it was decreed.

12 And Norman returned to Golda Meir, saying, We already cast the lead, but we will look after your grandson, plus tickets to the premiere for the whole family.

13 And Golda Meir looked askance, and said: So where's the Star? And lo! the Star, which they had seen in the east, when he opened on Broadway, suddenly appeared and stood before them.

14 And when they saw the Star, they rejoiced with exceeding great joy.

Whereafter the production team was set up, and many starlets came offering great gifts, but were turned down. And they were not let know.

2 And it came to pass that they were casting John the Baptist, and many great dancers came before them, and many great singers. And they were almost decided.

3 But they heard the voice of one crying in the wilderness: and the same John had his raiment of camel's hair and a leathern girdle about his loins; and his meat was locusts and wild honey.

4 And Norman smote his temple, crying, Get this nut off the set, we are trying to cast a movie, and the man answered and said unto him: I think you know my grandmother, how would you like two choruses of Goodbye Dolly Gray, also a soft shoe routine I do with a top hat?

5 And Norman grew calm, and said unto him, Thank you very much, please wait outside: and lo! a man stepped forward from among the multitudes and spake, saying, I am his father, the doctor, and this is

my beloved son, in whom I am well pleased, my name is Dr Meir MD, and I should like two seats in the centre, row B, next to Princess Margaret, if possible.

6 And the scribes waxed exceeding angry, saying: This guy is all wrong for the part, it is either him or us.

7 And Norman and Robert spake unto them softly, saying: Blessed are the meek, for they shall inherit the earth. And the scribes replied: Keep the earth, what about our ten per cent of the gross?

8 And so it came to pass that the role of John the Baptist did not go to the boy, but to a friend of the Chief Scribe, who jumped for joy even as the spring lamb, and kissed everyone, and went out and had a blue rinse, by way of celebration.

But the next day the Star came before them, exceeding low: in his left hand he held his douche-bag and in his right his prompt copy. And he spake unto Norman, saying: The foxes have holes, and the birds of the air have nests; but the Son of man hath not where to lay his head.

2 And Norman wished to know the reason for the Star's discomfiture.

3 And the Star cried out, saying: Get that bum out of my dressing-room.

4 And they went; and saw. And lo! In the dressing-room of the Star they found a boy, much like unto John the Baptist, and there was a woman with him, and she was feeding him soup. And Norman spake, saying: What manner of woman art thou?

5 And she answered, saying: I am Mrs Meir, the doctor's wife, and this is my son, the great film star, only who can eat the lousy rubbish they serve in the canteen, the boy needs to keep his strength up, you think Marlon Brando eats sandwiches, you think Richard Burton gets by on rice pudding, the skin sticks in your throat?

6 Norman wept.

7 And it came to pass that the Star had to be content with the second best dressing-room; and there was darkness over the face of the land.

Now it came to pass that Norman Jewison went forth the next morning, for he was much troubled. And the people had heard of the production, and wherever he went great multitudes followed him, eager to touch the hem of his garment, and he went up upon the mountain to think, with his accountants, and when he came down again, the multitudes were still there.

2 And, behold, there came a leper and worshipped him, saying, Lord, if thou wilt thou canst make me famous, I mean clean.

3 And Norman Jewison put forth his hand, and touched him, and lo! the leprosy came off on his fingers, and he saw that it was Plasticine. And he was much puzzled, saying, What manner of thing is this?

4 Whereupon the leper threw off his cloak and his hood, and stood before him in white tie and tails, singing, Nothing could be finer than to be in Carolina in the morning.

5 And Norman Jewison set up a great wailing, for they already had more singing lepers than they knew what to do with, and he informed the man of this: and the man said unto Him, How about the man sick of the palsy, who does this dance on a table-top, it was my grand-mother's idea?

6 And Norman spake unto him, saying, Let your communication be Yea, yea; Nay, nay, and maybe we can do something for you.

7 But the man replied, saying, What kind of a part is that, four lousy words, for someone with three relatives in the cabinet?

8 And Norman knew not what he should do: for was he not already beset with grave problems? And he turned aside in grief, and lo!

here were his disciples running to him, crying Norman, save us: we perish.

And first among them, a Second Unit Chief Disciple, let up a great shout, saying, We cannot work with the Special Effects Department, they are using the wrong wind machines and the wrong studio tanks and they are ruining the whole thing and we are two days behind already, and if this keeps up I and all thy servants will go into television.

0 And Norman went along with them to Lot Three, to where the Special Effects Department were setting up Miracle Shot Two; and behold, there arose a great tempest in the studio tank.

1 And his disciples began to shriek once more, and Norman saith unto them, Why are ye fearful, O ye of little faith? Then he arose and rebuked the winds and the sea; and there was a great calm.

2 And the men marvelled, saying, What manner of man is this, that even the winds and the sea obey him!
But even as the great tank settled, behold, they perceived a figure speeding across it; and there were boards upon his feet and a rope between his hands, tied in wondrous wise to a boat with motors that ran before him.

And he was singing.

And Norman shrieked out, crying, Who is that? And the disciples answered him, saying, Would you believe Golda Meir's grandson, who thinks he has a solution to the problem of walking on the water?

"Nonsense—we'll run for months."

Are You Going to Believe Raquel Welch?

when you could be believing Stanley Reynolds?

**TORMENT OF THE
WORLD'S No. 1 SEX SYMBOL**

RAQUEL: THE ULTIMATE WOMAN
"IT'S NO FUN BEING THE
WORLD'S
MOST BEAUTIFUL WOMAN."

Raquel Welch lay back on three pillows for support, looking pale, drawn but better without make-up. It was 12.30 p.m. in her villa in the South of France, where I interviewed her, and she had only just woken up... She wore a winceyette top that hugged her figure in the softest of caresses.
What kind of man turns Raquel on? "I like a man to be a man."

Day after day, the other week, Mr. Terry O'Neill, with a little help from the Ultimate Woman herself, was proving that the era of stardust glitter journalese is alive and gasping for breath in the *Daily Express.*

Glamour and heartbreak, the heartbreak behind the tinsel of show biz, the broken heart for every light on the old marquee, was Mr. O'Neill's strong card on the Raquel caper. When she developed what she coyly referred to as "the equipment", men, she said, started treating her like "a piece of meat", pushing her in front of the movie camera, telling her when to sit down, when to stand up, and giving her nothing but the dross of wealth and the pottage of fame as compensation. If it weren't for her kids, the villa in France, the cars, the diamonds, and the numbered bank account in Zurich and points West, she'd have given up the ghost a long time ago.

But somehow, I couldn't seem to get over the slight suspicion that Mr. O'Neill had been led up the villa path down there on the Côte d'Azur. Let's face it, this kid Welch has not only starred in, but also produced, *Kansas City Bomber* which is steaming the box offices coast-to-coast all over Yankland right now. This kid Welch is not just a star, she is a business tycoon. Ever since the *Express* series there has been appearing before my eyes a sort of a dream, in which, of course, any resemblance to persons living or dead is strictly unintentional.

The scene is the Riviera villa bedroom of that billion-dollar property, Annunziata Muldoon, she of the flashing Spanish gypsy beauty and the laughing Irish eyes. At curtain, Annunziata has just polished off a pair of brunch kippers and is lighting up a mid-morning cigar, pursuing the latest stock market results in the Wall Street Journal, Barrum's Weekly, *and the* Financial Times. *Telephones lie at the ready by each of her dimpled elbows. A worried frown knits her marbled brow.*

ANNUNZIATA: Up, up, up. All my stocks keep soaring. And this is supposed to be a recession. I gotta get me some kind of a nice tax loss but every lousy thing I touch turns to blue chip. (*Picking up a telephone*). Gimme Schnell, Raus, and Himmel in New York. Hello, Harry? Oh, it's Moe, Listen, Moe, what's this crud about me not being able to buy Uruguay for cryin' out loud? I own it already, huh? Well, listen, Moe, don't just stand there. Sell it. And buy Paraguay. Half a guay is better than none. And get me a nice tax loss, will you? How come I gotta tell you guys everything for cryin' out loud?

(*She replaces the receiver just as a man enters. This is Harvey Undergrowth, her new private secretary, a mild-mannered man in a chalk-stripe suit, tortoiseshell specs, his hair plastered back and neatly parted*.)

ANNUNZIATA: Who the hell are you?

UNDERGROWTH: Undergrowth, Miss Muldoon. The new man.

ANNUNZIATA: Yeah, well stop creepin' up on me like that when you burst in on me. When you burst in on me, make some noise.

UNDERGROWTH: M-m-m-m . . .

ANNUNZIATA: Come on, man, spit it out. Spit it on the wall, for cryin' out loud, so I can read it. I ain't got all day, there's a delegation of Swiss bankers coming here this afternoon for a laying on of hands and I want to run through them figures on Anaconda Copper. And frankly, I went over the books on Mesopotopian Gulf Oil this a.m. and I think the readings on the original bore drillings is a whole bunch of crud, Undergrowth. If I can't suck twelve hundred barrels a day out of that place, why, at $7\frac{1}{2}$ per cent repayment on the second mortgage, we won't be realising more than 5, $5\frac{1}{2}$ on a deal like that. I'd just as soon teach my grandmother to suck eggs as go into a crud set-up like that. And stop standing there so quiet, Undergrowth. And, Undergrowth, stop fidgeting.

UNDERGROWTH: It's M-M-M Mister B-B-B- Buck, y-y-y-y our p-p-p . . .

ANNUNZIATA: Yeh, yeh, Nimrod Buck, my press agent. They teach you to stutter like that at Harvard Business School, Undergrowth? What you wanna do is stick some rocks in your mouth and go down and shout at the swimming pool. It works wonders. Listen, Undergrowth, I know this winceyette top is hugging this equipment of mine in the softest of caresses and it troubles you. But, cryin' out loud, it's torment for me. You work around here you gotta get used to seein' the most beautiful woman in the world.

(*Nimrod Buck, the press agent with the eyes of a pawnbroker and the smile of a barracuda, enters.*)

BUCK: For cryin' outloud, Nunzi, what ya doin' ta me? I got a feature writer from the *Daily Express* waitin' downstairs an' you ain't even half-dressed. Get half-dressed quick. (*To Undergrowth*) Say, what the hell is this. Get them addin' machines the hell outta here, and clean up that ticker tape for cryin' out loud. (*To Annunziata who is getting back into bed*.) Nunzi, baby, how could you? To me? What wuz you before I took over? Runnin' that lousy loft in Wall Street, sellin' a little stock here, cornerin' a little wheat there. Strictly a nickels and dimes outfit. You wuzn't even listed on the big board for cryin' out loud.

ANNUNZIATA (*arranging an outrageous décolletage*): What the hell's with this *Daily Express*? Why can't they profile my holding companies or something really innarestin' like that Tanzanian zinc merger for gosh sake's?

(*Enter the Expressman.*)

ANNUNZIATA (*pretending to be only waking*): What is the hour? Yawn yawn, stretch, stretch.

EXPRESSMAN: Gone noon, Miss Muldoon. What's that top you're wearing made out of? Silk, huh? Or a sort of nylon? A sort of silky nylon you'd call it, I suppose? Boy, it clings to the equipment like the softest of I don't know what.

ANNUNZIATA: Gosh, noon already, and I been up filmin' onna location all night already and then chewin' my nails ha'f the night wunnerin' if it's worth all the heart break. If it wasn't fer them wunnerful kids a mine, Carlos and Sasha...

BUCK: Jake and Tom, for cryin' outloud, you dumb broad.

ANNUNZIATA: I wouldn't know what ta do with myself, honest ta God, fer Gawd's sake, I wouldn't, you know what I mean? It's called winceyette. Kind of hugs my figure sort of like the softest caresses don't it?

EXPRESSMAN (*writing*): W-i-n-c... Lots of heart break I'll bet in this sex symbol game, huh?

ANNUNZIATA: Oh, you betcha. Heart break ain't in it. It's more like torment, know what I mean? Say, you speak real good fer a ferriner.

EXPRESSMAN: Tell me, Miss Muldoon, what kind of man turns you on?

ANNUNZIATA: Well, right now I'm looking for an accountant who can cost a job right on the spot, no messing...

BUCK: Nix, nox, you dumb bimbo. (*To the reporter.*) Nunzi likes a guy to be...ah...a guy, like, don't you, honey?

ANNUNZIATA: Yeh, that's right. Speakin' frankly I like a man to

be a man.

EXPRESSMAN: How do you spell winceyette?

BUCK: An' the loneliness of bein' a top-flight sex symbol for all the chumps. That really bothers her. Don't it, babe?

ANNUNZIATA: I'll say. Yeh, loneliness ain't in it. It's more a kind of a torment. W-i-n-c-e—Hey, Undergrowth, how you spell winceyette? I got wealth and fame, diamonds and poils, three bootiful kiddies . . .

BUCK: Two, two bootiful kiddies. It's two. W-i-n-c-e—

EXPRESSMAN: Is that E, double T - E, or just one T?

ANNUNZIATA: But what does the world know of a lonely woman's heart behind all the tinsel? Two bummer marriages. An accountant who don't know double entry book-keepin' from a hole in the ground, and not a real good tax dodge in sight. Torment ain't even in the runnin'.

EXPRESSMAN: Maybe I ought to just make it "silky fabric". What do you think, Miss Muldoon?

ANNUNZIATA: I think there's a broken heart for every light on the marquee. Two E's.

EXPRESSMAN (*rising*): Thank you, Miss Muldoon.

ANNUNZIATA: Don't mention it, I'm sure.

(*Exit the Expressman in search of a dictionary.*)

ANNUNZIATA (*to Undergrowth*): Come on, get the lead out. I got the United Artist bankers skying in from New York tonight. Get me Kubrick on the phone. Sell my zinc, buy copper, and ask Steve McQueen what the hell he means holding out for ten per cent of the gross, who the hell does he think he is, Raquel Welch already? And by the by, call London, and buy the *Daily Express*; I think we might have a nice tax loss there.

(*During this speech Annunziata dresses in a plain, charcoal business suit, ties up her hair, puts on horn rimmed glasses. Nimrod Buck leaves in disgust, but the hitherto timid Harvey Undergrowth seems mesmerised. He walks towards her as if he were in a dream, as if he were seeing her for the first time*).

UNDERGROWTH (*lovingly*): Why, mm M-M-M- Miss M-M- Muldoon you . . . y-y-y-you're . . . e-e-e-e f-f-ficient.

(*Together they sit side by side poring over Anaconda copper while the adding machine plays.*)

CURTAIN

HOW TO MAKE EPICS
Alan Hackney

"Errol Flynn is dead, Ty Power's dead, they're all dead so you'd better listen to me. I'm the only one left," said Stewart Granger, and it was true and we listened. It was in Rome in the immediate pre-shooting period of *The Swordsman of Siena,* a period epic which was at last about to be brought to you, sitting at home in Ruislip, impatient for your next shot of glamour and swordplay. It was ten years ago but I remember it very clearly because it was one of those rare occasions when the star had got into effective control of the picture, for reasons of economics.

He didn't ask all that much, merely that his own part should be right. So for a week, the producer, director and myself had to sit and listen while he sorted it out. We were all slightly uneasy because lunch every day that week turned out to be about a hundred fried eggs on a couple of silver dishes, and I must admit, beautifully arranged. The trouble was, Granger wasn't interested in eating that week, and on the Monday when the cook asked what there should be for lunch, he'd said Fried Eggs, adding that he didn't want to be disturbed by trivial questions of this sort any more. His orders were obeyed.

When the bit in the script came up where Granger was stretched on the rack and taunted by an evil Spaniard dribbling wine from a flask over his anguished face I sought to cut in. The script, which I had rewritten, still had a hangover bit in it from the Hollywood writers who had the stretched Granger lick the dribbled wine tentatively and then say, to show he didn't care: "H'm—'05, not a bad year." I said, meaning to bring up a few other anachronisms while I was about it, that 1505 was ridiculously early for anyone to start vaunting their wine-snobbery. But Granger, evidently projecting himself into the part with relish, said: "Leave it in. I'm making a good joke there. And what will they care about anachronisms when they see it in Japan?" A practical philosophy, as you will see, so I didn't bring up other period gems like: "Maybe I'm getting smart like you, Orietta." I just changed them without saying anything. In the outcome, one or two things suffered. A wild boar hunt, echoing the picture called "A Hunt At Night" in the Ashmolean Museum, which was an element received with much enthusiasm when I wrote it, somehow got transformed into an indoor minuet scene which I was assured got the same point over equally well and more cheaply. Changes were introduced up to and after the last moment and my last glimpse as I drove away from the lot was of Sylva Koscina looking puzzled. I could understand it.

Normally, of course, the producer in this business remains very firmly in charge, which is only right and proper. He even hires (and can fire) the director, so when the film is shot (or sometimes, "shot and killed" as they say in the business) there is still someone to blame if it turns out to be a turkey. (The director is by now off somewhere else, practising his art for money, like the sensible chap he is.) Even the most successful producers have to temper their enthusiasm with caution. Michael Winner, with whom I jointly owned a script which he wanted to direct, negotiated long and hard with the producer, Charles Schneer, before he could get what he wanted. Mr. Schneer was for using another director to do the picture, as being safer and cheaper. At one point he said: "Michael, you *can't* be a

"The most offensive scene was your simulated disgust."

*"The other backers and I feel that you're attempting to incorporate
too many unrelated themes into one movie."*

great director. You haven't suffered enough.''

"Charlie," sighed Winner, "After all the hours I've had to spend talking to you, *how can you say that*?"

The same producer had one of those traumatic experiences that can come from picking a sunny location in a nice place. While his picture *Jason and the Argonauts* was shooting in a lovely bay in Sicily, a Spanish galleon came chugging into shot round the headland, carrying some of the unit of *Sir Francis Drake* and ruining an otherwise perfect Ancient Greek atmosphere. He had to leap in a jeep and call from the headland the immortal cry: "Get that out of here, you're in the wrong century!"

Another immortal cry, and as far as I know it's still in the finished picture because they couldn't take it out without losing a key shot, was emitted by Lionel

Jeffries. Dressed in full Highland regalia like the label on a Dewar's whisky bottle, he was supposed to escape from the maze at Hatfield House by doing a pole vault which landed him in a greenhouse. Preparing for his mighty leap, Lionel suddenly thought he ought to shout out some sort of war cry. "Here, it ought to be in Gaelic, though," he said. "Do you know anything in Gaelic?"

"No I don't," I said, refusing to take responsibility for what I could see was going to happen.

"I do," said Bernard Cribbins, and told him a phrase.

"What does it mean?" asked Lionel.

"I don't know," said Cribbins, "I think it's obscene."

"Good. Lovely," said Lionel, "Let's have a go."

When they called Action, Lionel howled it loudly and clearly as he ran up for his pole vault.

"Actually it *is* obscene," said Bernard Cribbins. "Still, never mind."

A long time later, when the film was out, the producer said to Lionel: "What am I supposed to do with . . . ?", quoting the irremovable phrase.

"Ah well, I don't expect they'll show it in Dublin," said Lionel soothingly.

"What do you mean? We're taking a lot of *money* in Dublin," said the producer.

"Ah well, there you are," said Lionel.

I can only suppose the censor didn't understand it. The trouble used to come when he did. Reasonable though Mr. Trevelyan has always described himself in the exercise of his duty, many were the angry cries of frustration that arose in his office when people would come to get their scripts vetted before shooting—an important precaution. It seems strange but it was only a few years ago that Mr. Trevelyan objected to the following. The scene, wartime Gibraltar, where the negligent Officer i/c Apes, played by Terry Thomas, is being closely questioned by his C.O. about them dying out while he was supposed to be in charge. The story was based on a real inquiry by Churchill, for the superstition was that if the apes should quit the Rock, so would the British. The sad reduction in apes might be a gift to enemy propaganda.

First the Colonel establishes that no remaining apes are pregnant, then:

Colonel: Oh. Well, when's the mating season?

Terry Thomas: 15th December, sir, to 15th January. Inclusive.

Colonel: We can't wait that long. Don't they mate any other time?

Terry Thomas: Not this species, sir.

Colonel (irritably): Well, what do they do all the rest of the year?

Terry Thomas: Well, they sort of just hang about, waiting for Christmas.

''Animals copulating,'' said Mr. Trevelyan, ''if you keep that in you'll have to have an X certificate.''

''What!'' cried the American producer, ''Jesus, that'd mean £40,000 off the possible take!''

The censor claimed that many markets, Canada for instance, might find the passage offensive. As we went down the stairs afterwards the producer fumed: ''Canada? By the time any print gets out to the sticks in Quebec it looks like shredded wheat anyway.'' Still, with a bit of horse trading we finally got an A. But a U certificate was out of the question if we dared to mention what children of all ages know—that animals mate.

It's a great life, really, but it all depends on constant collaboration. As Frank Muir has pointed out, ''collaboration'' is what people were shot for during the war. Or else they had all their hair cut off. Not to worry—in the business it just falls out by itself.

Robert Wagner and Natalie Wood
talk to
David Taylor

Images do count, I sense that. Whisked from the rehearsal studios directly to an apartment in choicest Belgravia by chauffered, indigo limo, Robert Wagner and his wife, Natalie Wood, smartly disembark, as if to camera. They beam, they clutch hands and eagerly sprint upstairs, say hi to the kids and to the nanny, beam some more, let in the man with the glasses and then order drinks, set fire to slim, 100mm cigarettes, beam again and flop at last on to the upholstery, pooped, but, well, they guess you could sum up, ever so happy. The image, glimpsed just so, is of panache.

The dazedly satisfied grin, the beam, which accompanies them throughout this trip comes from things around being swell in general and over-the-moon in particular, which is to say that they have arrived, both literally and figuratively speaking, to work along-side, whisper it, Larry. Sir Laurence Olivier, a while back, telephoned. He said hullo and this is Sir Laurence Olivier and how would you two like to come on over to London and work with me on a television drama special, an NBC/Granada tie-up for doing, lavishly, *Cat On A Hot Tin Roof*, Tennessee Williams? They were stunned. They were delighted and they were flattered and they were excited and started packing and beamed and now they can hardly believe all of it, being here already, learning lines, underway. They can't tell you what a privilege, how terrific it is. That man's only the best actor in the world, they'd say, that's all.

Have a drink, please and let's get this straight, properly structured. Natalie, ladies first, with those just outsize brown eyes, the three-times Academy Award nominee, of Franco-Russian descent who has, in her day, been voted Most Talented Juvenile Motion Picture Star by *Parents* magazine, has been away from the big screen for a little while, a conscious, thought-through decision, bringing up kid Courtney; and was last featured in *Bob and Carol and Ted and Alice*, but is still best loved as, for an instance or two, Maria in *West Side Story*, or James Dean's high school sweetheart in *Rebel Without A Cause*, a seminal film. And Robert, whom she calls R.J. He is dressed, without flaw, from head to foot in denims and is possessed of such assurance as to make Telly Savalas seem ill at ease and edgy, is known perhaps best for *Towering Inferno, The Longest Day, The Pink Panther* (in which Peter was, well, great) and for up-market, up-intellect detection series on TV, such as *It Takes A Thief* or *Switch*. Certainly he's been choosy. With the, well proliferation of detection formats, how could one do but otherwise? You need a feel. And, in other ways, too, he has that. A natural athlete, he plays scratch golf, once outclassed Sam Snead, if you please, and also steers one hell of a powerboat, it's relaxing.

It's just as well to get these facts down and down straight, they'd both agree, since we now spend a good half hour going over the way journalists make a habit of lousing up biographical data, which is just not right, it is wrong, but gets absorbed, repeated, part of the, well, legend, who knows why? It leads, from time to time, and right this other day is an instance, to litigation. How else to put things straight? He means that you just wouldn't credit what occasionally gets printed about him, about Natalie also, except that, para-doxically, you just might. That's what he's saying. Things warp.

And, I'd imagine, encourage a certain caution for our chat seems a little hedgy. They have a beautiful home, it comes out, just as you might expect that it would, and it's where they like to be. The furnishings are all out of storage and installed, plus Robert is testing his practical, household skills which have come on, well, since the days he put on rubber gloves to change a flashlight battery, can't be too careful, and hasn't yet been zapped by a shorted lead. They collect some. Not, aś tends to get assumed again, that Natalie is some totally-absorbed collector, but a while back they zeroed in, she puts it, on Indian culture through the Americas and found it absorbing. But with the kids, who has time? And if they do, who doesn't use it to work? They're professionals, after all, another reason why this opportunity to be working alongside is so much to be prized. *Cat On A Hot Tin Roof*: smouldering conflicts inside plantation Mississippi. In a shattering night of revelation, each member of a family, imprisoned by avarice and envy and self-delusion is forced to face reality. It's deep. It's, well, challenging. And, images apart, no question Robert and Natalie will do a good job. They're professionals, after all. And very civil company besides.

"It could be the memorial to Charlie Chaplin."

AUTUMN SONATA
LIV ULLMANN *and* INGRID BERGMAN

Cinema Drawings
ffolkes

NOSFERATU THE VAMPYRE
ISABELLE ADJANI *and* KLAUS KINSKI

MONTY PYTHON'S LIFE OF BRIAN
MICHAEL PALIN, GRAHAM CHAPMAN,
TERRY JONES, ERIC IDLE *and* JOHN CLEESE.

ISADORA
VANESSA REDGRAVE as
Isadora

NOUGHT'S HAD, ALL'S SPENT

Benny Green
on "The Story of O"
and the French
Cinema today

The pillars of the French film industry will sometimes tell you that they have half an eye on the British market whenever they mount a production. For many years I believed this to be a shameless lie. If the French film industry really cared a fig for the sensibilities of British audiences, it would produce pictures with English dialogue and stop this silly affectation of using a foreign language. Even the Rank Organisation uses what might be loosely called English in its screenplays, so why must the French persist with their anti-social behaviour? Once they reverted to understandable dialogue we could then hunt down and assassinate all those escaped juvenile delinquents who have made an occupation out of composing subtitles to foreign films, and who try to ram down our throats the spectacle of two people gabbling at each other for ten or fifteen minutes, while along the bottom of her bra there appears the line of dialogue, "Good evening". Only a few months ago we had the spectacle of Stavisky, in Alain Resnais's charade of the same name, mouthing the most violent epithets which came out in the subtitle as "behind".

Of course I realise that when the dialogue is incomprehensible, the temptation is to say that the whole thing is a masterpiece, which might explain why some of the most idiotic productions are so fulsomely praised. A few months ago I actually met a man who was able to take *Lancelot of the Lake* seriously enough to number it among his ten best films of the year, when the truth is that what Robert Bresson had done to poor old Arthur would not have passed muster as a music hall lampoon. *Stavisky* was only marginally better, and *The Sparrow of Pigalle* marginally worse, and yet almost nobody found himself constrained by the libel laws when these dreadful cinematic turkeys waddled across the world stage. I suppose what happens is that people get intimidated by anything they don't understand, which would explain, for instance, why they start laughing the moment I open my mouth to sing, but react to the warbling of Charlie Aznovoize with the gravity of bishops contemplating the Holy Grail.

My revolt against all this began many many years ago with a leaden-footed dance to despair called *La Symphonie Pastorale*, and has continued unabated ever since. Admittedly the responsibilities of being a movie reviewer make the task of avoiding all foreign pictures a little more difficult than it was before, but not all that much more difficult. Well-meaning people keep telling me that if I go on with this malicious attempt to ignore the existence of the French film industry as unreasonably as the French film industry persists in ignoring mine, my cultural life will wither away instead of being immeasurably enriched by exposure to the philosophers of the French cinema. It is quite true that about a year ago I stumbled by accident into a French movie and was elevated by the spectacle of a man farting himself to death, but enriching though such experiences are, I get the feeling that I can get by without them.

However, the French film people have now begun taking the British market much, much more seriously than was once the case. Roughly one third of all French productions are what you might call sexploitation movies, all of which are billed on the hustings as "The most scandalous pic ever to come out of France" or "The Hottest Thing from Paris" or some such junk. The bumph for *Emmanuelle* refers to the fact that it "makes you feel good without feeling bad", whatever that is supposed to mean, and the prefix "French sex" continues to mean more in the trade than, say "Swedish sex" or "German sex". So powerful are these connotations that the distributors of *The Story of O* omitted to bill the picture as "Swiss

"Has this film been heavily cut, or is copulation really that jerky?"

"OH, NO—SUB-TITLES EVERY TIME."

sex'', presumably on the assumption that in British minds there is something deflating about the thought of Einstein's countrymen trying to find practical ways of proving that the shortest distance between two points is very often curved.

As a matter of fact *The Story of Q*, a movie about as wild and woolly as the Chief Scout, was the first, although perhaps the unintended first, shot in the bloody battle staged around *The Story of O*, a French movie catering for men so timid in real life that they are obliged to fall back on fantasies of brutality and rapine. I happened to pass the Bloomsbury Cinema where *The Story of Q* was on show, and was I being unduly cynical to suspect that the curlicue at the bottom of the "Q" was truncated to the point where it might be mistaken by a myopic flagellist for the letter "O"? Only the fact that the movie industry is a noble one with a high moral tone obliges me to abandon that theory.

As to the longueurs of watching actresses pretend to be distressed by the attentions of unseen assailants, I am prepared to put up with that sort of thing at least in theory. What does genuinely distress me is the great cloud of intellectual flapdoodle which is hovering over our heads. Those connected with the book and the film of *The Story of O* tell us that the book is a moral work of the most intense severity, that it has philosophic overtones of the most profound importance to the survival of Christianity, that it is unquestionably art, despite the fact that Graham Greene says it is, that it is this and that and the other, but that of all the things it is not, it is not pornography. Why pornographers should be so coy about so ancient a profession I cannot understand. At last the French are making the sort of movies in which the British can show a sincere interest.

Enemy Within
Dilys Powell

Two of my un-favourite cinema themes are united in **Alien**: space-adventure and horror. Of course I struggle to overcome my bias. I make exceptions—an exception for *2001: a Space Odyssey*, an exception for *Solaris*. I am indulgent to horror movies in which Peter Cushing displays his beautifully straight face. But on the whole I find that Space does more than affect the sense of physical balance; on the screen it reduces the human being to a blank, and everybody comes out a brave bonehead. As for horror, it is the enemy of character, leaving no room for anything except prolonged screams. You might say that for me *Alien* has everything against it—well, nearly everything. How come, then, that I admire the film? It can't be (I must declare my prejudices) that a member of my family is associate producer. Clearly *Alien* must have more than a nephew to recommend it.

When it opens the cast are already in space, asleep but, in their regulated lives, about to be awakened by computer. An extra-ordinary set: the space-tug they inhabit, a warren of reverberating rooms and corridors and shafts, is taking back to Earth a valuable commercial cargo. Presently it is taking something else. In response to a mysterious signal the crew stop to investigate the source. What they find, or rather what, though they don't know it, attaches itself to them is a Thing, a Creature: as the title of the film puts it: Alien.

Much of the pleasure of the film depends on what happens next, so I will offer the barest details rather than pursuing the narrative. Pleasure? Yes: *Alien* is far from the customary exercise in disgust; it is a thriller which makes its points through passages of horror—by my reckoning three passages; and the tension is enjoyable because so much is left to the imagination. Indeed the one moment when I find the film falters, barely escaping the absurdity of most current horror bosh, comes when imagination is superseded and you are given a hasty look at the infant Alien as it explodes bloodily from what if I am to keep you in the dark I must call its nursery.

The preliminaries to the moment are OK: a scene of relief from fear, everybody on board en-joying a hearty meal—and then an eruption of agony. It is merely the spectacle of young Alien, a non-descript little bogey, scuttling off into hiding which shakes belief. Imagination is much better than the camera at creating the effect of horror.

For the rest, I am glad to say, you rarely see exactly what is happening. You rarely see Alien. Not until the end of the story do you get a full-length shot, and even then against such light as Space affords. Up to that you are limited to impressions, an impression of tentacles, nails, something that snatches, lurks, manages to be everywhere. And a fact or two. Alien can bleed, but bleeds acid. Alien grows fast. Alien is lethal.

Immured with this un-friendly passenger—and the film gains enormously from being for most of its length enclosed in the complexities of its space-tug—the cast carry on with persuasive acceptance of the situation. Ridley Scott, who directs (he made, you remember, *The Duellists*) has broken away from the familiar mood of heroics—indeed Dan O'Bannon's script wouldn't accommodate it. The players—Tom Skerritt, John Hurt, Veronica Cartwright, Harry Dean Stanton, Yaphet Kotto, Ian Holm (who, as you will learn when you see the film, is a bit different from the others) and especially Sigourney Weaver as the most level-headed and perhaps most cold-blooded of the voyagers—persuades because they behave, or so it seems to the non-space-traveller, like men and women experienced in space.

It is a happy change, and together with the use of suggestion rather than the precise close shot—not to mention the absence of the conventional type of robot—it makes for a movie one would gladly see again. Agreeable, by the way, to see for once a woman taking cool command. And one comes away strengthened in the conviction that if life exists on other planets or elsewhere in space one would really prefer to keep clear of it.

The Caine Mutiny
Richard Mallett

The box-office principle that *any* story must be treated as a love-story with merely decorative interruptions, that the treatment of any theme whatever has to be built on a foundation of boy-gets-girl, is taxed to the uttermost in *The Caine Mutiny* (Director: EDWARD DMYTRYK)—but they contrive that it shall hold. Indeed, it would hardly surprise me to hear that there are simple-minded fans who regard the film as an account of an episode in the life of Ensign Willie Keith, one that distracted him regrettably long from the important business of settling the situation between his mother and his girl, and that that is how they would summarize the story if asked what it was about. The truth—that Willie Keith is there at all only in the capacity of observer, as a technical device to help in the presentation of the real story which does not, in fact, very much concern him—if they could grasp the idea of it at all, would seem to them completely wrong.

But let us forget about them; certain scenes are point-lessly over-emphasized on their account, but not to a degree that spoils the picture for anyone a trifle more grown-up. The basic story of the mutiny and what led up to it—and above all the court-martial that followed it—remain as they were in HERMAN WOUK's novel and are quite admirably handled. HUMPHREY BOGART has certainly never done anything better than his portrait of Captain Queeg. In his

al scene, the mounting uneasi-
ess of Queeg as he testifies at the
ourt-martial, the way he feels and
eflects the changing mood of the
ourt, are conveyed brilliantly
nd—this is another thing that will
affle the simpler fans—quite mov-
gly. It is Mr. BOGART's triumph
hat he is able to carry out the
ovelist's aim and make us see the
oint of Queeg and sympathize
vith him even as we disapprove.

The court-martial, of
ourse, is the big scene, the focus
of the whole thing, as is indicated
by the continuing success in New
York of a stage version of that part
of the book and no more. But the
ninety minutes that precede it (the
whole film runs for over two hours)
are full of excellent, absorbing,
often amusing incident, none of
it—except the scenes concerned
with the private life of Willie
Keith—irrelevant to an understanding of the situation that the
mutiny brings to a head. And the
scene of the mutiny itself, when
the executive officer (VAN
JOHNSON) takes over command in a
typhoon, is made impressively convincing.

This is about the first time
the type-casters have allowed Mr.
JOHNSON outside the little en-
closure they long ago built for him,
and he makes the most of the
chance. It is a rare outing too for
FRED MACMURRAY as Keefer, the
irresponsible cynic. As nobody so
far has ventured to type-cast JOSE
FERRER, his performance as Green-
wald, defence counsel at the court-
martial, can be appreciated simply
as another different character
from his gallery. Mr. BOGART I have
already implied is first-rate. In fact
the only unfortunates are ROBERT
FRANCIS and MAY WYNN, who have
to appear as ordinary Young
American Lovers for the sole benefit of those members of the
audience who don't understand a
story about anything else.

The Deer Hunter
Dilys Powell

When, at the end of *The Deer
Hunter*, family and friends sit down
to a funeral meal a voice in the
background begins to hum *God
Bless America*, and the others take
up the song. Did you, I asked
Michael Cimino, director and part-
author of the film, mean this ironically? After all, of the three
Vietnam veterans, one is dead, one
mutilated, and the third haunted by
his experiences. No, said Mr
Cimino, no, he didn't; and it is true
that to draw back from the direct
approach of a film which depicts
horrors but gives no sign of resent-
ing them would disturb the
balance. At the same time there
seems little cause, whatever the
Almighty may decide, for the
characters on the screen to bless
America. The scene strikes me as
a falsity in a film which remains
otherwise true to itself.

The establishment of the
truth depends, of course, on script,
direction and the acting of the
principals; it depends equally on
the ensemble playing. *The Deer
Hunter* begins in joy: an Orthodox
wedding and a delirious party. The
community—a Pennsylvanian
community, by origin possibly
Polish but that is left vague—is
self-contained but feels itself
American, and the party cele-
brates something more than a
marriage.

Three young men, the
husband and two friends, are off to
Vietnam, and in an outburst of
dancing and drinking, with the
bride and the groom carried
shoulder-high, the heroes-to-be,
workers from a ferocious, satanic
steel-mill, enjoy their farewells.
People sometimes suggest that the
cinema is in decline. I doubt
whether it has ever produced a
crowd-passage more elaborately
organised, more brilliantly timed—
every figure in the excited throng
individually contributing—with an
effect of greater spontaneity.

One more fling before the
descent into war. The friends set
out for their favourite pastime, a
deer-hunt and a kill in the snowy
mountains; they will learn a lesson
about killing before the end of the
story. There are few links in the
film. It leaps without warning from
Pennsylvania to the battlefield,
from Saigon in flames to some
modest American household. But
there is a central theme which
links the shooting of the deer with
the savagery of fighting in Vietnam,
the fall of Saigon with the psychological problems of coming home.
It is the terrifying theme of Russian
roulette—or since the game of
chance appears so popular among
the Vietcong, who gamble lives on
it, who use it to torture their
prisoners, one might call it Asiatic
roulette.

And this is what I mean
when I talk of the film's own truth.
You are made to accept the lethal
game as a fact of existence in the
circumstances of this long film (it
runs over three hours). From the
festive opening, shadowed only by
the entry of the soldier back from
the war, you are led to the test of
courage in the Vietnam swamps.
Then the second crisis, the
revolver once again pressed to the
temples and fired; at last an end
which is muted—but has no
pathos. Pathos, again, would
disturb the balance. *The Deer
Hunter* keeps its own rules.

The detail is masterly: the
old women carrying the tottering
wedding cake across the street;
the horseplay among the friends
on the way to the hunt; the greet-
ings of acquaintances for the
returning hero. The details of
character for once are not
explained but left to speak for
themselves; thus one never knows
what buried animosity provokes
the angry set-to between two of the
hunting party. And this strengthens
the sense of truth. You are looking
at human beings who, as in the
course of ordinary life, don't
always behave logically, who
reveal quirks you didn't know
about.

A great deal is left not to
the dialogue but to performance,
and one is grateful to the direction,
at once sensitive and powerful, of
Michael Cimino. And grateful for
his splendid cast: Christopher
Walken and John Savage as the
Vietnam victims, John Cazale as
the friend who stays at home,
Meryl Streep as the bereaved
fiancée, especially Robert de Niro
as the chief survivor: the emotions
visible beneath the control, the
movements relaxed but purposeful
—and always the sense of leadership, of command. I was in Los
Angeles two years ago when the
film was being prepared. Though I
had admired Robert de Niro I was a
little surprised by the anxiety to
secure him for the role. Now I
understand.

THE HOUSE THE MOUSE BUILT

Alan Whicker
just back from televising
the wildest Disney show
on earth, comes up for air

How can you be mad at Mickey Mouse? Don't think it's easy. To restrain enthusiasm even slightly is not only unAmerican, it's kicking Peter Rabbit's cottontail—you feel such a brute; but fresh from Florida, I'm here to say: at close quarters Disney can cloy.

Now forty-two and very rich indeed, Mickey will move his billion-dollar business to the Sunshine State on October 1st to unleash a social revolution—a project of such magnitude it stuns even a State well used to space-billions, and moon shots departing on time from Platform 2 at Cape Kennedy, just down the road from the House the Mouse built.

For the first of our new *World of Whicker* series for Yorkshire Television I watched the birth pangs of Walt Disney World, largest private building project ever known, and was suitably staggered. Not yet publicised, but about to hit, its impact will register around the world.

Seven years ago Disney quietly bought-up 27,400 acres of swamp and woodland between Kissimmee and Orlando and set his "Imagineers" loose. Their incredible playground across 43 square miles is as big as Manchester or, for southerners, 80 times the size of Hyde Park. Against such a fibreglass fantasy-land, Blackpool is Lilliput.

Cinderella's Castle alone cost £2 million, and would make Ludwig even madder. The Haunted House is almost ready—they're just moving in the ghosts—near an idealised 1890 Main Street.

Thirty-seven lifesize Presidents "authentically garbed by Californian tailors" will be in action, computers controlling 24 body movements a second. Some of these grotesque living dolls also talk. Seven-foot audio-animatronic bears in Grizzly Hall sing how Davy Crockett "killed him a b'ar when he was only three . . ." Artificial lakes heave as artificial waves pound

manmade islands; and here Americans are *building* Cambodian ruins (while knocking them down elsewhere . . .).

This first phase is costing £125 million; Disney calculators expect more than ten million visitors the first year and by 1980 the equivalent of half the population of the United States. The average visitor to this global village should spend between £3 and £4—though a family visit will leave Pop's pocket £40 lighter, per day.

Walt Disney bought this vast spread because at his Californian Disneyland, opened in 1955 and toured by 10 million last year, outside promoters make four times his profit out of *his* crowds. Their motels, spaghetti-heavens, gas stations press-in and cash-in along concentric circles of ugliness.

In Florida, determined to contain his captive audience while they have any cash left, Disney

124

decreed they should stay, as well as play. Phase 1 has five giant resort hotels—the first so big that express monorail trains run right through a lobby big as a football field, silently disgorging passengers at Reception. Its 1,057 modular rooms, prefabricated down to wallpaper and bathroom mirrors, were just slotted in. Conventions already booked through to 1977 include the Catfish Farmers of America and the South-Eastern Peanut Association. Soon, another four motels, camping and trailer parks, hotel for pets, 200 ships on five lakes, a submarine fleet, two railways, park for 12,000 cars, golf courses, and eventually a Community of Tomorrow for twenty thousand people, living-in.

Though kept at a distance, developers fly towards Disney's honey: hot-dog-and-motel strips already surround his phantasmagoria. In satellite new-towns for 80,000 inhabitants, eighteen-storey motor inns are abuilding.

The gentle countryfolk of these ravished counties are still unaware, I suspect, of the magnitude of the coming blow. Kissimmee, once a trading post and the State's Cow Capital, had a gallop-in bar: "Bovine-orientated Kissimmee", said one magazine. There, and at the senior-citizens community of Windermere, residents are discovering Disney-land brings profit to promoters and real-estate men, but to others, just increased taxes, Cup Final traffic every day, roads jammed solid for twenty-five miles, crime, drugs and general disruption imported by the onrushing millions. "We'll be over-whelmed by people problems," said an official. "If everyone only drops a gum wrapper, we'll be knee-deep in gum wrappers."

So central Florida has had greatness, of a sort, thrust upon it. Now the fastest-growing part of the United States, Disney World brings the wildest statistics since space flight: to the Florida domain it will add £3,000,000,000; at least 1,000 hotels, restaurants and service stations; 80,000 jobs. A frantic landrush has sent promising one-acre sites up to £125,000.

Disney's take in the first year should be more than £40 million—much of it from concessions: the Florida Citrus Commission is paying £1½ million for the ten-year right to sponsor a pavilion selling orange drinks; Gulf Oil is putting up £7 million, Eastern Airlines £4 million. Big Business hopes some of Disney's whole-some mystique will rub off, that under his childish spell visitors will be in the right mood "to accept the Corporate message". Could be, for this international institution peddles instant happiness to a passive public which empties its mind and queues to buy.

Those "imagineers" are chillingly efficient; they improve-upon and tidy-up nature. On Swiss Family Isle the giant tree spreads magnificently; only when you touch do you find branches are fibreglass on steel, leaves vinyl. It's creepy. Clouds of pigeons will wheel-around sunset ceremonies, their primary feathers pulled-out until they learn to straighten up, fly right and *love* that place! Dissatisfied with available pansies, they bred a longer-lived strain that's *faceless*. There's Disney for you.

My reaction to his original Californian operation was, I think, typical: I went to smile tolerantly,

stayed to be enchanted. Florida will be the same, only more so; impossible not to succumb to such homespun charm, however phoney and oversweet. Not a child's world, but a middle-aged view of what a child's world might have been...

The man himself spun fantasies and relished an innocence that did not mix with the times. Walt Disney, a sort of genius, ignored the difference between children and adults; his sweet and harmless vision—mawkish, sugar-coated—reconciled generations and awakened old, warm dreams. The man-child who never tired of toys died of cancer five years ago, aged 65; he will not go short of memorials.

He escaped criticism by being resolutely cleancut and against sin; but his patriotic nursery whimsy is also waxen predigested nostalgia and a caricature of American history. The individuality of man and nature lies smothered by plastic, controlled by computers. Man dehumanised, nature defiled—but there I go again, being rude to cute mice.

At close quarters the

"Must be expecting trouble tonight, they've got the old balsa-wood furniture out again..."

insufferably sugary front displayed by this pushy industrial complex leaves me a trifle queasy. A sharp sense of double-entry book-keeping pervades, and all is artifical—even those inescapable white smiles, switched on and off with chill discipline. Over the whole dollar-hungry scene hangs a Jehovah's Witness sense of mission.

At the Disney "University" in California Hosts and Hostesses (in Euphemismland customers are Guests, uniforms Costumes, crowds Audiences) are indoctrinated and taught how to be "people specialists", which seems to mean frozen grins and canned answers. Simple mass psychology is aimed at keeping Audiences in a spending mood.

One of the Hostesses explained "When you work for Disney the glory falls upon you and you start to glow—it's pixie dust!" She didn't smile when she said that, unfortunately.

Meanwhile back in Paradiseland Walt Disney seems about to be canonized. Though far from popular in his lifetime, employees' eyes now light up at his name. Legends grow more loving as years go by and good works proliferate. In discreet corners throughout his growing empire, small portraits await their candles.

Our pilgrimage into his world was suitably humble, but we emerged perplexed; this was not only due to an alarmingly inept Public Relations department. We had driven five hundred miles to Orlando and received a guarded welcome from Disney's Marketing man Sandy ("This is a first-name operation, Alan"). They had their own television film to sell, he said, so although my thirty million audience around the world was acceptable, they preferred to control publicity. Indeed they do. Chosen groups are brought in for an organised tour, lecture, brief word with selected personnel—and away, clutching handouts. What they can't control, they fear. And there was this unchosen Englishman; when you wish upon Disney's star, it makes a *lot* of difference who you are . . .

After much charming

hesitation they allowed we might film, provided not more than ten minutes of Disney World appeared in the final programme. (We actually used seven minutes). We started carefully, to do the place justice.

Next morning a gritty PR man called Charles ("Now lissen here, Alan . . .") abruptly ordered us to leave the site by midday. I had mixed emotions: it was almost a relief to meet someone being thoroughly nasty—at least there was nothing bogus about *his* attitude.

He didn't say "These 27,400 acres are too small for both of us" but he *did* imply, with a stern stare over my left shoulder, that if we were still there, come sundown, we should be run out of town. It was High Noon in Fantasyland, and the pixie dust was coming down sour. We departed, meek but sorrowful. Our white hardhats were taken away, symbolically. Disney's private army of cops gave us brief automatic smiles as we drove into the sunset. Up music, run titles, fade.

Let not such curious incompetence, the unsure organisation man's fear of the committee above, cloud our reaction to a staggering achieve-ment. Disney's earnest army is making the world's major bid to solve problems of expanding leisuretime—and incidentally, problems of surplus cash.

Their organisation is whole-some, well disciplined and (usually) friendly. Within it the outsider will find no alcohol, no long hair, no drugs, no litter, no sex, no moustaches, no violence. Instead, a reassuringly bland blend of whimsy, brilliance of imagination, cunning crowd control; a senti-mental spread of antiseptic enter-tainment to delight those millions who love to get their teeth into a marshmallow-covered cream puff, artificially sweetened.

So—sorry to be out of step, but this Prole (one ten-millionth of the first year's throughput) can do without such manipulation, however innocent. I'll glow my own way, thanks, if it's all the same to St. Walt. Let's face it, there's something positively *inhuman* about Mickey Mouse.

OF MICKEY MOUSE AND MEN

Jonathan Sale celebrates the birthday of a rodent money-spinner

You've seen the film, now do the jigsaw, hop on the hopper, wobble the Wobbler, bend the Bendy Toy, munch the chocolate, slip into the mask and snip away with the pre-school safety scissors.

You knew about Mickey Mouse, but did you know about the Mickey Mouse Weeble, who comes with his chums Wendy and Willie Weeble (they all sort of wobble)? That's an Airfix product, as is the Mickey Mouse Bop-Bag, in hard-wearing polythene, with its three-inch high structure and weighted base, so that the kid can bop it but it never falls down, a bargain at £2.25.

When Donald Duck, Snow White, Dopey, Jiminy Cricket, Dumbo, Thumper, Lady, Tramp, Pongo Dalmation, Scat Cat and Robin Hood the fox take their bow in the final credits of their movies, this is not the end of the story. They are then on offer to manufacturers who want to market a jigsaw or hopper with a Disney character printed all over it.

Disney creations are not always ahead of the field. As a Wombles flannel currently providing a home for mould in our bathroom bears witness, the hairy things from Wimbledon have occasionally overtaken the American import. But what Disney has is staying power, so that its creatures are not flash-in-the-pans dependent on an ephemeral television series. They are backed up by films, which are around for three years, taken off the market for seven years, and reincarnated in time to catch a whole new generation. Last year Winnie the Pooh was the big money-spinner, but next year it will be the ultimate Disney creation that drags them in.

"He's got great big ears, a nose like a tennis ball and three fingers on each hand. But when it comes to shifting toys off the shelves, he's magic," is a testimonial from Mettoy Playcraft to the fun-loving rodent and his pals who have "been responsible for those extra noughts that make your sales figures look like a million dollars." Happy birthday, Mickey Mouse! Fifty next year, with a big splash aimed at the consumer in February courtesy of a national newspaper, a nine-week promotion starting in Easter courtesy of a grocery chain, and a television and cinema special organised by "Gus Zelnick, who heads up our film division". A David Cassidy song-writer has produced *Mickey Mouse, Donald Duck, Goofy and the Gang*, aimed to be released in August and to be a hit. There will be limited edition medallions and a golden commemorative paint box. A Mickey Mouse telephone is on the way.

"The spin-off to Mickey Mouse licensees will be tremendous next year," said Disney executive Keith Bales, though not to me (anyone who's anyone in the UK Disney business was watching the next new film, *Pete's Dragon*, in Monte Carlo last week) but to the prestigious journal that some time ago scooped an interview with him, *Toy Trader*. The principle of character merchandising, which last year brought Disney's international operations a revenue of over twenty-one million dollars, is that instead of making masks with goofy faces, you make masks with Goofy faces, like Reliance Snap Co of Bishop's Stortford. One day they were saying to themselves, "We've been in the business of making snaps for crackers for many years," next day they were going about like so many cloned Mickeys, Donalds and Plutos. They, like all other licensees, have to satisfy the quality control experts at Disney that they are not fly-by-night bodgers who will produce leprous mice with one ear and half a snout.

Once you have satisfied the chief executive (merchandising), you are guaranteed the exclusive rights in your part of the world to something that will sell, and possibly become an export, sometimes even to the United States. "The UK is in the top five Disney countries," said a girl they left behind in the Pall Mall headquarters of Disney's British operations last week.

Bell Toys of Ashford, Middlesex, can rest assured that their Pop Pals, "comic Disney characters retailing at 99p a pack," will be the only pals popping this side of the coastline of Britain. The same is true of the Trickey Trapeze set (60p), the Trickey Riders set in motion by pull ring action (85p), the Peppy Puppets (95p), the Roly Poly Donald Duck and the Roly Poly Mickey Mouse (75p) and the Disney Dancers (65p), all from the same Middlesex stable.

There is no conflict there with the products of another lucky licensee, Burbank Toys, based not, as its name suggests, in Los Angeles, but in downtown Wellingborough, Northants. "Each toy says many random phrases in its own authentic character voice," and don't sneer, I know people like that. These retail from £13.99, and the less well heeled might prefer the Mickey Mouse Bean Doll and

*"He was a potential liberator –
but the System bought him!"*

the Donald Duck Bean Doll at £3.75.

Even cheaper, and still from the Burbank production lines, are the "Disney Talk Ups". Why, even "the packaging has play value". The personae are Mickey and Minnie, Donald and Daisy, and they are "backed by extensive advertising support to create greater consumer awareness which is spearheaded by a compelling television commercial scheduled for the entire country." There will be "instore display material" announcing a competition, and a case of champagne for lucky retailers. "Retailing at £2.99, this quartet is an impulse buy for the pocket money market," say the manufacturers, who clearly are trusting on gaining the custom of the last of the big-time juvenile spenders; when I was a kid, three pounds wasn't loose cash for impulse buys, it was the sort of

money you needed to purchase the sole distribution rights for *Fantasia* and *The Lady and the Tramp*.

There comes a time when every variation of pull-along, talk-up Mickey Mouse has been spoken for, so that a go-ahead manufacturer has to look further afield. Cliro Perfumeries came up with Pooh Bear "in quality vinyl complete with tooth-brush and squeaker in an acetate drum presentation pack". They then put on the market another presentation box, this time of "Pooh Bear's peach shampoo and Tigger's strawberry bubbles," and, encouraged by its success, "finely sculpted figures of Pooh and Tigger in citrus fragrance soap," and the noise they hear o' nights is A.A. Milne turning in his tomb-sculpted, earth-scented presentation grave. Neither Milne nor anyone else could complain about the toothbrush, which every child is going to need, given the

choice from other licensees: Donald Duck cake from Angelo Granozio of Salerno, Italy; Winnie-the-Pooh Pudding from General Foods of Banbury, Oxfordshire, England; and Disney Bubble Gum from Anton van Zeyl of Amsterdam, Holland.

F. B. Gould of Kent came up with mobiles, not just any old mobiles, but mobiles featuring Mickey, Pluto, Goofy, Donald Duck and his three nephews, who are, as genealogists of the duck tribe will already know, Huey, Dewey and Louie. LSS Promotions have produced, rather rashly in view of the fact that children might decide to produce their own versions of Disney, a "How to Draw Walt Disney Characters Kit," and also the new Boppa Bat, laminated and crossgrained, in the shape of Mickey Mouse's head.

And so the list goes on, each sale presenting a few more cents in the Disney coffers: the

SUNSET LODGE RESIDENTS' LOUNGE

"He hardly ever has any visitors, except maybe once in a while a crabby duck comes in and starts slanging him..."

Disney Sing-a-Long radio from Hong Kong, the Donald Duck Sit 'N' Ride, Disney Honda Scooters, Mowgli Wobblers (to be fixed on the wall), Mettoy Hoppers (reinforced balloons for sitting astride), Bambi Stencil sets and Mickey Mouse nameplates with space for the buyer's own name (''Match the popularity of Mickey Mouse with a child's own name on an identifying nameplate and you've got yourself a quick impulse-selling, profit maker'').

Disney produces new characters all the time. On general release at the moment is *The Rescuers*, acclaimed for the fact that ''It introduces two *completely new* mice, an albatross called Orvill . . . and a completely new merchandising opportunity,'' according to Disney's Keith Bales. And he's right; there are Large Mirrors, Small Mirrors, T-shirts, PVC Stickers, Pyjamas and even—going out on a limb—Books, all devoted to those new-look mice (whose italics just there were my own, manufactured under licence, of course).

Coming soon is the movie that dragged the men from Disney to Monte Carlo, *Pete's Dragon*. Although *British Toys and Hobbies* doesn't reveal much of the story-line in its December issue, it does inform readers that the film has already produced its share of jig-saws (from Michael Stanfield Holdings), children's apparel (Tesco and Marks and Spencer) and Bendy Toys (from Newfield Limited). And Books.

Children's characters are, in fact, far from childish in their financial aspects. They are considered worth inspection by the *Financial Times*'s Arthur Sandles, who wonders if Mickey can stave off the merchandising attacks of the spin-offs from *Star Wars*, not to mention *Superman*, which features Marlon Brando and is said to be the most expensive film of all time. That last I can't say much about, but I have seen *Star Wars*. No, not the movie, just the list of merchan-dising, and it looks formidable. They come from outer space to bring you bubble baths, moulded marshmallows, character ice-creams, jigsaw puzzles, T-shirts, digital watches, Stormtrooper masks and hardware toys.

And Book.

CANNED FILM FESTIVAL
OLD DIRECTORS WHO WON'T FADE AWAY

Among the more noxious aspects of spring is the film festival. For those of us who won't be at Cannes, **DON LESSEM** provides a preview of what we can expect to miss:

HOLIDAY ON ICE—INGMAR BERGMAN. Bergman's first musical and a great one. Liv Ullman stars as a catatonic figure-skater who sees Death (Ryan O'Neal) in the cracks of the ice. She performs figure-eights until Spring (Max Von Sydow) melts the ice. Visually stunning in its stark contrasts and sparing use of color. Score by Lawrence Welk.

LA SAGNA—(THE BLOOD)—FEDERICO FELLINI. The savage depravity of the Visigoth conquest is revealed through Fellini's unique vision. The story centres upon a Roman circus troup which is captured and unmercifully booed by the invaders. Starring Anthony Quinn and Bozo the Clown.

YOU DIE, YANKEE DOG—AKIRA KUROSAWA. The director again examines the subjective nature of truth in *Rashomon*esque style. This time we see, through 24 sets of eyes, Babe Ruth's famous ''called'' home run in the 1927 World Series.

LE CHANDELIER (THE CANDLE-STICK MAKER). CLAUDE CHABROL. The debonaire young *chandelier*, masterfully played by Jean-Pierre Leaud, leaves work early one afternoon to go to the dentist. Chabrol, with his characteristic mastery of suspense and slow pace, has the audience on the edge of its collective seat throughout, as Leaud locks the office door, has difficulty starting his car, finally takes a cab.

THEY DIED WITH THEIR SOCKS OFF—NICHOLAS RAY. The foremost architect of the baroque Western has fashioned a bizarre oater concerning a calamitous fire in Bat Masterson's bordello. Also featuring the first shoot-out between blind cowboys. All five lines of dialogue are intentionally mumbled.

LA MALAISE DU PAP (THE POPE GETS A RASH)—LUIS BUNUEL. Once again the old master wittily satirises our religious institutions as the College of Cardinals visits the Rome Zoo. Watch for Bunuel himself in a rare screen appearance, beating a dead horse. With Fernandel.

LATE SUMMER, EARLY LUNCH—OZU. The traditional values of a Japanese rural family are shaken when an electrical fence is built around their farm. Gradually they discover that a chain-fence is only as strong as its weakest link. With Key Luke and Francis the Mule.

PASTA FAZOOL—(BREAD OF FOOLS). MICHEL-ANGELO ANTONIONI. A compelling tale of Moses's search for the unleavened bread. Filmed on location in the American Southwest. Antonioni's obsession with pure colour caused him to repaint the entire Painted Desert. Starring every Redgrave. In Italian with Italian subtitles.

THE POUR DEUX—(TEA FOR TWO)—FRANCOIS TRUFFAUT. A troubled adolescent, charmingly portrayed by Jean-Pierre Leaud, is ignored by his drunken father (Charles Aznavour) and beaten by his tyrannical mother (Jean-Pierre Leaud). Seeing no other recourse, the boy steals a gun and shoots them both. Taking to the streets, he is befriended by an eccentric millionaire (Jean-Pierre Leaud) and grows up to become France's greatest director.

HINTS TO FOREIGNERS WHO PRODUCE CINEMA FILMS FOR THE ENGLISH MARKET.

An English nobleman as a rule does not act in the above manner during a misunderstanding with a lady who has engaged his affections.

English sportsmen and sportswomen are seldom as decorative as this.

When the Earl of Wessex meets an ex-officer of his regiment in the desert they are unlikely to behave like this.

When the notice preceding the picture definitely states that the action takes place in Piccadilly the above doesn't look right somehow.

HOME MOVIES

And it's in your neighbourhood NOW!

"But aren't you going to rather a lot of trouble... just for our home-movies?"

A critical guide to current releases in the wonderful world of eight-millimetre domestic production...

KODAK: A remarkable achievement, this one-reel silent account of a day in the life of an ordinary, lollipop-sucking New York street photographer. Though clearly made with television audiences in mind, it looks good if a little fuzzy on the Boots Super Pull-Up Home Screen and one hardly misses the sound at all. Colleagues tell me there could be a series in this, though from what I was able to lip-read of the dialogue, phrases like ''Sell me something, sweetheart'' and ''What's this cab?'' will need some explaining to English audiences. It also seems a pity that the hero should be portrayed as a bald Greek sex-maniac: that's the kind of image which gets amateur photography a bad name anywhere in the world, even New York.

ON THE BEACH: Another lyrical tribute to family life from the fertile camera (believed to be a Fujica Single 8 Colour) of Mrs C. B. Potter of Littlehampton. This year she has chosen ''holiday time'' as her theme and the shots of little Celestia Potter being buried in sand by her fun-loving brother as in the background the tide comes even closer to the beach are cleverly built into a most suspenseful sequence. Sadly the end of the film is somewhat confused—at one point the camera appears to have been hurled into the sand and there us a curious shot of Mrs Potter's left ankle as she runs towards her daughter. This may however be intended as an indirect tribute to Antonioni and his views on the uncertainty of all human life, though one feels he would have ensured that the lens of the camera was facing upwards as it hit the sand.

EUROPE HERE WE COME, Part 17: Mr and Mrs Chislehurst of The Laburnums, near Bromley, are again delighting neighbours and friends alike with film of their foreign travels, and this year's movie has some extremely witty sequences including one hilarious shot of Mr Chislehurst apparently propping up the famous Leaning Tower of Pisa! But the film has something serious to say as well; in the shots of traffic jams in downtown Milan is an all-too-clear warning of the dangers of joining the Common Market, and it is obvious from the commentary given live at each performance by Mrs Chislehurst that she didn't really care for Italy at all. Next year, the Chislehursts promise us ''A Return to Blackpool''.

GIVE MY REGARDS TO EALING BROADWAY: For tube lovers everywhere, this hand-held account of a journey on the Central Line taken by E. J. Knoakes will hold considerable fascination, although it is inclined to get a little monotonous in the tunnels. It is also a pity that Mr Knoakes had to shoot it in the rush hour, since for a considerable stretch of the film the picture is obscured by what appears to be the City Prices edition of the Evening Standard held by one of the other passengers. Enthusiasts are however eagerly awaiting Mr Knoakes's companion work filmed on the Northern Line on Sunday afternoon and due for release towards the end of 1976.

ABOVE US THE WAAFS: Real nostalgia, this, since it has been transferred to Super 8 from the original 16-millimetre print filmed during the war by Warrant Officer Hebblethwaite, now of course Mr Hebblethwaite of The Larches, Surbiton. One or two visitors to the Hebblethwaite home have complained that the film is pure pornography, but Mr Hebblethwaite prefers to consider it his own special contribution to the war effort, a patriotic masterpiece indicating the ability of the British to carry on regardless. Some of the characters in the film have now acquired a kind of period charm, and two or three are believed to be in touch with their solicitors.

ZOOMING ACROSS THE CHANNEL: Unfortunately this is not the speedy, all-action travelogue promised by the title; instead Mrs J. G. Arbuthnot has been content to station herself on a bench just outside Eastbourne and point her camera out to sea; unhappily for her, and for viewers of her fifty-minute documentary, the zoom lens on certain home-movie cameras is not as effective as some advertisements would have you believe. Still, there is a most interesting albeit accidental close-up of a seagull in the thirty-seventh minute, a shot which should come as a timely warning to all in the habit of standing bare-headed on the decks of cross-channel ferries.

THE NIGHT MY NUMBER NEARLY CAME UP: A searing, adult human drama set in the Palais de Bingo at East Croydon where clever tracking shots establish our hero, Rodney, just as he is about to call Full House; the atmosphere here is positively Dostoievskian, and in the fanatical attempts of Rodney to cover his last number with the side of his thumb we are all given a little insight into the private hell of the gambler. This film is not recommended for the susceptible.

A SMALLER SPLASH: M. J. Whittle's deeply touching account of what life is like for a talented but intellectually disturbed house-painter in contemporary Sydenham; the scene in which the hero is abandoned by his tortoise, Albert, and finds himself unable to carry on painting the back door of No. 17 Crystal Palace Parade until he's had a bit of a sit down, will live in the memory for well over twenty minutes.

For many amateur film-makers, mere ciné-snap-shooting is not enough: they want to make **movies**. HEATH has been on location with some of them . . .

"OK, let's get the day rolling."

"Come back later, the wife's busy right now."

"It's a wife swapping party."

"I'm going to make this movie about a husband who leaves his wife for a young girl and finds true happiness."

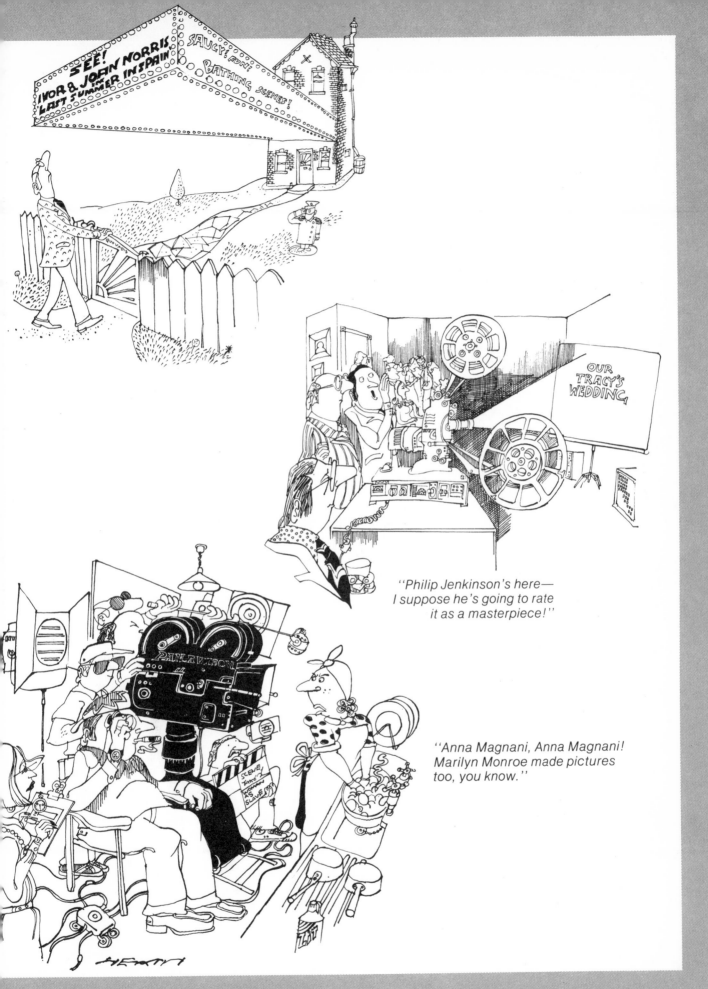

"Philip Jenkinson's here—
I suppose he's going to rate
it as a masterpiece!"

"Anna Magnani, Anna Magnani!
Marilyn Monroe made pictures
too, you know."

Home Movies for Abroad
Jonathan Sale

Interior, Dalston Garage, 5.25 am. Enter, right, two men in off-duty bus-drivers' suits. Voice: ''The day starts early.'' Men look at watches.

It's not often I manage to get a jump ahead of the Sunday film critics, the habitués of cinemas showing nothing but Chilean allegories with sub-titles (or, more impressive, without sub-titles), the fans of eight-hour epics on the rise of Fascism in some parts of Italy, and those who can't say Nō to a Japanese season at the National Film Theatre. Yet how many subscribers to *Cahiers du Cinéma* have sat through *The Nine Road*, the searing documentary of a day in the life of the Number Nine Bus? Certainly none of them was sitting in the stalls last week when it had one of its screenings; in fact, no one was sitting anywhere in the film theatre of the Transport and Travel Film Library theatre except for myself and the man from British Transport Films.

Movie-making in Britain is not dead. It is alive and flickering hard by Marylebone Station, where the film unit has made, or commissioned, over 1,100 short films, strips and commercials. These are not likely to have a long West End run (they ''must NOT be exhibited on any occasion when an admission fee is charged'') but they are shown abroad when two or three travel agents are gathered together, and have a larger part in spreading the image of Britain than *Sweeney 2* or *Jubilee*. They can be hired in this country for around the price of a couple of seats in the commercial cinema—£2.50—and to me, a film critic for the afternoon, they were free. I even had the pick of the catalogue and the chance, never to be repeated, of choosing my own programme.

Back in Dalston Garage, they are four men short. ''Is this something that happens quite often?'' queries the Peter Snow-type voice. ''I'm afraid it does,'' answers the man in the suit behind the desk labelled ''Garage Manager''. Talk about lifting the lid off London Transport! *The Nine Road* goes on courageously to show how the staff cope with the shortages, the traffic, the route changes and the passengers.

We see a conductor taking fares, a driver driving and an Inspector putting a pencil behind his ear. Sometimes the bus goes round Hyde Park Corner, sometimes down Fleet Street. We see queues at bus stops, and roads empty of buses. And this honest and compelling movie concludes with another astonishing touch of *cinéma vérité*. ''This is One Zero,'' snaps the driver into his radio-telephone, ''I am in Cannon Street and boiling over.'' Just like the passengers.

Interior, Dalston Garage, midnight. Close-up of buckled fan. Voice: ''The trouble was a buckled fan.''

Final chords of music, which is, like the bus, in the middle of the road. Credits roll. The Peter Snow-type voice turns out to originate not from ITN but from Douglas Cameron of LBC.

There may not be Snow in *The Nine Road*, but there is certainly snow in my next movie. There is a train in the snow, a snowed-up notice saying ''Refreshments'' and men in the snow. It is entitled *Snow*. A snow-plough with a great beak scatters snow like a speedboat racing through the waves. The driver of a passenger train looks ahead, passengers look out of the window, the driver stares ahead, passengers gaze out of the window. Is this some kind of socio-political comment?

Later a fireman shovels coal (this collector's item dates back to 1963), passenger eats, labourer shovels snow, passenger stuffs face. Yes, this is very powerful Marxist stuff. As is another film in the same genre, *Snowdrift at Bleath Gill*, which dates back to the Golden Age of movies about snowdrifts, 1955. Although this is longer—it lasts a good ten minutes—it has the same theme of Them and Us. Men shovel, cough, swear, walk about with lanterns; supervisors give instructions. Finally, as the music on the soundtrack crashes and the film becomes poignantly under-exposed, the stranded engine eaks free.

No film show is complete ithout an earlier (1952) and nger (16 minutes by the clock, ice that by the mind) film, *Train me.* This is a no-holds-barred ama of extra trains laid on to ppe with the broccoli harvest in rnwall which cause a shortage stock for the tinplate factory ade of South Wales. Meanwhile in erdeen at 12.30 fish board the ndon train, and cattle from eland are too sick to travel. ecutives argue over routes, coal tipped into wagons, the evening ift takes over. The film ends in e dawn of the next day, eliberately leaving us in suspense out the precise quantity of occoli needing shipment from e West Country.

The shots of the Toton arshalling Yard alone make this

much sought after in railway enthusiasts' circles, but there is a whole new generation of films that home in on separate aspects of life in Britain today and are perhaps more useful to the foreigner wondering where to spend his currency. He should not miss *Boardroom of the North*, an introduction to Harrogate, or *Gateway to Opportunity*, which is an eyeball-to-eyeball confrontation with Kings Lynn. You can guess the subject of *A Fine City, Norwich*, and the only surprise with *Leicestershire—A Heritage at Risk* is that they actually have one to lose. I think that *This is Bournemouth* says it all, as does *Window on Weymouth*. I like the harsh directness of *Thanet*, available from the Amenities Department of Thanet District Council.

Most of the local movies are available from the local councils, but British Transport Films have made their mark on this market as well. *The Port of Grimsby and Immingham* is 18 glossy minutes of "There is more to Grimsby than fish—wood-pulp, for example"; pilgrims, I learn, left Immingham for the New World. One of the attractions of Glasgow is, according to *Glasgow belongs to me*, the ease with which it too can be left for the surrounding countryside; these seventeen minutes of cliché are worth £2.50 for the theme song alone, coming from Glasgow Police Choir. If that doesn't get the tourists' jumbos speeding towards Britain (the audience reflected as the house lights came up and it stumbled out into the Marylebone Road) precious little will.

THE FAMILY ALBUM: NEW STYLE.

ostess. "Now I must just run through one more for you. This is my brother Archibald having breakfast in the arden, in two reels."

THE ACTORS' SYMPOSIUM
The Celluloid Cafeteria

CLOSE ENCOUNTER
Alan Brien

Having spent a lifetime rejecting the comforts of unreason, and resisting the lures of the supernatural, I still have to report that the crowd of gossip-column names last week leaving the packed press show of *Close Encounters of the Third Kind,* and blinking in the unexpected sunshine of Leicester Square, seemed very near transfigured. Particularly the women. It was as if its climactic finale, with the blinding arrival of visitors from outer space, had put them through a sauna with their clothes on, meanwhile shampooing their hair, polishing their cheeks and Sanforising the fabric.

In the trade, science fiction is usually considered "spotty b.o. for fem auds". But *Close Encounters*—if nothing else, the decade's most resonant film title—looks like being the first of its kind to attract women back to the cinema. Even the *New Yorker*'s choosy and cool-eyed critic, Pauline Kael, described the end of the film as "one of those peerless moments in movie history—spiritually reassuring, magical and funny at the same time".

I was not surprised, then, to meet two women friends shortly afterwards, both of whom claimed recent personal experiences of extra-sensory phenomena at work. There was the film critic, returning early for the press show from the Berlin Film Festival, who had fallen asleep on the airport bus and dreamed of a crash on the road when broken glass from the windscreen hurtled directly at her. At that point, she struggled awake and realised the bus was about to collide. Still in the grip of her nightmare, she crouched on the floor and the glass passed over her head.

Then there was the journalist whose likeable but strange twelve-year-old son is given to hypermanic bursts of speeded-up activity when it appears as if he is mainlining electricity and his hair stands on end like a fright wig. At these times, she said with a doubtful, hesitant smile, almost every working machine around the house packs up suddenly—the washing machine, the Hoover, the mixer, the radio, even the car. I pointed out gently that her car anyway was notoriously unreliable as her colleagues would witness from the number of times she called the office to report herself stranded in the back of beyond. As for her domestic gadgets, she was not exactly the most mechanically-minded of part-time housewives.

"No, no," she said. "It's not just our place, but all about us in our little part of North London. The neighbours have been calling in and pressing copies of *The Exorcist* and *Audrey Rose* on me. They're not complaining. They all like my son. But everything is packing up in their households too, cars and all. There's no way he could be doing this by any ordinary means. It has to be something like a poltergeist, or an effect of electrical brain activity that nobody knows about so far."

As someone who fights off the universal London cold every winter by the exercise of mental obstinacy (operating on the analogy that if a couple of German nuns could get the stigmata through faith I could surely drive off a few sniffles and wheezes by anti-faith) I have no doubt that mind and body are interlinked in close psychosomatic sympathy. But I also take the line that, when faced by an apparently insoluble puzzle, the sanest reaction is to establish that the facts have been correctly recorded. Many mysterious happenings only appear mysterious because some part of the pattern has been left out of the description. In a choice of explanations, I prefer the methods of Sherlock Holmes even over those of his fairy-loving, spiritualist creator, Conan Doyle. So far I am not convinced there is any convincing evidence for distant encounters of the first kind. But the investigation continues.

BANX

"Maybe you'd like something to drink, sir, before the mirage starts."

REVIEWS

Close Encounters Of The Third Kind
Barry Took

The word around Wardour Street about **Close Encounters Of The Third Kind** has been that it's a cross between *Gone With The Wind* and the second coming. Come to think of it, I suppose it does have elements of both. It's certainly long and it is about a strange, unearthly visitation by, well, scarcely a flying saucer, more a flying three-hundred piece dinner service. An immense piece of special effects that I suppose at a pinch is worth the two-hour build up to its appearance.

Before we see it, or indeed those who inhabit this space Leviathan, we've seen funny lights shining on Indiana homes, the electrical equipment in said Indiana homes going berserk, heard a tune repeated by many people none of whom have any connection with each other except, that is, a crowd of some hundreds in India (not Indiana) who rush about humming it in a giant *Sing Along With Outer Space*. Not only that but we've seen the materialisation of aeroplanes that disappeared in the Bermuda Triangle back in 1945, and other manifestations that were they to happen to you and me would have us as an additional burden on the already overstretched Health Service.

Sturdy but sensitive scientists led by François Truffaut, unravel the mystery of the flashing lights, strange manifestations, etc., and arrange a rendezvous with the extraterrestrial beings in Wyoming. There they play the tune—the space ship answers fortissimo on what sounds like a tuba, (clearly brass playing is well advanced in the galaxy) and lands. It then disgorges the pilots of the aforementioned aeroplanes lost in the Bermuda Triangle in 1945 plus other humans from other times (we

don't get to see them too clearly—they were presumably a sub-plot and that got lost in the editing) and a little boy who's been removed from his Indiana homestead after a good deal of special effects, but who seems quite cheerful about it all when reunited with his mother. There's more, lots more but I don't want to put you off the film altogether.

Frankly, I thought it was tripe designed and made quite brilliantly for an audience of village idiots.

There are good performances from Richard Dreyfuss, Teri Garr, Melinda Dillon, and François Truffaut, but the biggest contribution is from Douglas Trumbull who created the visual effects, and which are very special indeed.

One last point—it's not a bit like *Star Wars*. That amiable film appeals to the child in us—*Close Encounters* appeals to our credulity.

Facile Concoctions
E. V. Lucas

I spent not a little time at the FRED ASTAIRE picture at the Carlton Theatre in wondering why it had been called *Top Hat*. I guessed at first that it was because FRED ASTAIRE has evidently been looking at MAURICE CHEVALIER and MAURICE CHEVALIER has made the straw hat famous. But since there is no longer in the film any insistence on the top-hat and its potentialities are not allowed to enter into the final grand ballet, I must suppose that the idea of rivalry was allowed to drop. But what's in a name, anyway, and peculiarly so when FRED ASTAIRE is dancing? Yet, although his feet consistently charm and bewilder, I thought his songs deplorable.

Once again I have to reco a division of allegiance. A consid- erable section of the audience at the Carlton, and particularly the gentleman with a loud and too-lor laugh just behind me, thought more of ED. EVERETT HORTON than of FRED ASTAIRE or GINGER ROGERS They waited for his each appear- ance, greeting it with such delight that the succeeding sentences were lost: a consequence which makes one realise that Holly- wood's timers, or whatever the attendant laugh-measurers are called, had been unimaginative. I am not denying that ED. EVERETT HORTON is mildly funny, but his habit of always misunderstanding the first remark to him, and momentarily taking an insult for a compliment (his principal title to eminence), can become tiresome Also it persuades one very quickly that such a stupid listener would never have reached his position a a theatrical *entrepreneur*.

Going Pop
Dilys Powell

Difficult, really, to know whether to congratulate the pop stars or to commiserate with th In the past, before they were ca pop, one knew they would come out OK. They would have a Busl Berkeley-type finale, or if they w unlucky enough to die in obscur there would be a celebratory concert at Carnegie Hall. But al that is changed now. They may enjoy success. But after succes all they can hope for, if one may judge by Brian Gibson's **Breaki Glass**, is a chair in the psychiat clinic.

It begins, of course, in th same way, except that nowaday as time goes on the performand becomes a shade more polishe (in the old American musical the singer or the dancer was livelier before celebrity was achieved). There is the humble start in the back yard (a variant in British movies: instead of the back yard London pub). A group is formed The audience grows. A tour is arranged. The audience is enthusiastic. There are appearances in major halls. The udience is hysterical. A love affair intervenes. Then things begin to go wrong. Commercial backing destroys the purity, artistic, moral and spiritual, of the performance. There is a rift in the love affair. The group disintegrates. And here comes the fashionable new element in the plot: drink persists, but drugs are added.

As a matter of fact in the British pop musical something else has been added: protest. The British pop movement does a great deal of protesting. It protests about people who have the bad taste not to belong to its generation. It protests about the police. Kate (Hazel O'Connor), central figure of *Breaking Glass*, protests, if my stunned ears did not mislead me, about racialism. She half-owns to anarchism. And wherever she goes she is accompanied by violence.

The glass of the title is broken not by the force of the human voice (you remember the shattered chandelier in *Le Million*?); it is pub glass and it is broken in a series of brawls. There are peaceful intervals. Jon Finch, masterful as the records producer, presides over temporarily lowered voices. Phil Daniels, persuasive as the group's manager, occasionally able to keep the glassware intact. A deaf saxophonist (Jonathan Pryce) contributes a few moments of quiet. For the rest, Miss O'Connor shatters the eardrums. At first she sings with blonde hair in a pudding-basin clip, with glistening maroon lips and the smudged eyes of a giant panda. With success the words of the songs are tamed, the blonde hair is oiled back, and the lips pass through crimson to electric blue. But the mouth still opens in a savage rectangle, the shoulders still march, the whole body is still alive with aggression.

It is an exercise in menace; it is a *tour de force*; one has to admire. But a character in the film remarks: ''Somehow this new music gives me a headache.'' The pop audience, I suppose, don't have headaches. Nevertheless I can't help fearing that they are in for a deaf old age.

Screen Pantomimes
E. V. Lucas

...the place

the place of the very young I cannot describe their reaction to *Snow White and the Seven Dwarfs*; but at the New Gallery the other afternoon, which seemed to be full of children, I heard no cries of distress. Nor, on the other hand, did I hear many gurgles and chuckles of delight; and if this was so, it is, I fancy, because GRIMM has been rather roughly handled and Americanized. *Snow White* herself, whom we have always thought of as a charming little girl, wavers between the naïvest simplicity and adult sophistication, and speaks in a voice in which the accents of *Betty Boop* are far too prominent; the *Prince* is sheer pasteboard; the hard-boiled *Dwarfs* are a shade too realistic, and the *Queen*, as the jealous grandmother, is of malignity compact, and, as the witch, an unholy terror. But whether those of tender age can get any harm from all this is doubtful.

And the story, I think, is too long. DISNEY films must not be full length.

But the woodland creatures! Here WALT is at his best. Those that we saw in his *Little Hiawatha* are now carried out to their highest power: the rabbits, the squirrels, the racoons, the owls, the pigeons, the blue jays, and above all the timid inquisitive deer. I can think of nothing that the screen has given us more charming than these frolicsome knights-errant coming to the rescue of *Snow White*, leading her to security, and then helping her again by cleaning up, the final triumphant touch coming when two of the birds, who have been busy in hanging out the clothes, descend to imprint with their footmarks the edging of the gooseberry-pie.

Lord TYRRELL, I suspect, when he refused the full licence to

Snow White and the Seven Dwarfs boggled at the preparation of the Apple of Death; and the steps are fairly gruesome. But he was probably being too sensitive for others. The modern children can be hard-boiled too. If, however, WALT is thought to have gone too far here, he struck one as having tried insufficiently when the *Princess* receives her awakening kiss. That, surely, should have been a more terrific moment.

Esprit De Corps
Richard Mallett

It seems odd—I was about to write—that nobody before *Stage-coach* (Director: JOHN FORD) should have thought of applying what I may call the ''people-thrown-together'' idea to the past rather than the present. I was about to write that, and of course I have now written it; but I imagine that some correspondent is already putting pen to paper to tell me that it has been done. Never so well, I insist; for *Stagecoach* is extraordinarily good. I read two laudatory notices before I saw it and I was all ready to disagree with them, but I don't. This picture, with no big names (except the director's) and a collection of what may not unfairly be called stock characters, is raised by direction, acting, camera-work and sheer atmosphere into the top class.

The period is 1885 and the story is simple enough: basically it deals with a coach-full of people travelling from one frontier settlement to another across wild country in which the Indians have risen. The characters too have been chosen with that eye for an easy contrast and that liking for the obvious point that always seem to influence the choice of characters designed to be thrown together for the purposes of fiction. But although they may be type-parts they are all admirably taken. The most spectacular, from an acting point of view, is perhaps the drunken doctor (THOMAS MITCHELL); but there is hardly any point in singling out one player from the eight or nine, for all have roughly the same amount to do, and together with the wild country, the wild riding and the excellent detail they make *Stagecoach* one of the most absorbing and exciting films I have seen for some time.

There is a good deal of very effective musical accompaniment, based on American folk-tunes (the cheerful air that symbolises the progress of the coach has been in my head ever since); but I ask you to notice particularly the brilliant use, here and there, of absolute silence.

"Nay, lad, you're holding her all wrong!"

BEYOND THE Y-FRONTIER

Going it alone on film
by Benny Green

It was when I saw that interminable film *The Left-Handed Gun* that it first occurred to me that when a Man Keeps His Own Counsel and is clearly a Loner, it is probably because his breath smells. The deduction was certainly true of *The Left-Handed Gun*, a pretentious attempt to romanticise a grubby little homicidal lunatic called Billy the Kid, whose code of honour would have gone down big with Attila the Hun. The same is true, I suspect, of all those big, bad, mean and moody Western hombres who personified law and disorder. They were all men who found it much more congenial to clean up a town than clean up themselves, and once you start to think about it, you realise that the real reason why no gunfighter would go within fifty paces of Wild Bill Hickok was that Hickok hadn't washed his neck or changed his socks in twenty-five years, that Cole Younger was Tall in the Saddle and short on toothpaste, that Jesse James was too preoccupied with holding up trains and not nearly preoccupied enough with holding up his underpants. Not for nothing is the polecat so prominent in the mythology of the Frontier.

It is also sadly true that the man who Walks Tall has almost certainly been fitted out with a pair of lifts by the Wardrobe department, a device which has the added advantage of appearing to tilt him forward into the sunset at an angle of elevation which would give any ordinary man a hernia. There is probably no substance to the rumour that when Alan Ladd made Westerns, in order to convince the audience that our hero was tall enough to see over the top of the bar counter all the equestrian work was done using Shetland ponies, but that is one of those canards with more than a grain of truth to it. The urban hero presents many more difficulties, of course, because if you shoot a man against the background of those big lumps of rock which always kept getting mercifully in the way of John Ford's actors and then tell people that this is *The Philadelphia Story*, your chances of closing the credibility gap will not be much improved.

In any case, although the man who Does His Own Thing is acceptable enough while he is actually doing it, what are we supposed to make of him once he has done it? The trouble with being True To Your Code is that you can only be true to it once; after that everyone else starts being true to it and nothing is ever quite the same again. I have often wondered what Wyatt Earp did the day *after* he cleaned up Dodge City. (There will always be those cynics who wonder what he did the day before he cleaned it up too, but there is nothing to be done for such people.) Surely he woke that morning, took his head out of the spittoon and sighed for the good old days when the Caughnawaga Kid had only to show his face in town for Consolidated Coffins to rise fourteen points and the typesetters down at the Sentinel to shoot themselves. Try to imagine what Grace Kelly's life was like after *High Noon*, once she settled down with that chatterbox Gary Cooper. Men who are sufficient unto themselves are invariably insufficient for the rest of us, because having obeyed their Inner Voice for all those years, they have become the biggest bores in creation.

Of course people who go to the pictures don't give a fig for all this. They like to go on dreaming of a world whose problems are so childish, whose courage is so raw, whose moral issues are so clearly defined, that it needs only one brave man to turn the tide. They like the idea of big John Wayne firing a single shot and making thirty-six extras fall off their horses. They love the suggestion that big James Stewart can still buck City Hall. They positively squirm with rapture when big Bob Mitchum is shown to be a man of Few Words, and it never enters their heads to wonder what those words are. Walkingtallsberg is like the land of pornography in that it relies for its effect on the real world never getting in on the act. We have only to imagine the arrival of a Keynesian economist at the OK Corral, or a Union card in James Bond's pocket, to see what irreparable damage ambiguity may do to the tissue of our dreams.

But what about Going It Alone *inside* the movies? The genuinely heroic attempts have taken place behind the camera rather than in front of it. Until not so long ago the great Renaissance man of the movies was Orson Welles, on the strength of *Citizen Kane*. For thirty years it had been assumed that Welles conceived the film, produced it, directed it, wrote it, starred in it, polished the camera lens each morning and swept the locker-room each night. Then in 1971 there appeared on the bookstalls Pauline Kael's brilliantly seductive *The Citizen Kane Book*, which proved beyond reasonable doubt that Orson Welles was really Herman J. Mankiewicz, having for twenty years clearly hidden his genius from everyone in Hollywood, including himself, by writing hundreds of dreadful scenarios and drinking a lot, had suddenly revealed himself in his true colours with *Citizen Kane* and then carelessly forgotten to tell people who he was. That was the end of one myth, and only the other day there was a blow struck at another when a man appeared on the radio explaining how he had written down all the music which Charlie Chaplin was thought to have composed. To date nobody has come forward to claim authorship of the lyrics which Chaplin is thought to have written, although one of the most effective antidotes to insomnia I know is to lie there in the dark trying to imagine the expression on Irving Berlin's face on the morning he first heard *I'll be loving you eternally* and thought back to the good old days gone beyond recall when he had written *I'll be loving you always*.

To what extent Von Stroheim Strutted Tall when he made his movies, what Jehovah would have to say about Cecil B. De Mille's faith in himself as an original story writer, whether it was because he was consumed by idle dreams of Walking Tall that Von Sternberg persisted in turning up for work wearing his sister's riding boots, all these are vitally important cinematic questions to which the Pauline Kaels of the future will surely have to address themselves.

However, in the meantime, there is still one way left in which beleaguered modern urban man, beset by pestilential bureaucrats and fishbrained architects, can still experience the sensation of Going It Alone, of Being Seen Against the Skyline, of Coping with Destiny Single-handed, of Outfacing Destiny in Lonely Isolation. All he has to do is to go to the pictures any weekday afternoon.

CAST NOW WHILE COUCHES LAST
Stanley Reynolds

Switch on the television or go to the cinema, look at the stars on the screen and you can guess they are there because of—a woman. In the past ten years there has been a quiet revolution in show business. The casting couch has been thrown out of the window; women casting directors have walked in through the door. There are 72 casting directors in Who's Who. Fifty-four are women and only one man has come into the business in the past eight years.

—Daily Mail, March 4

Some of Hollywood's prettiest starlets are compiling a blacklist of directors who still use the casting couch. A special Moral Complaints Committee formed by the Screen Actors Guild is currently taking evidence from actresses who say they were promised work and success in return for bedroom favours. Actress Diana Silliphant revealed what happened when she went looking for work. He was lying on his back on a couch and said, "I'd like a massage." When I asked if it would get me a part he replied: "It would help." She told him: "You have the wrong girl." He replied: "You weren't right for the part anyway."

—Daily Mail, March 9

Well, you don't know me but you might just happen to know my face. A lot of people do. It's surprising because I've had the worse kind of luck which is hitting the acting lark just enough so your foot is always in the door, and what with the dole and one thing an' another you can get by, without never actually ever getting inside the door, know what I mean? Well, a gizzer in a pub or a little old lady or something will come up to me—it happens maybe twice a year—and say, "You're 'im ain't ya?" Of course, they don't know who the 'im is. Nobody knows my name.

Let's face it I got one of those faces that looks like it ought to belong to a film star. That's how I got into the show business. A lot of people think this is something what can only happen to a bird with a pretty face. But it can happen to a bloke likewise. A bloke who is, well, let's face it, devilishly handsome, can get hisself in as much dead lumber as a bint who is a looker when it comes to the show business.

If I hadn't been so good looking I might never have started in the acting lark or I would of quit a long time ago an' gone into the haulage with my brother Ted an' been a lot better off than I am right now. But always you dream of the style you could have if for once that door would open and you could walk right in, know what I mean?

Girl (leaving cinema after ve'y pathetic film, to weeping friend). "BEAR UP, DEAR; IT'S ALL OVER NOW."

Anyway, I am sitting in the caff waiting for my agent to come in like he always does of a morning on account of I'm dieting aren't I—that's what you got to go through in the acting—an' I can't manage the seven flights of stairs to Moe's office since the lift broke, not on grapefruit an' one slice of dry toast. Anyway, I'm perusing the *Daily Mail* when suddenly I read in this item that there has been a revolution in the casting game an' it's now practically all birds who are running the show.

Well, I tell you, grapefruit an' dry toast or not I felt like running up them seven flights of stairs an' strangling the agent, Moe, on account of for years now he's been sending me to the ordinary sort of casting directors an' me an' the rest of the blokes spent the afternoon kicking our heels like in a dentist's surgery listening to the screams and moans an' then the giggles—like they was using laughing gas in there—an' then some starlet comes out adjusting her mini-skirt—I mean I'd go back that far, far as the mini an' further too, back to the days when they used to come out adjusting their seamed stockings—an' the casting director shouts, "Next!" an' then he looks around an' sees it's all blokes out there waiting an' he says, "Sorry boys, we ain't lookin' for your types; we're lookin' for the new James Dean", an' we all go home an' practise looking sulky in the bathroom mirror until it's time to go out an' drive the radio cabs.

Well, anyway, I look at this article in the *Daily Mail* an' I can't believe my luck. I practically start rubbing my hands together in anticipation of me actually getting inside the office with one of these new female casting directors and I am practically laughing out loud thinking of the birds an' starlet bints sitting outside kicking their heels an' having to listen to all the giggling emanating from the vicinity of the ol' casting couch. I think of all the suffering I done over the years of anguish standing with my foot in the door so it is practically taking root. Always thinking that maybe it was my image an' name that was wrong an' constantly changing my name, like from Lance Gauntlet, which was my first stage name when the costume epic was all the go, to Rock Tab an' a Tony Curtis hair cut an' blinking eyes, an' then to Tuck Buick that time when Moe said they were casting for a spaghetti Western an' I paid my own fare to Rome, an' then to Harry J. Bleeder when it became all the go to be dead common an' sort of ethnic, know what I mean?

Anyway, I can see now none of that matters. It was the plain an' simple fact that in those days there weren't any birds flying the casting couches an' I might as well call myself Soft Joe for all the good a star quality handle an' a flashy set of capped teeth are going to do me when it came to those old time bloke casting directors. Now things, as they say, ain't what they used to be.

Just then Moe comes in for his morning cuppa an' he sees me an' he says, "Whadda ya say, Lance?" See, I told you, nobody knows my name.

"I haven't been Lance since 1954 when they were casting Ivanhoe over here, Moe," I tell him.

"Yeh, well, ah, er," Moe says, "only jokin', pass the sugar." But instead I pass the *Mail* to him an' shove that article under his nose.

"What have you been doin' to me all these years, sendin' me to them sex fiend casting directors when there has been a revolution in the business an' it's now loaded with undoubtedly randy bints give their right arms away to get a crack at a bloke like me, an' don't tell me different haven't I been on the mini-cabs of a night all these years?"

Give Moe his due, he's cool. Got a bit of the couch system going for himself, too, in the agent lark; but he's getting on, Moe, an' looking at the age on some of them starlets Moe is pulling these days, well, it kind of makes your tongue coat up; they must have been in rep with Dame Edith, half of 'em. "That newspaper's five days old," Moe says. An' I look an' he's right.

"So what?" I say.

"So this," he says, an' he shoves that morning's issue of the *Mail* under my nose an' I see that the ol' Lance Gauntlet-Rock Tab-Tuck Buick-Harry J. Bleeder—and whoever, Watchacallit, yours truly's luck is still running dead lumber. For there before my very eyes is a shattered dream—out in Hollywood some kind of nutty Moral Complaints Committee is going to get rid of the casting couch.

"That's the trouble with Yanks," Moe says, "they got no respect for tradition."

"Get me in to see one of these bird casting directors, Moe," I say, "quick!"

"Bad news," he says, "travels fast."

"Not five days fast," I say.

"With your kind of luck, Tab, it does," Moe says. "But," he says, "I might just have something for you." An' he passes me a name on a card an' what do you know first thing the next day I'm walking into my first ever female lady casting director an' she is all narrow jeans an' four-inch heel cowboy boots an' I flash her the big

"We pay for their medical training and the Yanks get the benefit."

smile like I do some nights on the mini-cabs when you pick up a bird an' it looks a little lost an' lonely. An' there is a couch just made for casting standing in a darkened corner. Next thing you know it is pulling its four-inch heel cowboy boots off an' thumbing me towards that dark corner. "Weird," I says to myself, "weird." Listen, I know this is the place where they used to put the three dots in the old-time books but here, I'm sorry to say, it will not be necessary. Have you any idea of what six weeks of grapefruit an' dry toast can do to a bloke?

Then suddenly this bird casting director is throwing its four-inch heels at me, lacin' itself back into its jeans an' using the sort of language at me which a man of my age shouldn't hear from a girl young enough to be his daughter if I ever actually got caught for some of the things I did when I was this girl's age. "What's your name, creep?" she screams. "I'm black-listing you!" she yells as I beat a hasty out an' round to the caff where I stoke up a meal that's got me middle-aged spread in about forty-five minutes. "Just my luck," I think, "to get landed with a Woman's Lib nutter looking to get her own back."

Well, the upshot is I'm on the mini-cabs that night an' I picks up this classy bird in St John's Wood an' she all of a sudden leans over into the front seat an' says she's So-'n'-So the famous lady casting couch person an' she says, "Don't get offended but I'm trying to cast this part of a middle-aged, randy mini-cab driver. It's not the star role but, take it from me, it's the best part in the film." An' she starts shovin' her card in my face when I stop the cab an' say, "Missus, I've just had a sudden urge, kind of like St Paul on the road that time, to go into the haulage business," an' I stop the mini-cab right there an' get out an' start walking saying a silent farewell to Lance and Rock, Tuck and Harry J. and what'shisname.

The Casting Couch ffolkes

"But, Mr. Wirtz, I'm only applying for a job as usherette!"

"Er, hello dear, Miss Preston seems to have a nasty nosebleed."

AN IDEAL CINEMA
Barry Norman

Let me say for a start that anybody trying to introduce an ideal world around here is going to meet with my implacable opposition since there's a very fair chance that in an ideal world I'd be out of a job.

In an ideal world, after all, there would hardly be any need for film critics, would there, and what sort of ideal world would that be? I mean, look at it from my point of view—out there starving on the streets with a wife and mortgage to support, to say nothing of two dogs, two cats, two daughters and, for all I know, a long-lost, free-range guinea pig still roaming the local fields and liable to turn up again at any minute demanding its rights.

No, in an ideal world all films would be, by definition, ideal

and that being so I can't see anyone being particularly anxious to employ me to announce this fact to a viewing public that knew it already. The basic problem, you see, is that one man's ideal world is another man's penury.

Mind you, the prospect suggested above—the prospect of the total disappearance not only of me but also of every other film critic—probably comes as close as it's possible to get to Wardour Street's version of an ideal world.

Wardour Street, which is where film distributors, exhibitors and publicists have their lairs, hates film critics. Film critics, says Wardour Street, are snide, though it doesn't use the word in its *Shorter O.E.D.* sense of counterfeit, sham or bogus.

What Wardour Street means by snide, as applied to film critics, is sarcastic, cynical, underhanded, dishonest, sadistic and quite incapable of recognising sincerity, true beauty and the producer's undoubted altruism.

"Don't you realise," says Wardour Street, usually represented at such times by a publicist

"What are you trying to get into, Miss Murchison, the movies or the Olympics?"

"Sit over here with me, duckie, and let's talk about my contract or something."

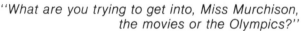

with a large scotch in his hand, "that Herb Omlet, God bless him, gave a year of his life to this picture? A whole, goddam year. And he did it for nothing—a lousy quarter of million up front and ten per cent of the gross. Then guys like you come along and piss so much ice-water all over it that he'll be lucky if that ten per cent brings him another couple of million."

It does seem a very small reward for a whole year of a film producer's life and in an ideal world no critic would have to face that kind of accusation or bear the heavy responsibility of knowing that a chance remark tossed into the public prints or uttered lightly on the airwaves had caused Herb Omlet to delay his move from the foothills of Sunset Boulevard to a mansion in Bel Air for another year, another film and another ten per cent.

So then for obvious reasons an ideal world is simply not good enough. Let us therefore project the idea a little further and consider an ideal, ideal world with room for us all—producers, publicists and critics alike. In such

a world every film would be *Citizen Kane*, or possibly *La Grande Illusion*, or, if you like, *Ninotchka*, or . . . .

Really I can't imagine anything more boring. It's not just the great films that make a critic's life supportable; the very bad ones play an equally important part, for there is nothing quite so satisfying as a truly rotten movie.

Does anybody remember *Zarak* and Victor Mature saying to Anita Ekberg: "It is written that a man must not marry his father's wife"? (I'm not entirely sure where else it's written but it was certainly written in the script of *Zarak*, thank goodness). Or Anthony Perkins renaming Diana Ross *Mahogany* in the film of that title because "I can't think of a better word for something soft and warm and brown"? Search *Citizen Kane* as diligently as you like and you won't find more pleasurable dialogue than that.

So in this doubly ideal world there would be a place for really awful films as well as very good ones. But, great or dreadful, what would they be about? Well, they

would be about conflict rather than violence, people rather than things, love rather than sex. You may think, because you probably don't go to the cinema very often, that that's what films are about now but, generally speaking, they're not and haven't been for some while.

It often seems to me that the ultimate in contemporary movies will concern a murderously psychopathic android from another planet which alights from a space ship a mile long and proceeds to rape every woman on earth, having first brutally kicked to death any man with the temerity to oppose it.

The cinema's current obsession is with science fiction; its permanent obsession is with violence and sex.

Now I have no objection to sex in the cinema—not on the screen anyway, though in the auditorium it can be a trifle distracting. But I don't necessarily want to watch sex all the time.

Apart from anything else it's much over-rated as a spectator sport since the most dramatic result that can be achieved is a

149

one-all draw.

Once upon a time in the cinema actresses remained vertical and fully-dressed from reel one to end credits, screen lovers were allowed to kiss for no more than eight seconds at a time (and then with their lips zipped up) and you only knew a seduction had taken place when a train suddenly thundered into a tunnel.

I miss those trains thundering into tunnels. I haven't seen one in years. Nowadays you get the full, heaving seduction, usually in close-up. I know many an actress whose pubic hair is more easily recognisable than her face and I sometimes believe that the last leading lady permitted to keep her knickers on for the entire duration of a film was Greta Garbo.

What's more in those old days when the lovers moved into their final—and quite possibly their only—embrace you knew they were at least temporarily in love. Today as the picture fades out on the umpteenth act of copulation and the background music swells up over the heroine's last climactic moans all you can be sure of is that, in the modern idiom, they're getting their rocks off together.

No, hold on. I'm beginning to sound like Mary Whitehouse. What I mean is that a little bit of sex on the screen, like a little bit of SF, is perfectly acceptable. Violence hardly ever is. Explicit violence in the movies is not only brutalising but, even worse, shows a depressing lack of imagination on the part of the film makers.

Thus in my doubly ideal world the movies, great and lousy, would occasionally deal with science fiction (or whatever the latest trendy genre happened to be), occasionally with gentle and erotic love-play and rarely, if at all, with violence. Unfortunately that would mean the cinemas would be virtually empty since box-office returns indicate that the patrons are very fond of violence, even more fond of violent sex and probably most fond of violent sex among the crew of a spaceship involved in inter-planetary warfare.

Well, in an ideal world you couldn't have empty cinemas. I think we'd better start again. In a *trebly* ideal world . . . .

SEATS IN ALL PARTS

Charles Reid analyses the cinema's ills . . .

The cinema iş in decline, they told me. From every five bob the Chancellor milks two and a halfpenny, from every two-and-nine, elevenpence. I am infatuate. As an infatuate I grieve and rage.

The seed of my infatuation was thus. The tram route to our suburb originally ran a mile and a half from the centre of our town. A tram shed stood at the end of it. When the route was extended the tram shed was abandoned. After two months a man with white spats, a waistcoat slip and a port-wine complexion bought the shed and turned it into a picture palace.

This was about the time when, Henry Herbert Asquith being the Prime Minister, early newsreel cameras were taking shots of siege-smoke adrift across the roofs of Sydney Street. The new picture palace had ventilation holes in its sidewall. By standing on two bricks, cricking necks and shutting one eye, small proletarians in Eton collars that were washable because made of celluloid could see a quarter slice of screen with W. S. Hart, la Pickford, Lilian Gish, John Bunny, Ford Sterling, and Charlie himself partly out of view. For a total spending of fourpence I saw the first *Les Misérables* and the first *Quo Vadis?* with Mounet-Sully leading in the one, Amleto Novelli in the other.

There was acting for you; for anybody, at all events, with a heart, a pair of eyes and some hankering after the sublime (all rare endowments, when I come to think of it). Not that people really had to act. Just to *see* people and planked sidewalks and sunlit streets and railway lines was felicity in itself. Reduced to a patterning of shadow on light, the external world took on, or I'm a Dutchman, a new and noble beauty.

To-day, unhappily, the mode is for cubby-holed men and women cut off at the breast-bone acting in small, bluelit refrigerators full of tonic water, with the bubbles flowing horizontally.

"But perhaps I'm merely being quaint and archaic," I reproved myself. "Perhaps my cinema-love and TV-hate are the aberrations of a sentimental old highbrow. I must seek another opinion."

I sought it in S.W.1. In S.W.1 stands a vintage job—The Luxuria. It was so named—in all innocence—when opened in 1930. Architecturally it is of the banana layer-cake school, grimy and scowling rather after twenty years. In the upstairs foyer the manager lined up his linkmen, checkers and usherettes for my benefit before they went into battle.

"Do you all watch TV?" I asked.

"Yes," they chorused.

"Which is the better entertainment—TV or the cinema?"

"The cinema every time."

"But why shouldn't you prefer the cinema?" I objected. "After all you're cinema employees."

The house engineer spoke up. He is a stocky man with folded

arms and often says this is a free country.

"The thing people don't like about the cinema is the prices," said the engineer. "Man takes his wife and two kids to the pictures. What with fares and chocs, he spends twice more in one go than a week's telly instalment—and the telly's at his fireside all the time."

There in a nutshell, I should say, is why accountants at circuit headquarters are beginning to worry about The Luxuria's future. I worry myself. My affection for the place is deep and moist-eyed.

I remember well the evening paper pars The Luxuria made when building. Site diggers uncovered a mediaeval wharf and traces of a Thames creek the archaeologists didn't know about. Two balcony girders a hundred feet long were inched, eased and threaded, nobody knew how, through the streets of S.W.1, making hay of other traffic.

Up in the dome magic lanterns made ever-changing conflagrations, cloud pageants and snowstorms. The back of the stalls was an undersea cave, glowing and seaweedy. It dripped incandescent stalactites. Such effects in the early 'thirties were intended to allay the *angst* and panic we were all feeling about hunger marchers and the Wall Street crash. They were ripped out or de-wired years ago. The giant organ, so thunderous and tinkling a bore in its day, is now silent except once every six months when a man comes in at ten thirty in the morning to tune and true it up. He usually rounds off with a page or two of "In a Monastery Garden", once a loved syrup.

Changing tastes apart, a resident organist would cost The Luxuria another two thousand pounds a year, and The Luxuria cannot afford anything like that. In 1949 admissions were around a million and a half. Last year they were down to less than a million. They are dipping still. There is a tendency to draw tensely on cigarettes and bite finger-nails.

A gilt-edged double bill—*End as a Man* and *Full of Life* (Judy Holliday)—recently pulled in eighteen thousand in one week. Not bad. But look back to 1946. In a single week that year there were forty-five thousand admissions. At that time it was a regular thing for four queues to overlap each other round the nose of the building and down the pavements on either side from late afternoon well into the night.

The Luxuria has been through much. Bomb-blast jammed its window frames, brought plaster down and put out a lot of lights. More recently there have been Teddy Boys. Hundreds of them used to take over the back circle every Saturday night. If they didn't care for a film they would toot rhythmically on bike horns. There is a special way of doing this. You hold the bulb against your ribs and toot with your free elbow. Nine weeks ago firecrackers were thrown into the gangway and among neighbouring seats during a Lana Turner-Jeff Chandler dalliance. With three husky attendants and two policemen fetched in from the street, the manager turned out three rows of hooligans. They deflated at the first flash of his torch.

Who or what is going to deflate The Luxuria's money and patronage troubles? The manager is sure means will be found. So is Bertie, his head projectionist. In a converted hotel smoke room at Richmond, Bertie, then a boy, ran the first *Les Misérables* and *Quo Vadis?* from a booth hung with wet asbestos blankets. Among his regulars was ex-King Manoel, who used to scatter cigarette stubs on the carpet. Kings come, kings go and, having gone, they don't come back, says Bertie, but the cinema is now part of human nature, and human nature will take a bit of rubbing out.

. . . and **Sprod** draws his own conclusions

152

Dear Bryan

Barry Took

A letter arrived in the *Punch* film office recently addressed to Bryan Forbes, whose work is currently enjoying a season at the National Film Theatre. Rather than send it on, we thought we'd publish and be damned.

The Enchanted Cottage,
Wood Green, N. 22.
Wednesday.

Dear Bryan,

Me and my mate, Mike, went along to the NFT a couple of weeks ago to hear you telling us about your career in the movies. Well, Bryan, I must say you seem to have seen it all and done the lot, acting and directing and producing and writing and being an executive and everything. What with one thing and another you can't have had a moment to yourself.

Whistle Down The Wind is my favourite of yours. I thought it was smashing, and that bit they showed at the NFT where the vicar was going on about vandals stealing the lead from the Church roof for poor Hayley Mills, who only wanted to know if her kitten would go to heaven, was dead good. Ditto *The Angry Silence* with your mate, Richard Attenborough (now *Sir* Richard, of course. Any chance of a tickle in the direction for you?). Your Hollywood film, *King Rat* was a good one and all. Likewise many others. And I see we've got *International Velvet* to look forward to in the near future. You told us at the NFT that it might be Nanette Newman's best film yet, and said how she came to you and said, "Tatum O'Neal is a natural", which is very generous from another actor and must have knocked you all of a heap. I mean to say, film stars are not noted for their generosity usually being on a big ego trip and tend to be a bit out of touch with reality. Come to think of it, you have Nanette Newman in a lot of your films. I suppose that her being your wife it could be embarrassing if you used some other actress, and besides the extra income probably comes in handy when, as you said, you often don't know where your next job is coming from. My mate Mike thinks she's smashing, and I say good luck to you.

It was interesting at the NFT when that lady in the audience said you weren't very good at comedy—and you sort of bristled and said, "What about *Only Two Can Play*?" Hear hear. And, of course, *The Wrong Box* where Peter Sellers used a kitten as a blotter.

Still you can afford to smile when you're criticised because you don't have many flops do you, and I admire the way all through your career you've been able to step into the breach at a moment's notice—like you were telling us about how in *Cockleshell Heroes* you were re-shooting the same scenes that the proper director Jose Ferrer had just done. I didn't quite get the point of that. Was he a rotten director? Then there was *Whistle Down The Wind* where you stepped in for Guy Green, and *The L-Shaped Room* when you obliged when Jack Clayton dropped out, and *The Mad Woman of Chaillot* which John Huston was supposed to have done. Hence the expression "well that's show business", I suppose.

You mentioned film critics once or twice in your lecture at the NFT and it sticks out a mile you don't like *them* very much. What was that phrase you used about your friend's film *East of Elephant Rock*? Oh yes, you said "the critics urinated on it". Well Bryan, I suppose they've got their job to do. After all they're not employed to go round saying that *everything's* good, and I might add that I saw *East Of Elephant Rock* myself and think that whatever the critics did on it was well deserved. Of course you're quite right to say that television has killed the cinema and, as you pointed out, TV can get good writers. Now why's that do you think?

All in all it was a good evening. It's not every day you get a chance to hear the personal views of one of our leading film makers. Come to think of it, you're about the only leading film maker we've got.

Yours truly,
Aubrey Greenspan.

P.S.
Me and my mate Mike managed to creep into the preview of **The Stepford Wives.** Well, Bryan, I thought it was smashing and my mate Mike did a drawing of it.

You directed it, of course, and very nice too. Katharine Ross as the wife who leaves New York and goes to live in the suburb of Stepford is very good—almost as good as Paula Prentiss as her friend, Bobby. Nanette Newman is in it too but didn't have much of a part really, being more on the edge of the action as you might say. In it but not *in* it, as it were. You're in it too if I might make so bold, rather like Alfred Hitchcock used to walk across in *his* films. It *was* you wasn't it in the mac outside the pharmacy?

Well, *The Stepford Wives* has been waiting a long time for a showing over here, being made in America in 1974, but it's been worth waiting for. Mind you that William Goldman who wrote it is no mug, and I should think the pair of you got on like a house on fire.

Well, anyway, I liked it very much, even if it is a bit long—and if I may say without causing offence, very well shot.

Of course the story's tripe but then what isn't these days, but wouldn't it be a laugh if it was a really *big* success. Well, here's hoping. One way and another, Bryan, what with your NFT season, *The Stepford Wives*, and *International Velvet*, this could be your year.

The Rhinestone as Big as the Ritz

Alan Coren

Ah, Time, Time! Can it really be thirty-five years since a little girl changed her name to Beryl Taylor and tiptoed into all our lives with her extraordinary performance in *Lassie Eat Up*?

True, she hadn't managed to get the juvenile lead; but the three minutes she made all her own as the waif to whom Lassie gives rabies were enough to bring her to the attention of the legendary Sam Goldblatt, wisecracking head of Tantamount Studios, which operated out of a disused navy yard in East San Diego.

Sam was looking for someone to play the daughter of Harold Gable in *Local Velvet*, a picture which, though it broke a few box-office records, was nevertheless as good a movie as has ever been made about a broken-down carthorse which a little girl rides to failure in the annual East San Diego Knackers Derby. The closing sequence, in which little Beryl Taylor holds up a bottle of the impact adhesive she once groomed and cherished, her eyes filling with glycerine, rightly earned the film a nomination for a Sammy in the 1944 Goldblatt Awards, though it was narrowly beaten for the un-coveted statuette itself by Tantamount's other blockbuster, *The Burmese Falcon*.

When her contract with Tantamount expired, the studio having merged with Twentieth Century Dingo to form Sam's Used Trucks Inc., Beryl was instantly snapped up by Warnold Brothers, who were looking for a new star for their 1949 epic, *A Plaice In The Sun*, the film which ultimately said all there was to say about the two great and ruthless families who between them controlled the wet fish trade in Peoria, Illinois, during the closing years of the nineteenth century. Beryl played the part of Jock, the flame-haired Aberdeen whaler, since no actor on the Warnold books was prepared to appear in a kilt. These, it will be remembered, were the early days of the notorious McCarthy Era.

Still, she managed nevertheless to catch the eye of young Conrad Fulton, heir to the Fulton hotel empire; or, more precisely, the Fulton Bide-A-Wee Motel, an establishment on the outskirts of Cleveland where local construction workers could, for a mere five dollars, get a square meal, an hour's bed, and Mrs Fulton.

The marriage was not a success. Beryl was too young: still only eighteen, she was naïve in the ways of the world and did not know how to handle a middle-aged playboy who thought she was an Aberdeen whaler called Jock.

The marriage was annulled in 1951, and Beryl immediately married Malcolm Wilding, a dapper English actor with a tattersall waistcoat and a two-tone Vauxhall Ten who had nearly appeared in three Sid Field movies. For a time, they were a typical glittering showbiz couple, their twin careers in temporary abeyance as they travelled the well-worn muscatel circuit, their names never very far from the gossip columns of a dozen countries: there was the time Malcolm fell down in the car-park of Ted's Elite Roadhouse, Luton, and his name was splashed all over page eighteen of the *South Bucks Licensed Victualler*; there was the occasion when both their lives were almost wrecked in Flatbush, New Jersey, after eating the three-dollar seafood platter at the Ptomaine Dinette; there was the narrowly-avoided scandal on the shimmering French Riviera when Beryl's hand was discovered in the coach-driver's trousers during the tour's visit to a nougat factory in Montelimar; and finally, of course, early in momentous 1955, there was her affair with, and subsequent marriage to, dynamic midget tycoon and impresario, Mike Toad.

Toad, 49, had made hundreds out of the construction business, and, restless for fresh fields to be conquered on, he invested the money in the legendary movie of which he was producer, director, screenwriter, lighting cameraman and man taking tickets, *Around Minnesota In Eighty Days*. Beryl, sadly, did not star in this picture, since she had just signed a contract with Kwiklean Karwash and April was their busy period, with everyone wanting a full wax job after the winter's ravages.

The film was a limited success, but this did not faze the irrepressible Toad; when it closed on the Tuesday, he still bought Beryl a fabulous set of non-stick saucepans. "Easy come, easy go!" was, he told the press, his philosophy.

It was perhaps the only period in her life when Beryl Taylor was truly happy; tragically, that period was cut suddenly short when two of the film's other backers, Toni and Luigi Frascati, caught up with Toad in an alley behind the Roxy Bowl 'n' Nosh, Spokane.

A widow at twenty-three, Beryl went back to Hollywood to try to forget. Hollywood tried to forget, too, but Beryl had influence; two of her friends from the early days who had become starlets and had then gone on to make fantastic marriages to powerful and wealthy men rallied to her support. Ruby Hayworth, who had married the Brian Khan, and elegant Grace Melly, now the wife of Prince Monolulu, went to bat for Beryl and brought pressure on the newly-formed Metro-Goldblatt-Dingo studios to put her in *Similar To Cat On A Hot Tin Roof*. Although her sequence ended on the cutting-room floor, so, by great good fortune, did she, and Sam Goldblatt thereafter agreed to star her in *Butterfield 6*, a fifteen-minute musical remake of *Alexander Nevski*. Since Beryl had no singing voice, her songs were dubbed by Eddie Frischauer, the Singing Austrian Journalist. The outcome was, of course, inevitable: by the end of shooting, Eddie had become Beryl's fourth husband.

Once again, their careers cast a blight upon their romance: while Eddie's went down and down, so did Beryl's, and pretty soon they found themselves competing for the lousiest parts in Hollywood. The crunch came when they both turned up, each having neglected previously to inform the other, to audition for the part of the horse in Warnold Brother's *Shine*, the low-budget western about a lone negro gunfighter, tragically lost when someone inadvertently opened the dark-room door.

In 1962, Beryl and Eddie divorced.

It was also the year Joseph L. Mankiewicz made *Cleopatra*.

The rest is practically history.

It was on the set of *Cleopatra* that Beryl first met Dai Burton. Burton had grown up in the Rhondda, in an ordinary acting family; his father was an actor, and Dai's six brothers were all actors, too. Dai was the only coal-miner among them. In consequence, family relationships were often strained to breaking-point, mainly due to the great disparity of incomes. The Welsh film industry had been in the doldrums since 1909; every day, Dai's father and his six brothers would get up at five a.m. and set off for the studios, hoping against

"Of course, it was nothing like that in the Good Book."

"It's the tee-shirt of the film."

Coming Home
Barry Took

hope that someone would want to make *How Green Was My Valley* again. Every night, they would all trudge home once more.

Dai, however, was not only a former faceworker, he was also local branch secretary of the NUM. He had a green Volvo, and was bringing home £64.32, after stoppages. Jealousy was rife; the situation could not go on. Dai left home, and went to Hollywood on an NUM fact-finding mission.

It was here that Fate played her trump card! Beryl had been signed up by Mankiewicz to stoke the Fox boilers; she was working the March 14 day shift when Dai Burton walked in with the president of Coalworkers Local 54. She looked up from her shovel. Their eyes met. He recognised her at once.

"Al Jolson!" cried Dai. "It's a great honour, look you!"

She showered; they fell in love.

From then on, the couple all Hollywood came to love were inseparable. Together, they ran the central heating system on *The VIPs*, supervised the natural gas conversion on *Who's Afraid of Virginia Woolf?*, and, after one of their many tempestuous rows, burned down *The Taming of the Shrew*.

They married in 1964, divorced in 1974, remarried the same year, and divorced for the second time in 1976, while all the world wondered. Back home in Britain, both sorrow and anger raged in the breasts of Burton's millions of fans, who felt that he had thrown away a career which might have taken him to the very top, made him another Arthur Scargill, even, some said, a new Joe Gormley.

Inevitably, the backlash of this resentment struck at Beryl Taylor. On both sides of the Atlantic, her erstwhile fans were growing sick of the endless public exhibitions of outrageous behaviour, and pretty soon studio bosses, ever on the *qui vive* for signs of discontent likely to damage an already ailing industry, were looking elsewhere for boiler maintenance forepersons. There were rumours of her unreliability—stars shivered while radiators clunked feebly, or broiled while ill-regulated thermostats sent set temperatures into the nineties—until, at last, Beryl had it made clear to her that it might be time to call a halt, hang up her goggles, retire to a less ostentatious life beyond the public glare.

In 1976, accordingly, she married for the seventh time; her new husband was Geoffrey "Geoff" Warner, a quiet New England businessman with his own van. Little has been heard of them since their wedding: just one interview, published in *Coke & Derivatives Monthly*, when lovely Beryl Taylor, a little sadly perhaps, told the world that "if I had to do it all over again, I guess I'd choose to be a little more successful, you dummy!"

It's an odd sensation to walk through the dusk of a small French seaside resort and suddenly hear as you turn the corner of a dusty street the soundtrack of *Star Wars* booming out at you through the twilight. The cinema at Argeles— and the number of people who ask "where's that?" pleases the one-uppish side of my nature—is called the Vox, is about the size of an average scout's hut, and during the season shows two different films every day. As you can imagine, there was prodigious variety: Fassbinder and Disney, Louis de Funes and Woody Allen, *Monty Python* and Bertolucci, John Travolta and Richard Dreyfuss, plus an array of mysteries of the sort that you only ever see on BBC2 after midnight.

I can report that the Vox was full for every performance, and that the audience, by and large, were young. The simple fact is that the Cinema is alive and well in France, indeed in continental Europe as a whole, and it's puzzling that the Cinema in Britain, with the exception of big films in major cities, is not. At least it hasn't been. The reason is fairly clear. Where a country has good television, there's little incentive to go out and pay for inferior entertainment. French TV is of an awfulness it's hard to imagine in Britain, and with notable exceptions TV elsewhere in Europe isn't much better.

Admittedly there are pockets of excellence and European TV stations show their quota of American and English imports, but British TV, patchy though it is, is staggeringly better. That is to say—it has been.

There are signs, disturbing for TV addicts and heartening for film buffs, that things are changing. Films are getting better, TV is getting worse. Being involved however peripherally with both I can be

157

fairly objective. I can think of twelve films released here during the past twelve months that have been superb. I can't think of twelve television shows or series of comparable excellence.

What are my top twelve? Well, in no particular order there's *Annie Hall*, *The Turning Point*, *Star Wars*, *Assault on Precinct 13*, *Pardon Mon Affaire*, *1900*, *That Obscure Object Of Desire*, *The Lace maker*, *The Duellists*, *Dersu Uzala*, *Oh God*, and *Providence*. Admittedly in the same period there's been *The Comeback*, *The Swarm*, *Herbie Goes To Monte Carlo*, *Holocaust 2000*, *Salon Kitty*, *Viva Knievel,* and *The Choirboys*, But I cannot think of anything on television that had the class or the breadth of say fifty per cent of the films shown in the cinema 1977/78, except possibly Dennis Potter's *Pennies From Heaven*, *The Muppets*, and *Out*.

Looking to the future the prospects for the Cinema are bright but unless we get a Fourth Channel fairly soon, television is going to become even more dire.

It could be that the trouble is money. British television is suffering from too much money, the film business has to make ingenuity and novelty a virtue. Not that the best films are necessarily cheap but it's my experience that the best film makers are not the biggest spenders and, of course, all the good films around are going to turn up on television sooner or later. In the end everybody benefits from good, well made films, a healthy box office and the work of alert and energetic young film men.

What's good for Wardour Street today will be good (eventually) for the TV moguls of Shepherd's Bush, Golden Square, Euston Road, Leeds and Elstree. Without movies where would they be?

THE MOVIES IN THE MORNING
Robert Robinson

The first time I went to a Press Show I was thrilled to bits at the prospect of meeting film critics, and I nearly burst into tears when I was made to shake hands with the first one and he was carrying a string-bag full of vegetables.

When he sat down he pushed his hat to the back of his head but didn't actually take it off until after the credits. Culturally speaking, I was feeling pretty insecure; I knew I didn't have to go to the Press Shows because the editor I was working for thought reviewing was no substitute for the real business of life, which was interviewing film stars, and I daresay this made me demand more of film critics than they were going to be able to offer. I wanted to feel I'd made it with the intellectuals, but this man's string-bag had two marrows in it, and when the lights came up I could see he was also carrying a cauliflower and a packet of Tide.

I could have murdered him. When he got up I saw he hadn't bothered to take his overcoat off, and there were deep transverse creases in the herringbone that suggested years of creative sitting. I got the feeling that films were incidental to his real purpose in life, which was to persuade onlookers that they were honorary members of his own household. When he walked out into the street I looked sharply at his trouser-bottoms to see if he'd got his pyjamas on underneath.

ECONOMY AT THE CINEMA DE LUXE.

Mrs. Jones (completing her fourth hour). "I USED TO STAY ONLY TWO HOURS; BUT ONE 'AS TO MAKE THREEPENCE GO FURTHER THESE DAYS."

I must have been feeling fairly paranoid at the time, because I found myself extending this principle, and every morning at the Odeon or the Empire would descry hidden motives as the critics came in through the cold swing-doors. Something about the satisfied way one of my colleagues took his seat made me know (a) he had never doubted that life was meant to be lived on the feet, but (b) no marks were deducted if you could prove you'd done the resting in cinemas. Another man had taken up film criticism because of the unrivalled opportunities it afforded for barking like an Alsatian. Trained to a hair on Capstan Full Strength, he was in a marvellous position to kid people he was only coughing, but he didn't fool me. Barking against time, he could get in twenty or thirty in the course of an average-length feature, and the last as fresh as the first.

Some days you had the Alsatian, and some days you had the man who came along to spot bad lines and get his laugh in first. Some days you had both, of course—woof, woof, ha, ha, and over everything a dense pall of after-shave, bursting silently from the pores of someone I could never quite locate, who had carefully marinated himself in Old Spice for the three days previous.

Of course, it was just me feeling persecuted. I knew the editor didn't give a damn if I pirated the reviews from a one-eyed sailor-man, as long as they fitted into a panel two inches square, and didn't make his wife feel challenged. No wonder I went round suspecting everyone of wanting to beat me to death with rolled-up synopses. Nowadays, it goes without saying, my colleagues are some of the suavest, handsomest devils you could hope to snore through ten reels with. But the actual occasion stays very cold.

No one likes to be sat next to at Press Shows—every man keeps an empty seat between himself and the world, and sits suspended in a caul of solitariness. The people who make the films get very worried about the glacial climate that prevails at Press Shows, and sometimes go out into the street, importuning old ladies to come in and do a bit of chuckling. They hope the chuckling will make the critic worried about not chuckling himself, and perhaps nudge him into suspecting his own responses rather than the film's.

Not a bad scheme in theory, but it never seems to work. For one thing, the undeclared reason a critic puts up with having to give coherent accounts of films not themselves coherent (apart from the fact that it's better than working) is that he's never got over being allowed into a cinema for nothing. If he finds the place swarming with old ladies who not only haven't paid, *but don't even have to form an opinion*, it makes him very sensitive. The old ladies rustle contentedly, and at the end clap enthusiastically even if the film has been run backwards. This, and the presence of ice-cream girls, makes a critic savagely indignant, as though a role he'd taught himself to experience as more or less in the star class, had turned out to be below-the-title after all.

I think I miss a lot not going to the lunches. Press Shows are islands surrounded by lunches, the lunches being given by the film people in the interests of cheering the critics up. I don't go, because I can't muster the metabolism necessary for talking to a man with that special sort of animation which stops him wondering why you haven't said anything about the film you have just seen, which he directed. But in the early days I could do it without getting out of breath, and while eating and drinking free, felt relaxed enough to take in the anthropology.

The lunches looked human enough, but there was always one element which let you know, as it were through a megaphone, that the whole occasion had been flown in complete from Selfridge's grotto. Once it was a man who produced a pigeon from his shirt before the critics had finished their mussel soup. He'd been hired to put everyone in a good mood for the film they were going to see, but the pigeon got away before he could make it do what he wanted it to do, and it flew up on to a gilt mirror and sat there arranging its feathers. The man did a few tricks

"Remember when women's films used to be weepies?"

with burning paper, and kept on chatting about how he liked a good gangster picture and did anyone know what had happened to Veronica Lake. But he couldn't take his eyes off the pigeon. When people tried to get the bird down by throwing it bits of bread, he said irritably "Leave it alone, it'll come down when it's ready." It was a terribly melancholy occasion, and in their hearts all the critics knew no film was going to be able to match it.

Perhaps half past ten in the morning is a funny time to go to the pictures. It's the wrong hour to be looking at those bas-reliefs of females and chariots, left behind on the walls of cinemas as emblems of a civilisation that perished in 1937. Sometimes they even haul in a man to play the Wurlitzer, and he tinkers away at strange old tunes as if he were trying to reproduce in laboratory conditions a happy outing of thirty years ago. No good in the morning. Critics leave Press Shows with a faint metallic taste in their mouths, as though the machinery which processes the fantasies had slightly tainted the product.

159

Garbo
ex-Greta
E. V. Lucas

Films have come to a sad pass when RAMON NOVARRO goes blind and GARBO'S shot at dawn. Realism no doubt would be the excuse; but who wants realism when lovely woman is under sentence? Reprieve is what we want. As, however, the picture is called *Mata Hari* and as *Mata Hari* was a spy and was found out and executed, GARBO must be; but as, on the other hand, the story of *Mata*'s career and character has been much distorted, it would have been simpler and more in accordance with the rules of the cinema game to give her another name and a happy ending in the arms of her lover, with an oculist in the background prepared to renovate the hero's eyes.

Such a solution would have improved this picture in other ways too, for the melancholy concluding passages are far too long and very monotonous, with GARBO as a tragic figure with much too high a forehead and no chance to get another hat. Her ordinary allowance of hats has, until her arrest, been one for every ten minutes; but with gaol comes a head-dress more suited to a broken-spirited Magdalene than a still defiant traitor, and not what GARBO'S admirers expect or desire—at any rate for so long at a stretch.

It will perhaps already have been observed that I call the lady GARBO, without any ceremony whatever; and I must admit that each time I have done so my pen has baulked. But I am merely following the METRO-GOLDWYN lead, which has cut out the GRETA. Henceforward the world has to say GARBO only: not even the GARBO, which would be a shade less familiar and abrupt.

So let it be. Homage to GARBO, who is a beautiful creature with many gifts and graces, although perhaps always, in this film, a shade too languid and serene. It would be interesting to see in the same part her closest rival, for, though she is in the main also passive—more loved than loving—there would be some differences very well worth watching. Different hats to look out for too, although DIETRICH—no, the DIETRICH—no, MARLENE DIETRICH, in *The Shanghai Express*, confines herself to one.

Considering *Mata Hari* as a sensational talkie, one can say that it holds and excites and that it has been very well cast. Any film with LIONEL BARRYMORE in it is assured of a measure of success, and here, as ever, he is steadily virile and persuasive until the inevitable moment when he is shot. No one has been so often shot as this excellent actor. LEWIS STONE, another sterling support of any film, always to be relied upon, is excellent too as *Mata Hari*'s pitiless employer; but exactly what all the spying was about and what was done with the information I could not discover, nor could we work up much sympathy for RAMON NOVARRO as a flying-officer in war-time with no sense of duty whatever.

It will give some idea of the receptivity of a cinema audience and its simple tastes when I say that on the same evening that I went to the Empire, with thousands of others, for the thrills and emotions of a GARBO spy-drama, there was shown an animated photograph of the domestic life of the nightingale, with snatches of its song and the house was spellbound. I never saw a prettier film, or a curtain-raiser so unlike what was to succeed it.

Mae West
E. V. Lucas

The distinctions of type can sometimes be puzzling. Thus, in the programme of that excellent piece of tough life in the New York Bowery in the eighteen-ninties, *She Done Him Wrong,* the largest letters are given (after those of MAE WEST, the heroine) to three actors whose work is comparatively lifeless, whereas the burden of the play is borne by such old friends as NOAH BEERY as the saloon-keeper, and DAVID LANDAU, who for once emerging from the police-force becomes *Dan Flynn,* a crook, and is bumped off; but as to whether "bumped off" and certain other phrases used in this film are as old as the eighteen-ninties I am doubtful. As a whole, however, the reconstruction seems to be sound. *Dan Flynn's* top-hat, frock-coat and the cigars in his waistcoat-pocket inspiring profound confidence.

As for the central figure, MAE WEST, as *Lady Lou*, the star singer and power behind the throne in *Gus Jordan's* saloon, she is a terrific personality with something of the frank audacity and "twiggy-vous" expression of MARIE LLOYD, some of the massiveness of BESSIE BELLWOOD, and much that is commanding and sinister of her own. It is odd that with all the emphasis that is laid on her singing, the songs chosen for her in this play should be so inferior and to too large an extent inaudible.

As a whole *She Done Him Wrong* is so exciting and amusing that the feebleness of the end is the more of a shock. Detectives should be detectives, above the ordinary emotions which sway poor human nature, so that to see this super "dick", having arrested all *Lou's* old associates, carry her off and slip a ring on her finger is to cause much rubbing of the eyes, particularly as she has just stabbed *Russian Rita* to death and will have to "go up the river" herself.

Tallulah
E. V. Lucas

"She talks so enthusiastically," says the Carlton Theatre programme about Miss TALLULAH BANKHEAD, "that the muscles of her neck often reflect her earnestness." This idiosyncrasy I did not notice during the actress's first talking film, *Tarnished Lady*; but, for the rest, the management's account of her is accurate, although the thousands of her London admirers, and in particular the ecstatic young women who have made a habit or rite of waiting outside the stage-door on the first nights of her new plays to express their adoration, will regret the use of the past tense: "In London Tallulah Bankhead *was* the darling of the footlights"; "during the eight years she *spent* in England", and so forth. One cannot read sentences like that without realising that the Paramount studio has very definitely made a capture and means to hold to it. TALLULAH has widened her sphere; she can appeal now, through the medium of the talkies, to all the world at once instead of to a single audience; but she has lost her emotional allies; and they have lost her—for I suppose that even such allurement as hers, when translated into photography and phonography, lacks most of its appeal. The gallery may still be crowded by sympathisers and devotees, but there is no communicating current. TALLULAH is no longer *en rapport*; she is thousands of miles away across the sundering sea.

But when her contract with Paramount is finished and she returns to the London stage—if to one who will then be a millionairess such a course has any attraction—or if during her cinema career she makes, like one CHAPLIN, a personal visit to inaugurate a new picture, how the streets will be congested, how the doors will be besieged, how those long-suffering servants of the public, the London police, will be called upon to exercise firmness with tact!

In *Tarnished Lady* TALLULAH has been fitted very carefully with a part. Every mood in her not extensive repertory is provided with material, and by turns she is insolent, pitiful, reproachful, disdainful and, if not loving, desirous. But always—as I used to find her on the stage—tragic. I can remember no face, certainly not the face of any actress playing in tragedy, so tragic as hers. The bitter words, "Vanity of vanities, all is vanity", are written all over it, and Mr. GEORGE CUKOR, the Paramount producer, is, I fancy, going to have some difficulty in diversifying her roles. But perhaps he will not try. "The mixture as before" is a time-honoured prescription.

Marlene Dietrich
E. V. Lucas

The beautiful spy is always an alluring figure, even though there is the risk that our natural hostility to her calling may cut across our sympathy. When, however, the motive of love is country is insisted upon as strongly as it is in *Dishonoured,* our sympathy can be kept in order; and, although we may regret that she allowed a kiss to interfere with business, the new film-star, MARLENE DIETRICH, holds it to the end.

She begins, this beautiful spy, very well and almost too easily. Her first victim is an Austrian General supposed to be in traitorous treaty with the enemy. The duty of *X.27*, which is MARLENE'S name in the secret service, is to test that supposition. The *General*, by falling in love with her, makes it very simple, she discovers his treachery and he obligingly shoots himself. Good. Now, having proved herself, she shall have a real task: she shall go to Russia in disguise and ascertain the intended movements of troops; so off she speeds in an aeroplane, but very foolishly accompanied by her black cat: one of the best screen-actors I have yet seen, but an embarrassment in the higher spheres of espionage. In the barracks, where she stations herself as a clumsy housemaid (but she can't be clumsy for long, this German enchantress), is the Russian officer, also, as it happens, a spy, known as *H.14* (VICTOR MCLAGLEN) who had met both her and her cat under compromising circumstances when on his secret service mission to Vienna—who, in short, was the sharer of the fatal kiss.

The rest of the story becomes a duel between these two. So long as *X.27* can keep her country's needs uppermost in her mind all is well, and *H.14* is first drugged by her and then through her instrumentality captured and imprisoned and condemned to be shot.

Had there been no kiss *H.14* would have died the death. Love, however, conquers all; *X.27* asks to be allowed to question him in private and, after weakening her case by kissing him again, lets him escape. Dishonoured! She had been a good spy until then, but she could be trusted no more and there was nothing for it but a firing-party.

We all sat on the edges of our seats hoping and even expecting a reprieve. Yet it did not come. She was dressed so exquisitely, her composure was so complete, her smile so bewitching, that surely help must arrive. But HERR JOSEF VON STERNBERG, the author, is pitiless: bang went the rifles and the lovely *X.27* was dead, *soignée* and self-possessed to the last.

HERR JOSEF VON STERNBERG (every one is German these days!) knew what he was doing when he prepared and produced this story for his fair compatriot. Leaving aside for the moment her really extraordinary physical charm, her slow candid methods are perfect for such a role. No one can look so persuasive, so true; no one has a voice so well modulated and controlled, and it is not the less pleasant to the ear for the slight foreignness of it. Another of this new actress's notable qualities is her sense of time and rhythm: she never hastens and yet is never slow. Her strength is in the deeper emotions, but her mischievous moods are a delight. There are a few moments in this picture when you see only her mouth beneath her mask; but what a mouth! I urge you towards that glimpse.

"There's somebody in there at the moment – when he's seen it, you can go in."

HEATH

Per Ardua ad Hollywood

The RAF is using battling old war movies as motivational training films Stanley Reynolds wonders about the lads out there

I calculated we might be home by six when the trouble with the port engine started. There was a violent shudder.

"God, what was that?" the navigator said.

"Could be a broken air-screw, skip," the co-pilot said.

I was silent, my cheek muscles twitching all down one side of my face just like Gregory Peck's in *12 O'Clock High*.

"Not an air-screw," I thought, "not a broken air-screw. Not on a lousy, penny ante run like this, not after all the big trips like Bremen and Cologne, Mannheim and Schweinfurt."

"Bandits at two o'clock," the co-pilot said. I put her into a dive, the old bus shuddering every inch of the way, I listened only to the sound of the engines: in reality, to the sound of one engine; the port had gone.

"Wanna ice-cream," the tail gunner said.

"Made it, skip," the co-pilot said, "jolly good show."

Behind us the bandits had been halted by the red light. "Ha ha," the co-pilot said, "a three-litre Rover and a brand new Marina and they couldn't beat us in an old thing like this. Ha Ha." The co-pilot was only twelve and could not remember the great days the old bus had had on the bad runs over Bremen and Cologne; it was just probable that the co-pilot had never even heard of Schweinfurt.

"Rat-a-tat-tat," the tail gunner said. 'Wanna wee wee, wanna ice-cream.'' The ball turret gunner was getting his nappy changed by the navigator.

"God," I thought, "I ask for men and they send me boys."

How surprised all we motorists were last week to learn that the RAF had only just now realised the worth of old movies. *12 O'Clock High*, the World War Two bomber pilot film in which Greg Peck's cheek muscles twitch all over Schweinfurt, Cologne, Bremen and Mannheim while the sound track is loud with the noise of exploding 50 cal. machine-guns and calls of "Bandits at two o'clock," had just now been accepted as an official RAF training film.

"It is what we term a motivational film. It shows pride of service," an RAF spokesman said. Well, we motorists have known all about that motivation stuff for years. How else do you think we go on piloting our old wrecks week-end after week-end? To the sea, into the mountains, picking up all sorts of flack from passing juggernauts, getting strafed by high-powered Jags and Mercedes Benz, knowing all the time that the fan belt is worn wafer thin and is likely to go any moment, that the exhaust pipe is held on by wire, and the tyres haven't got a snowball's chance in hell of doing another hundred miles.

But we are motivated. We have seen all the old war movies on TV and we head for the sea coast as if we were carrying the bouncing bomb. Everybody knows this. How come the RAF didn't? Funny, I would have thought the RAF would have been filled with adventurous fellows like us motorists, chaps with their heads swimming with scenes from *Dawn Patrol* and *633 Squadron*. Just the sort of chaps to dive through a cordon of ME 109s or panda cars with breathalizers and think nothing of it.

Maybe the RAF has been advertising itself the wrong way around all these years of the technological revolution? I don't pretend to know all about it, but it sounds to me as if those adverts in the newspapers which spoke of A levels and presented the job as if it were like driving some kind of glorified computer have got the wrong sort of bod into the old RAF.

Well, it must have or else why are they worried so much about motivation that they are showing them old films like *12 O'Clock High*? They've got themselves a pack of glorified computer operators with those adverts and now they find they'd actually rather have someone a little bit more like Erroll Flynn and David Niven in *Dawn Patrol*. Taking off bareheaded into the wind with the aeroplane trembling under hand like a living thing, flying not on beams and beacons and radio fixes but by the seat of your pants, diving headlong, guns stuttering, into the Richthofen Circus or crashing up a one-way street the wrong way like Binkie Ainsworth did the other night while the little barmaid from the cricket club cried "You fool what are you doing?" "Listen," Binkie said, "When I see a hole in a cloud, I dive." Binkie came down from Oxford last year and has been selling soap every since. Why isn't he taking kites up for the RAF and throwing them about?

"Well, we don't want dangerous drivers, old boy, we want...er...ah...the sort of chap with two A levels who's interested in computers and...ah...er..."

In my own fleeting romance with the US Navy air corps I learned that one of the chief reasons pilots crashed on take-off was that they liked to do that look down as the plane lifted into the air off the edge of the carrier deck. You know the look down, you've seen it in all the movies and you can do it really good with these new head rests they have in all the new cars nowadays. Evidently that look

"This is her first serious part."

"Of course, the drink ruined him as a stuntman."

down—John Wayne had it to perfection in both *The Flying Tigers* (a remake of *Dawn Patrol*) and in *Flying Leathernecks*—is death or disaster in a jet lifting off a carrier deck. I resigned from the naval air corps. What was the use if you couldn't do that look down like in all the movies? Leave the fleet air arm to the sort of chap who likes to play with punch cards. Give me an open car, a panda on my tail and nowhere to dive but the hind end of a one-way street. Jets never really interested me. What half lured me was the fact that the jets landed at 120 mph and did a dead stop at 90. If you snapped the wires you crashed into all the other wrecked planes piled up at the end of the carrier deck. I'm sure some psychiatrist slipped up when they let me through the net, but that was what really got me about the whole thing.

Now, with the cost of these modern jets you cannot really blame the RAF for looking for the careful sort of chap who envisions a long range career. These planes are no longer made of canvas and plywood and held together by piano wire and chewing gum. They are the jet-age latests, but I'm not letting my boys go up in computers like that.

Of course Greg Peck in *12 O'Clock High*, with the small-seeming B-17 Flying Fortresses and their pop-gun armament, has about as much relationship to the modern air force as Errol Flynn in *Captain Blood* would have to today's Navy. But it is nice to know that the RAF realises there is something missing up there in today's computerised blue yonder.

One note jars, however. Greg Peck, as the dynamic General Savage who restores morale in the American bomber squadron, has a nervous breakdown at the end of *12 O'Clock High*; he starts twitching in both cheeks and has to get sent stateside.

"I must admit," the RAF man said, "that is, unfortunately, a weakness in the film."

I should say so. Rather like using Alastair Sim as Scrooge in the movie of *A Christmas Carol* as a morale booster for hard eyed merchant bankers or Victor McLaglen in *The Informer* to promote more co-operation between the Roman Catholics and the Army in Northern Ireland.

I was sent by Zanuck in 1938 to write a movie based on anecdotes Lord Castlerosse had told him on a flight over Czechoslovakia. Zanuck's man took me to Brook's for lunch with Castlerosse and I found myself confronting all three hundred pounds of him, staring me down with a wild look in his eye. He ordered up a huge lunch from the blackboard, as did Zanuck's man. I ordered pineapple. "Pineapple?" queried Castlerosse. "Pineapple," answered I. Not another word was spoken during lunch but an occasional "Pineapple?!" from Castlerosse. At the end of the lunch he said, "I like you, Blum!" and told me to fetch up an airplane and a beautiful secretary because next day we were going to his estate in Ireland, which included one of the Lakes of Killarney. Next morning I went from Zanuck's suite at Claridge's to Castlerosse's suite at Claridge's and told the man all was ready for our sojourn.

"What sojourn?" he asked.

"Lake Killarney."

"Oh, that!" He tossed me a telegram. It read: "DON'T COME. YOU KNOW WHY. FATHER."

"Why!' I asked.

"I was disowned twenty years ago."

I began to see I was dealing with a rather unique man. It turned out that he couldn't remember telling any anecdotes over Czechoslovakia, and insisted Zanuck did all the talking. I ended up staying three months at Claridge's trying to find out who told whom what, and during those three months I was contantly with Castlerosse. Every day and every night. I took him to lunch and I took him to supper and I paid all the bills. Faint beeps began to flash in from Hollywood that I was spending more than three Zanucks, to which I cabled back "CASTLEROSSE IS THREE ZANUCKS." One night I thrust a huge supper check over to Castlerosse and said, "Why don't you pay this one, Valentine?" He glared at me and said, "Are you *mad*?"

Every night he would

164

The Film That Darryl Zanuck Never Made

A true-life story of corruption, splendour and Lord Castlerosse, now turned into a major magazine article by **Edwin Blum**

come to my suite with two or three girls he was presumably keeping (I never could find out because they couldn't talk English) and I would order up a bottle of hundred-year-old brandy from Claridge's cellar. Sometimes two. We'd argue drunkenly about politics, sports, food, women, anything. I began to note that some of my lines were popping up in Castlerosse's column in the *Express*. I accused the man once of "stealing" my stuff without pay. "Are you mad!" he exclaimed, "Didn't I spend the whole morning taking you down to the docks to find you coffee that would taste like that damned American swill?"

"It all tastes like British swill."

"Didn't I take you to the fights with Lord Astor and didn't he take us to Cliveden? Didn't I take you to play golf with Joe Kennedy?"

"What good does that do me when you know I'm for Churchill?"

"So am I!" he thundered.

I stared at him incredulously. "And you write all that crap saying Chamberlain saved the world?"

"I'm writing a column for Beaverbrook, you fool!"

I refrained from saying *I* was writing some of that column. Not out of tact or pity. The doctor had warned Valentine off brandy and he was on his thirtieth whisky and soda. You can't be hard on a man when he's switching drinks.

I finally caught on to Castlerosse, and it happened this way: every day at the same hour he would drop in at his bridge club, and every day the same three Etonians would be waiting for him and knock him back for two or three hundred guineas. One day I said to him, "Valentine, can't you see those guys are taking you for a pigeon?" He glared at me wildly and said, "I am taking *them* for pigeons!"

"With all those chits you sign? That mountain of due bills?"

"They can't cash them in. They don't *dare*!"

"Why not?"

"Because I owe one hundred and fifty thousand pounds all over London! I have created an edifice, and there is not one man among them brave enough to test a stone!"

"I can't speak for the sex but the violence was terrific."

A week before I was to return home I suggested to Castlerosse he wouldn't get paid anything by Zanuck if I didn't bring back a story. He told me to write one, and he would co-sign it. I wrote a story outline in which Burton of Arabia turns against the British Empire in the Indian Mutiny.

Castlerosse read it and had fifty copies published as a book. The title read Burton of Arabia by Lord Castlerosse and Edwin Blum.

"Valentine," asked I, "what will Beaverbrook say when he sees this movie?"

"He'll never see it, because Zanuck made *Lloyds of London* and *Disraeli* and he'll never go against Empire."

"Then what makes you think Zanuck will pay you for writing it?"

"Because, old cock, Zanuck told me he loves first editions!"

And Zanuck did pay him.

So now you know why I often gaze fondly on the two sterling Georgian wine-coolers Valentine gave me as a parting gift. What I like most about them is that the American customs inspector told me I'd have to pay duty on them because they were not antiques.

Where are they now?

THE FIRST TARZAN

HARRY AND LESTER PLIMSOLE
Pioneers of the soft shoe shuffle

"I've got news for you guys . . . . I'm no longer an agent."

ORGOTTEN IDOLS OF THE ILVER SCREEN

ANDA GLAMAL
p of the Silent Era

CARL (KNUCKSY) BLOHEIM
Warner Bros. star gangster hoodlum

AMON LE CHERE
greatest of the Latin lovers

AND FRIENDS...

Moviemakers' Lib

HEATH puts an end to
sex discrimination on the
film-set

"You come into the room, you see her lying there naked, you revolted with yourself for seeing her as a sex object..."

"Make-up room! What ake-up room?"

"What d'you mean, I'm not to be rescued in the nick of time?"

"Has anyone ever told you how attractive you are with your glasses on, Ms Banson?"

"But I don't remember being castrated in the script!"

NO CANNES DO

As another
film festival opens,
Barry Norman
reports

Cannes, they say (and by they I mean the old-timers of the movie industry, bottle-scarred survivors of a hundred film festivals and similar boozy junkets), Cannes is not what it was. There's no answer to that, of course, except the silent nod of sympathy and the unspoken thought that very possibly the Cannes Film Festival is the sort of function that never really was what it was.

What the old-timers have in mind, I suppose, is the Cannes of legend, the Cannes of the early fifties when movies were the world's most popular entertainment and the beaches throbbed with hungry little starlets whose bikinis never got wet and who were bought by producers at so much the dozen.

Those were the days when a British starlet called Simone Silva hurled aside the top half of her swimsuit and had herself photographed with a bemused Robert Mitchum who, sitting there minding his own business, was at least mildly surprised to find a camera and a ripe boob thrust simultaneously into his face.

Ah, but it's not like that now. The starlets have gone, their race having vanished as mysteriously as the Etruscans, and these days the best-looking girls at Cannes are the visiting hookers down from Paris to enjoy the sea air and turn a profitable trick or two—elegant, arrogant creatures strolling languidly along the Boulevard de la Croisette, closely followed by a large cigar clenched between the false, but manly, teeth of about 5ft. of rotund movie magnate, himself a vision in Bermuda shorts and a shirt inspired by Van Gogh's palette after a bad day at Arles.

And yet...the starlets haven't entirely disappeared; an endangered species they may be but they're not quite extinct. I remember, a few years ago, Lindsay Anderson pausing on the steps of the Palais des Festivals on the night his film was shown and striking a pensive, dignified pose for the photographers. His chagrin when he discovered that the cameras were aimed not at him, the director, but at a perfectly unknown though delicious girl who was certainly not in his film and probably didn't even have a ticket to the cinema was moving to behold.

"This festival," he said, "is becoming vulgar." And he swept off. Well, it wasn't a total loss—if you looked closely you could just see him lurking in the background in one or two of the pictures—but there was no denying his verdict.

Cannes *is* vulgar. Any marketplace is vulgar and Cannes is a marketplace, a hustler's hunting ground where movie moguls buy and sell films (and each other) under the astonished gaze of about 35,000 visitors lured there by a rumour that Bardot and Burton and Taylor and Newman and Redford and McQueen will all be present, mingling intimately with the populace.

They won't, of course. Mostly they emulate Dirk Bogarde who lives up the road at Grasse and avoids Cannes at festival time on the grounds that it's his idea of hell, being full of all the people he'd hoped were dead—an understandable attitude when you watch some of these people scuttling about, wheeling and dealing and flogging hard-core porn and very likely, given a reasonable offer, their sisters.

Yet there is something about Cannes, not glamour exactly but a lingering possibility of glamour, that sets it apart from similar affairs in Berlin and Venice (now, alas, no more, its festival having fallen victim to a political quarrel of such inscrutability that even the Italians couldn't understand it) and Moscow and Mar del Plata and

San Sebastian and Cork (an agreeable festival, I understand, held together by a shoestring and kept afloat on a sea of Guinness) and London and New York and Karlovy Vary (wherever that may be) and Los Angeles and Edinburgh.

Most of these rival festivals are earnest functions where films are shown out of competition for the benefit of dedicated movie buffs. Cannes is not earnest, bestows prizes on the deserving and undeserving alike and is more concerned with businessmen than movie buffs.

Mind you, I'm not saying you can't see films at Cannes, good heavens no. To some extent seeing films is what it's all about. Even one or two of the less decisive moguls have been known actually to view the occasional movie before buying it, although they're more likely to make a bid on the strength of a one-page synopsis, so long as it's not in joined-up writing.

If you're totally out of your mind, or a critic, or probably both, you can easily watch six films a day and some do, poor fellows. But the price they pay is heavy because they miss most of the parties and parties, along with buying and selling, are what Cannes is really all about.

With regard to these parties, however, certain important points must be kept in mind. For instance, you never, save in the last resort, attend the parties to which you've been invited as a party to which you've been invited can hardly be worth attending in the first place.

Instead you gatecrash the parties from which you've been excluded. This is easily effected, particularly if you have a champagne glass on your person, for an ostentatious twirl of this as you pass the man on the door leads him to suppose that you've already been in once and are simply returning for a refill.

It's inside that the real danger presents itself. Remember, the party is celebrating some film or other and the people who made it will be there and will certainly accost you, seeking your opinion. Tricky this, because even if you saw the picture you very probably disliked it.

So what you say is..."Charlie," you say, assuming the film-maker's name is Charlie, "Charlie..." And here you sigh and shrug helplessly as if in the grip of some emotion too deep for mere words. "You've done it again, Charlie. You've just done it again."

Or else..."Marvin, that was, gee, that was one hell of a picture," or... "Homer, it was...it was a total experience, Homer", or... "Only you could have made that movie, J.J. I mean that sincerely, J.J." And so on. And since nearly all film-makers are certifiable megalomaniacs they will happily interpret these ambiguous remarks as fulsome compliments and press another glass of champagne upon you. So long as you keep to the formula you're perfectly safe but on no account must you ever tell the truth unless you really did like the movie and the odds are against that.

I learned this lesson from a man from the *Daily Express* who went (by invitation, actually) to a formal supper after the showing of the official French entry, a film that created much fuss since it combined sex and excrement with such ingenuity as not even a Frenchman had been able to achieve before.

Well, he'd just arrived when the producer fell upon him, asking what he thought of the picture and he, being taken by surprise, absent-mindedly said it was decadent and disgraceful, whereupon his invitation was snatched away and he was ejected forthwith. At moments like that Dirk Bogarde is quite right—Cannes is hell. But it doesn't have to be, not if you play your cards right.

R. G. G. Price
reports from the fest

I missed Bali, as it clashe with Blenkenberge, but I hear goo reports of the new Fassbinder, *A Mother's Tears*, one of his deeply committed weepies. There is said to be some marvellous dun photo graphy.

The Belgian festival was chiefly notable for the Spaghetti Easterns, society comedies set o the WASP end of Long Island and produced on a shoestring by Italians. On the last day, one of these contributions to polished humour began at dawn and was followed by a champagne break-fast with Zsa Zsa Gabor and a cheerful, middle-aged woman sh introduced as her grandmother. I could not wait for the programme of instructional shorts organised the Liège Co-op as my flight to Taos was due.

Here nearly every film stuck to the Mexican party line an was visually influenced more by Sica than by Eisenstein ... all rain on half-built housing projects. The longest film—*Eviva Speranza*—lasted $5\frac{1}{2}$ hours and never moved from one corner of one room.

The most enjoyable item was the delightful Albanian cartoon, *The Wolf Who Learned Skate*. I loved seeing it again, though I had enjoyed its simple, lively fun and its simple, lively drawing and its simple, lively colours at Aix-les-Bains, Ploesti, South Shields, Addis Ababa, Darwin and Innsbruck.

I had to cut the Grand Farewell Banquet, with a two-hou speech by Lindsay Anderson, because of the cross-country journey to Bergen. The theme thi year was "The Dawn of the Film" and the organisers had strung together some marvellous mater from the earliest days—a man walking along the Rue de Rivoli, a rowboat on the Yser and a hanso in Park Lane. Sometimes the

FAR-FLUNG FILM FAN

...heraman had forgotten which
... up the film should be inserted.
...ny of the shots were completely
... of focus. There were a good
...ny sequences showing just
...e-tops and there was one
...xplicable frame with Lord
...dolph Churchill pointing at a
...r saying "No Visitors". To
...ke the opening of St Tropez, I
... to miss a picnic at the
...hplace of the man who wrote
... first subtitle, "Father, don't
...p!"

This year the official events
...t Tropez were rather over-
...dowed by an Anti-Festival,
...minated by the Neo-nihilist
...up. Their manifesto begins,
...polish the screen and save the
... from being structured in the
...rests of the capitalist power-
...ck." They believe that, instead
...he audience's passively
...tching whatever the financiers
... to project onto the fourth wall,
...y should move about, relating,
...ng. Films should be projected
...o naturally occurring
...faces—people, furniture, food,
...embly-line etc. Any loss in
...mmunication, they claim, is
...re than made up by the gain in
...evance.

I found the official
...gramme more interesting. Its
...me is the rediscovery of the
...lier talkies and most of the
...ries are remakes. I did not
...ch care for the *Carry On* team's
...sion of the Marx Brothers'
...imal Crackers*; but Twiggy was
...e in Ken Russell's *Congress
...nces* and there was an
...eresting *Blue Angel* with Mae
...est.

This is one of the most
...ish festivals and, as well as five
...six full-length films a day, there
...re non-stop parties. One
...morable binge combined shark-
...ning, a discussion of non-
...presentational documentary and
...plendid seafood and Chablis

lunch.

During the week I had an
illuminating talk with Clint
Grabopotocki, the Idaho cult
director, who was trying to drum up
finance for his Rabelais in a mid-
twentieth century setting, with
Jack Nicholson as "Craps"
Panurge. He keeps being turned
down because Andrew Lloyd
Webber isn't writing the score: he
wants to use the Auric music from
early René Clair.

I was sorry that I couldn't
wait for the Redford-Hoffman
Raffles; but I only just made it to
Stoke-on-Trent for the twelve-hour
screening of Anthony Powell's *The
Music of Time*. To get an American
release, Losey had to use
American box-office stars. Simon
Raven's screenplay does what it
can by intermarrying the Four
Hundred with the British
aristocracy; but the disparate
accents jar. As a British actor,
Malcolm McDowell, is used for

Widmerpool, it seems a naked
concession to the front office to
make him talk Brooklynese. In any
case, surely Groton would have
been nearer?

One of the most enjoyable
fringe events was a Press
Conference given—or
lavished—by Zsa Zsa Gabor, who
loudly confided to us that she was
writing a film for herself—the story
of Lady Jane Grey. She is such
good value on these publicity
jaunts that somebody should build
a film round her conversation.

I did not stay for the Free
Lithuanian "satire-opera" as it was
time to leave for Darjeeling. On the
plane, Trevor Griffiths told me that
he is hoping to sell his script for
Kipps to . . .

NEATH

*"We're making a sort of 'Easy Rider' but for
the older generation."*

DEATH IN VENICE
BJORN ANDRESEN as Tadzio
DIRK BOGARDE as
Gustav von Aschenbach

Cinema Drawings

ffolkes

INADMISSIBLE EVIDENCE
NICOL WILLIAMSON as
Bill Maitland

BLOOD FEUD
SOPHIA LOREN

LOST AND FOUND
GEORGE SEGAL *and* GLENDA JACKSON

MOTION PICTURES
H. F. Ellis

I once was Spencer Tracy in a storm at sea. That is to say, I was in the storm. Spencer Tracy was on land, with only one arm, at a place called Black Rock. Evil men with secrets to hide obstructed his honest purposes, refused him answers, tripped him up, and poured tomato sauce into his coffee cup. These humiliations he accepted with dogged perseverance. The ship's cinema, which was really, I suppose, the lounge, moved up and down. When the ship rolled, screen and audience tilted together, so that we seemed to be cornering at speed. The bows rose steeply upwards, and Tracy with them, so that one had a sensation of lying on one's back to see, as in the Sistine Chapel; then down they plunged, and it was hard to resist the belief that the top of Tracy's head must come into view. No actor ever had a tougher task. Sooner or later he would break out. This meekness could not last. The great big bully with the sauce bottle had as sure and terrible a retribution coming to him as was ever meted out to a bad man on the screen. But meanwhile Tracy had to portray a craven submission, a willingness to take it all, a massive inertia that must yet carry some hint of a tightly coiled spring within—and all this to the satisfaction of an audience that dipped and soared, that swung about him in great arcs like so many wind-blown herring gulls.

Some few great actors have the power of riveting the attention when doing nothing in particular, even when absolutely still. To achieve this when the audience itself is in motion is perhaps a unique jewel in Spencer Tracy's crown. Nobody left or was sick. Our instability, I think we all felt after a time, added a new dimension to the film. "Surely he will hit him *now*?" one said to oneself and instantly, with the heart already in the mouth in anticipation, fell fifty feet towards the bottom of the sea. But he didn't. He shuffled off again, with that pitifully empty sleeve tucked into the pocket of his coat, and our outward breath of exasperation coincided with the rocketing lift of a mighty wave. This admixture of mental and physical sensations produced feelings of extraordinary intensity, akin to death. The suspense was terrific. When you are gripping the arms of your chair to control your over-mastering excitement *and* to save yourself from falling clean out over the side, life has not much more to offer. The nearest equivalent I can think of in the realm of entertainment would be to watch the duel scene in *Hamlet* from a Giant Switchback; but the opportunity has never come my way.

The cinema, in its long struggle against adversity and bingo, has attempted many innovations. Sound and colour and wide-screen and 3-D and puffed-out smells—these have been tried. But no serious effort, as far as I know, has been made to get the audience on the move. The Metros and the Goldwyns, the Hustons rather and the Bergmans, the Antonionis, the Kramers and the Zeffirellis have strained ingenuity to the limits in the matter of camera angles, visual surprises, unheard-of viewpoints; it never seems to have occurred to them to try the effect of swinging the stalls through an arc of thirty-five degrees during the battle in *The Shrew* or suddenly tilting the cheaper seats over backwards at the crisis of *High Noon*. Or, if it has, they have timidly baulked at the mechanical difficulties. It is time the Swinging Cinema came to London.

The other arts are no more enterprising. What a to-do there has been about mobiles in the plastic and old-scrap-metal fields. Thin rods oscillate in currents of air and bicycle wheels rotate. Kinetic art employs machinery, mirrors, kaleidoscopic lights to introduce a semblance of stir and bustle and to promote vertigo in the spectator. Infinite trouble is taken by op artists to produce an illusion of movement, to make lines and squares recede and bulge, disappear round non-existent corners and reappear the other side. But always there is the hidebound assumption that the viewer will be rooted to a single spot; he will take up a position and maintain it, or at best will walk slowly about the object, strictly on the level. So advanced, so forward-looking and original they think they are, these artists. They make bold statements in print, as well as on canvas or with wire. The *Sunday Times* conveniently listed some of them in a recent magazine.

"I forced myself to contradict myself so as not to follow my taste," remarked Marcel Duchamp in 1946. 'Naked men in sculpture are not as handsome as toads," said Brancusi a little earlier. "When one chooses a couple of old iron rings from a hub of a wagon," observes David Smith, "they are circles, they are sums...They have sentiment and they also have the geometry." "Sometimes I see it and then paint it. Other times I paint it and then see it. Both are impure situations, and I prefer neither."—Jasper Johns.

These utterances may satisfy the reactionaries. I find them self-centred and frumpish. They do not invite or involve the co-operation of the public. "I do not paint for the stationary"—this is the kind of pronouncement I should like to hear—"nor to be hung on stable walls. My work is intended to be seen while travelling obliquely through space at speeds in excess of thirty to thirty-five miles an hour."—Paul Glisch (1967). "Moving abstractions contradict their own inherent rigidity. It is the floor of the Tate that should jiggle about."—Hilary Muttonhouse.

Something should be done, too, to promote the Theatre of Oscillation.

But I was writing about Spencer Tracy. He cut loose in the end, of course. It was the tomato sauce that did it; and to the best of my recollection, he simply threw his large opponent three times running in as many seconds—bang! bang! bang!—with his single arm. Once over his shoulder, once in a kind of lightning loop through the air, and the third time, just as the ship fell sickeningly into a trough, clean through the glass door of the establishment. One remembers these things, and him.

"Look out, it's...God, I'm awful with names!"

REVIEWS

W. C. Fields
E. V. Lucas

The case of W.C. FIELDS is a hard one. He is full of gay and insouciant absurdity; he has an incomparable voice in which to be comically sententious; his nose blossoms like the rose; his movements have the grace of the trained performer; his general appearance, though genially grotesque, is benevolent; and we all long to see him and hear him again; and yet no sooner does he enter a film than that film ceases to be, except as an impossibility.

Take *Poppy*, his latest, as an example. *Poppy* is the thin enough story of a "carnival girl" of much charm and beauty, who, after a hand-to-mouth life with a showman. *Professor McGargle*, or W. C. FIELDS, her putative parent, to whom she is attached as *Little Nell* was attached to her grand-father, is discovered to be really the daughter of another man and a rich runaway woman, and thus to be heiress to the Putnam millions. It is poor threadbare stuff, but it might be made acceptable. Yet it could not be so as long as the *Professor* is played by the incredible FIELDS—by this plump seamy elf who appears to belong to another world; this spoilt child who learns his lines with difficulty, says them without proper stress, and appears always to be longing to be following his bent elsewhere.

As it is at present, in order to give our old friend the ex-juggler sufficient chances to be funny, of which he does not enough avail himself, the plot totters and succumbs. Some of the jokes with which he has been supplied, including the ancient one of the ventriloquist selling a dog, and a memory of CHIRGWIN with his one-string fiddle, would have yielded more had he thrown himself into them; but the claims of that other land, that fairyland of misrule from which he came, are too much for him; while his efforts to extract laughter from bad croquet are both incredible and pathetic. Someone realising the limitations of this truly remarkable comedian should take him in hand and fit him.

Cyrano De Hollywood
E. V. Lucas

The true SCHNOZZLE addict, I take it, goes to films that have JIMMIE DURANTE in them, in order to gloat over his huge nose. But if I became one of his fans it would be far more on account of that triumphantly snapping eye which he flashes at us with a sideways thrust of the head. Noses can become tedious, and I rather fancy that this one is on its way in that direction; but no one can deny that its owner is at the moment making the most of what Nature so oddly and lavishly provided. He is following his flag. This organ gives the name to his latest film, in which he is by no means the most important character—*The Great Schnozzle*—and in America you cannot escape from it, even though far from cinemas, for repre-sentations in coloured cardboard and plaster-of-Paris are employed to advertise and prove the value of a score of commodities.

But SCHNOZZLE is as a matter of fact greater than his nose. I have spoken of his swift challenging eye. He has also a voice all his own and a voice-production all his own, and either he himself or the authors of his films are careful that he has plenty of things to say. Some of his phrases have entered the language: "Am I mortified?" for

which he draws attention to his "poisonality"; and in the new film, where he has, as a crooked prize-fight manager, to become more than usually explosive and voluble, some of his phrases are terrific, whether in the heights or depths, the two extremes between which he moves like a shuttle. "It's a neclipse!" he cries at one moment and the next he is on de top of de woild. Although over here he is not exactly, as in America, a national hero, the faithful are a powerful band, and you never heard such laughter as in the Leicester Square Theatre when he makes his final entry and it is discovered not only that since we saw him last, ruined and fleeing from the rogues he has swindled, he is rich and splendid, but that he has married the girl over whom the two champs had quarrelled and the preposterous couple have been blessed by a first-born the very image of its father. That this infant should also have the nose is the crowning jest. But isn't it a prospect to make the brain reel—SCHNOZZLES in perpetuity?

The Marx Brothers Again
E. V. Lucas

There is a pleasant surpr[...] in the first few minutes of *Anima[...] Crackers* at the Carlton. After it depressed our spirits by startin[...] an all-singing musical comedy, song suddenly turns to speech choruses give place to antics a[...] all is amazingly well. Just as on[...] was fearing the worst too.

"If you can't laugh," sa[...] Chinese proverb, "don't open [...] shop." If you don't want to laug[...] advise, don't go to *Animal Crackers* at all, for, funny as th[...] MARX BROTHERS were in *The Cocoanuts*, they are now funni[...]

ll, in exactly the same way. It
ay be the fun of the asylum, but it
ordered too and gets its full
fect. An idea of the insane
onsense that inspires their acts
nd words may be conveyed by the
urlesque of a detectives'
onference between GROUCHO, the
ARX with the spectacles and
oustache, and CHICO, the MARX
ith the Wop accent and hat.
ROUCHO has undertaken to find
e thief who stole the picture, and
hico offers his advice. "You must
o to everybody in the house," he
ges, "and ask them if they stole
" "Vell, and if they are all
nocent?" "Then you must go to
verybody in the house next-door."
But there isn't a house next-
oor." "Then we must build one,"
the devastating reply; and the
vo idiots sit gravely down and
an the new house, even to the
athroom decorations. Pure
onsense is so rare that *Animal*
rackers should be seen if only for
e five minutes occupied by this
ntastic duologue.

According to the
rogramme the original play was
e work of four authors, but, if
ver words seemed to proceed
om the actors themselves
pontaneously, these do. Not, of
ourse, that HARPO has any.
ARPO, the fool of the family, is still
umb and still a thief, even to the
tealing of a birthmark from the
icture-dealer's arm.

The MARX BROTHERS are of
e school of LENO, their
consequence is radiant. That is

to say, GROUCHO'S, CHICO'S and
HARPO'S is. But what of the fourth,
ZEPPO? ZEPPO is a problem. In fact,
the only serious moments in this
revel of madness are when we
ponder on his place in it. In *The
Cocoanuts* he had little enough to
do, but here he has less, and if
GROUCHO did not dictate a travesty
of a business-letter to him he would
not exist. Is he ever funny? Or is he
perhaps the cement that binds the
brotherhood together, the power
behind the throne? If not, how
more than fraternal of GROUCHO,
CHICO and HARPO to let him in on an
equality.

The Left-Handed Woman
Dilys Powell

The Left-Handed Woman is
written and directed
by Peter Handke, the Austrian
novelist and playwright who
has been screenwriter for
Wim Wenders; it is about loneliness, self-inflicted loneliness. A
wife, married in reasonable happiness, has a blinding revelation. She
must live alone; she wants, I
suppose, in the time-dishonoured
phrase, to find herself. Most of the
people in the cinema who want to
find themselves don't search in the
right direction; they don't look at
themselves. To do Peter Handke
justice his heroine (incidentally she
has her little boy to keep her
company) is inclined to self-
examination. And the director,
watching the isolation of women in
the area where he lived, began by
conceiving a film about a general
solitude.

The narrative is made up of
tiny incidents, images of isolation
and human reactions. The woman
works as a translator. She suffers
interruptions from her son and his
friends; has moments of rage;
listens to the remonstrations of her
husband and the advice of her
father. Nothing decisive happens;
it is a chronicle of the everyday. In
its soft colours it looks beautiful;
and it is beautifully played by Edith
Clever and, as the husband, Bruno
Ganz (they were the couple in *Die
Marquise von O.*). I respect the
film. I am driven to admire the
sequence of significant narrative
detail and the slow, pause-filled,
often dislocated dialogue.

That said, I must confess
that I find the film interminably
boring.

Just For The Record
Richard Mallett

Believe me, I don't pretend
to think that any words of mine will
by this time have any influence on,
or even be of particular interest to,
anybody who either has or has not
seen *The Great Dictator*. I should
like to get away from all this talk
about Mr. CHAPLIN's speech at the
end of the universally-praised
excellence of the film as propaganda and consider it merely as
entertainment. Great stretches of it
are perfectly brilliant, unbeatable
entertainment; for all of which the
old CHARLIE and not the new
serious-minded Mr. CHAPLIN is
responsible. The dance with the
balloon-world, the Brahms-accom-
panied shave, the Hitler speeches
that sound like duets for pig and
banjo—such scenes are first-class
and beautifully funny, and there
can be few people who would not
be delighted to see them again.
The serious stuff, on the other
hand: the Ghetto scenes, the
scenes of straight, as distinct from
comic (and defeated), stormtrooper brutality, and similar links
with the world of abominable
fact—these are less successful,
because of the old-fashioned,
almost "period" approach. Either
they are meant to be convincing or
they aren't; if they are, they fail to
convince an audience used to
more efficient methods of film-
making, and if they aren't there
was no point in including them at
all.

. . . And how many pursuits
are there more futile, do you think,
than the application of logical
methods to the discussion of a
Chaplin film? Of course you will
see *The Great Dictator*, and of
course you will enjoy it, and of
course nothing that anyone else
has to say about it matters at all.

Charlie

Barry Took

When Sir Charles Chaplin died on Christmas Day 1977 it was almost as if it was an afterthought. He slipped out of the world as un-obtrusively as he'd lived in it for the past twenty years quietly, in Switzerland. In his life he'd been loved and loathed, fêted and vilified, subject to villent abuse and praise that verged on deification. A contemporary of Henry Ford and Pierpoint Morgan, of Hitler and Mussolini, Stalin, Churchill, Roosevelt, Mao Tse Tung and General Franco, he was more famous and better liked than any of them and survived them all. Indeed Chaplin will survive as long as film survives and will be making people laugh through whatever eternity awaits the human race.

He came into films before anyone really knew how to make them and left the world at a time when all but a handful had forgotten. In between he made half a dozen great films, many good films and a few stinkers. In recent years it became fashionable among the reach-me-down pundits who scrape a living from the rim of show business to compare Chaplin with Keaton to Chaplin's detriment, which is as pointless as arguing about who won the battle of Jutland. In *Limelight* the two masters played a short scene together with such harmony and timing that you held your breath never wanting the scene to end.

When someone is great comparison is irrelevant and Chaplin was a great comedian. Not only that; he was a great teacher. His only tragedy was that so few bothered to learn. Vic Oliver, the Austrian comedian, used in his act to play a few notes on his violin, stop and say, ''all the great musicians are dead. Beethoven is dead, Brahms is dead, Mozart is

dead . . . I'm not feeling too good myself.'' With the passing of Chaplin you get a sneaking feeling that all the great English film comedians are dead. Stan Laurel is long gone although his films are always with us. Hancock and Sid Field died before they could develop. George Formby, Arthur Lucan and Will Hay were too idio-syncratic to do well in World cinema. Who's left? Well there's Terry Thomas, but he's settled for

character cameos. Peter Ustinov does voice-overs for Disney and appears to work for anyone who asks. Marty Feldman was quoted in the *Daily Mail* recently as saying he's going to spend '78 watching circus clowns in an attempt to build a screen personality (which is rather like watching the Muppets every week because you want to be a frog). Peter Cook and Dudley Moore spend more time out of the cinema than in it, although I have a hunch that Dudley is going to be very much in demand when their recently completed *Hound Of The Baskervilles* is released.

Then there's Monty Python as a group and John Cleese—solo. I have a feeling that Cleese is going to be the next big English film star.

John Cleese is intensely individual. He's extremely clever and extremely funny. He's already accepted as a TV star in England and is sufficiently experienced in film making to be able to make the jump from TV to film (and it's a big one: if you don't believe me, ask Morecambe and Wise or Charlie Drake) and determined enough to make sure that things are done his way. Let's face it, the man is obsessed and in the long run it's obsession that makes stars. Where would Chaplin have been without obsession or Garbo or John Wayne or Hitchcock? Obsession doesn't mean mania, although it hovers close by, obsession is the over-riding conviction that you are right. Cleese has one other quality that makes him an ideal hero in contemporary society. His work totally lacks sentiment. Not for him the tear behind the smile, the hint of tragedy behind the belly laugh. You feel that there may be razor blades in any custard pie he throws and that a slip on a Cleese banana skin could be terminal.

If I had a talking picture of you

Alan Coren

The survey revealed that the three films most often video-taped and most often re-run were Casablanca, The Sound of Music, and The Wizard of Oz.

US News & World Report

He swung the car into the garage too fast, partly because he had been concentrating on his mocking chuckle, partly because he was still not too good at driving with one hand and leaving the other draped nonchalantly across the back of the passenger seat, and he ran into the geraniums stacked, dormant, along the back wall.

He got out of the car and hurled the door shut with that cynical unconcern for material objects which he had really been working very hard at lately; but the wing-mirror fell off, and he could not suppress the wince which wiped out what remained of the mocking chuckle. He would have preferred not to have shut the door at all, he would have preferred to have left the engine running and tossed the keys to the saluting doorman, but they did not have a saluting doorman, and, anyway, he was not too good at tossing. The reason he was not wearing his new high-crown trilby with the steamed-down brim was that when he had walked into his office at the Trustee Savings Bank that morning and tossed it casually towards the hat stand, it had sailed out through the open window and been run flat by a Number Eleven bus.

He shoved his hands deep into his trench-coat pockets, em-bedding his fingers in a pork pie he had forgotten to eat at lunch-time, and stared at the ruined plant-pots.

He sucked his upper lip over his top teeth.

"Of all the garages in all the towns all over the world," he said softly, "she puts the geraniums in mine."

Then he removed his upper set to enable him to get his top lip down again, and went towards the house.

As he turned his key in the lock and pushed open the stained-glass-panelled door (it had a little mis-shapen palm tree on it, and a yacht, which always brought to him a poignant pang) of 14 Baluchistan Terrace, his eardrums vibrated with thirty wattsworth of *Over The Rainbow*. He glanced into the living room; the twin decanters of Cyprus Brown were jumping up and down on the walnutteen sideboard, and three chipped mallards were trembling on the regency-striped walls, the leaded lights were rattling in their eau-de-nil frames, and his three small children sat glued to the television set, impervious to the cannoning decibels.

He wondered, bitterly, whether Rick had had kids. He had run the cassette—what? Fifty times? but there had been no references to Casablanca Road Comprehensive, no complaints from the night club next door about offspring climbing over their fence and stoning their cat, no wellies, dead frogs, bits of Lego or satchels strewn all over the dance-floor. How had Rick got to forty without accumulating the genetic detritus that had come, willy-nilly, to everyone he knew?

"Cut the noise!" he snapped, rocking slightly on his

"*Relax everybody! It's only someone impersonating King Kong!*"

heels, leaning forward a degree or two from the hips, bunching his fists.

"We won't be able to hear!" screamed his son.

"We won't be able to learn the words!" howled his daughter.

The baby threw up, into the plum moquette.

He stared at them, trembling.

"The problems of three little people don't amount to a hill of beans in this crazy world," he muttered, "someday you'll understand that."

He turned on his heel.

The three children turned briefly from their devotions to watch him go. His son put a forefinger to his temple, and began to screw it in.

The baby laughed.

The daughter said:

"I wish we were orphans like Dorothy."

"Yes," said the son. "I'd rather have a scarecrow than *him* any day."

"Or a tin man," said his sister.

"Imagine being brought up by a *lion*!" cried the little boy. "Fantastic!"

The baby stuck his face in his Paddington, and began to sob.

She was staring out of the sink-window, towards Austria, when he walked into the kitchen. She wore a dirndl; she had put her hair in braids; but she could not see Austria for the rear wall of the Kumfisnugg Double Glazing factory at the end of their tiny garden. Not could the garden itself be said to be exactly alive with the sound of music: the lawn was churned mud, with the grass no more than sporadic verdigris among the weals of football boots, in the centre of which stood a rusted climbing-frame and two black apple-trees ineptly pruned to moribund stumps. It was the sort of view one might have had from a Passchendaele trench.

She did not turn when she heard the door close, because she knew that the kitchen had not been

entered by a lean-limbed smiling aristocrat in a green hunting coat and a feather in his hat.

He, for his part, was not particularly concerned at her not turning, since it was exceedingly unlikely that she had, in his absence, become a soft-mouthed Swede with eyes like Bambi and an imperceptible nose.

So he opened the larder, and he poured himself two fingers of Wincarnis, and he raised his glass to her back, and he said:

"Here's looking at you, kid."

The crash made her turn, finally.

"What was that?" she sang, projecting well, her mouth working like a Li-lo footpump, giving, as she turned, a little dancing skip.

"I walked into the larder door, kid," he muttered, dabbing the Wincarnis frantically from a trenchcoat that was as moisture-proof as you can get for £17.95, mail order warehouse.

"But That Is What Happens

"Well, I'm going upstairs to have a look at the shirts and socks... if you want anything, just whistle."

When You Do Not Wear Your Spectacles!'' she trilled, enunciating each word as if she were slicing cucumber.

"I see all right, kid,'' he grunted. He looked into his drink, swirled it around the glass, thought about curling his upper lip again, then thought twice. He did not want her to be there if his teeth fell into the Wincarnis. He wondered why her accent was getting more and more clipped. He wanted it to get more and more Swedish, it might help. He glanced up: maybe if they sold the video-recorder, he could buy her a nose job. Or, at least, a camel-coat, a big felt hat.

But how could he sell the machine? What would he do, nights?

She walked to the fridge, wondering why his accent was getting more and more American. She wanted it to get more and more Austrian, it might help.

"I Am Sixteen, Going on Seventeen!'' she carolled.

He banged down the empty glass. Why was it always the wrong women who ran off with Victor Laszlo?

"When do we eat?'' he said. Caviare, he thought, maybe a duck or two with cherries on it, one of them bottles of the Good Stuff you used to be able to get in Paris, a long time ago.

"I'm Waiting For The

Faggots To Thaw,'' she sopranoed atonally, momentarily drowning *The Yellow Brick Road* from the room next door, and he went out again.

He walked back slowly from the pub, ignoring the stars. Clear nights, who needs them? Fog was what you wanted, soft grey melancholy fog, with senior policemen materialising out of it, full of cynicism, who would tell him that it might be a good idea for him to stay out of Pinner for a time. These days, all you saw of cops was an arm throwing a crumpled crisp packet out of a Panda quarter-light.

Dinner had gone even more badly than normal. He had changed into a new white genuine ex-officer's tuxedo that had arrived only that morning, and the baby had thrown Miracle Whip all over it, and when he tried to mop the raspberry stain at the tap, the lapel had come off.

The older children had sung *Over The Rainbow* all the way through the meal, eighteen times in all, and his wife had encouraged them, since her pervading dream was of a choral family picking up cups and rosettes at every turn.

The centre of his faggot had been chill and hard, and when he pointed this out to her, she had thrown her head back, tossed her

hair seven or eight times, laughed gaily, and replied to the effect that doh was a deer, a female deer, and ray a drop of golden sun.

He had wondered, briefly, where Rick had managed to lay his hands on the Luger.

And then he had left them, and gone down to the pub, because it was his wife's turn on the video machine once more; so he had shrieked PLAY IT AGAIN! with all the sarcasm he could muster, and slammed the front door so hard that the yacht fell out.

He asked for a large rye at the Cock & Weasel, and the barman invited him to piss off, this was not a bleeding baker's, so he had mooched back into the night to walk around until *The Sound Of Music* had run its appalling course and it was his turn to run *Casablanca*, and now here he was at the gate of Number 14, and time had gone by, and there was, thank God, no flicker behind the front-room curtains, no tonic horrors as he opened the front door.

He did not take his trench-coat off. He inserted his cassette, and lit a cigarette, and let it hang in his mouth as he sat back in his chair, narrowing his eyes.

Upstairs, his wife lay staring at the ceiling, thinking of lederhosen; while, in the room across the landing, his children dreamed of Oz.

THE ROUGHEST CUT OF ALL
Larry Gelbart

Summer of '77. I'm on the beach at Honolulu, when the phone that always rings, rings. I am asked by David Merrick to write a screen-play called *Rough Cut*, which he is producing for Paramount. Blake Edwards to direct. Burt Reynolds to star. It's a sophisticated diamond caper movie, very much in the Cary Grant mould. Terrific.

Someone has already written a screenplay based on a novel whose name escapes everyone. I'm told I can use whatever I want of either. I read both, several hundred pages of paper, and weep for the poor trees that died in vain. While I am reading, my manager makes my deal with Merrick. I look forward to meeting with Blake in LA to discuss the screenplay. The next day my manager calls back. We no longer have a deal. Merrick does not want me to write the film. Why not? To this day I don't know. One day he loves me, the next day he hates me. What I also didn't know was how lucky I was, being out of the picture, figuratively and literally.

A few days later, another call. Merrick *wants* me to do the picture. I begin to feel I have a three-picture deal with Merrick—all to write the same picture. (I was later to find out that a team had been hired to write the screenplay after Merrick called off my first deal. Reynolds, who at that time, had writer and director approval, said he wanted only me to write the script and so the team was dropped. As of this moment, nine writers—if you count me three times—have worked on the film. But more of that later.)

Back in LA, Blake can't meet. He's off to Europe to look for locations for *The Pink Panther's Revenge.* We begin the first of many trans-Atlantic, trans-Pacific, trans-Sylvania phone calls in which I invariably wake him at three in the morning. Finally, we make a date to meet in Paris to lay out the outline. He can give me two days. Two nights, actually. Turns out to be more like two hours.

Blake is staying at the Bristol Hotel in Paris. In a duplex apartment with its own elevator. Very appealing to deposed dictators and film directors. By the time we meet in his private dining room, I have a galloping case of Napoleon's Revenge. After a superb dinner, which I wash down with a Mylanta suppository, we go to his study and chat for about an hour about the screenplay. Same thing, the next night. (Blake is busy with ''Panther'' business during the day.) What we decide is that I should go back to LA, work out my own outline and just start writing. Blake expresses his total confidence in what a great job I'm going to do.

So I write it. I deliver the screenplay to Merrick in January, '78. He sends it off to Blake, who is now in Hong Kong (naturally).

In February, I'm off to Fort Lauderdale for a month of rehearsals with the Jackie Gleason company of *Sly Fox* (that's another article—I'm only giving you one heartbreak at a time). Via phone, Blake and I try to figure out when would be the best time for me to meet him in Hong Kong. We decide that the best time would be never. We agree to meet in London in several weeks' time.

The meeting takes place in Blake's suite at the Dorchester. It has only one floor—he's roughing it. I'm feeling rotten again, terrible jet lag—the Wright Brothers' Revenge. Merrick is there, too. Blake's read my script. He loves everything up to and including the Main Titles. That is to say, he loves the first page. He tells me how he sees the rest of the picture. It's another movie, not the one I wrote, nor one that I can. An honest disagreement. Directors are the money. Merrick honestly sides with Blake. I'm off the picture. I've been in the business a lot of years. It always hurts.

I learn a few weeks later that *Blake* is off the picture. Merrick is looking for a new director. It seems Burt Reynolds wants to do *Starting Over* before *Rough Cut.* Merrick is willing. All Burt has to do is give up writer and director approval on *Rough Cut,* which he does.

(A word here about Mr Reynolds. When the Indians speak of a man of substance, they say he casts a shadow. Burt has the best shadow I've met in a long time.)

There follows a long period during which I have no idea of what is happening with the screenplay. In June of '79, Merrick asks me if I will go back to work on it. It is then that I learn at least four other writers have had a go at it. I then did three re-writes of the screenplay, working a good deal with Reynolds and Don Siegel, who was hired as director. And later fired as director. And then re-hired as director. After a couple of weeks of shooting in England, Siegel was taken off the picture by Merrick. A British director replaced him, but apparently that didn't work out. Blake Edwards flew in from his home in Switzerland to offer his services. One of his conditions was that he be allowed to do a re-write of my re-write of the various re-writes. Are you still re-with me?

Siegel came back. Anthony Shaffer, the English playwright, was hired to work on the script and is probably doing that, even as you are reading this piece—which Merrick will no doubt ask him to fix after he finishes the screenplay.

In 1960, Charlie Feldman hired me to write the screen version of a play called *Fair Game*. Written by Sam Locke, it ran 187 performances on Broadway, chiefly because of the popularity of its star, Sam Levene. Charlie had me write the Sam Levene part for William Holden. When I finished the First Draft, he told me I'd have to re-do it because instead of Holden, he was signing Jeanne Moreau for the part.

I really should have gone into real estate right then and there.

DOWN MAMMARY LANE
Barry Took

The first film I ever saw was either *Green Pastures,* or *The Lives Of A Bengal Lancer.* At a distance of forty years it's difficult to remember every detail, but as far as I can recall the film was about a negro family serving in the British Army on the N.W. Frontier. One son was called McGregor and was a rotter, the other was Mose, a swashbuckling roué who came up to scratch at the right time when the Regiment, owing to a timely intervention by someone called De Lawd, won the battle of Balaclava. The Colonel of the Regiment was

"He was one of the best stuntmen in the business."

183

played by C. Aubrey Smith and was called, as I remember, Catfish.

That's nostalgia for you; Instant Garble.

Because it's what you want it to be, the past is usually all good news, and I would be tampering with my own right to self-deception if I looked back at my cinema going with anything but pleasure.

Cinemas were built in the 30s, as were gin palaces a generation before, as somewhere to go that was better than home, and the Picture Palaces of my youth, the Gaumonts and the Ritzes and later the Odeons and Granadas, were marvels of comfort and excitement. Sitting round a coal fire listening to Harry Hemsley on the wireless was all right in its way but the cinemas had organs that rose up through the floor bathed in multi-coloured lights, and ice cream girls shining torches on their specialities, and usherettes in uniform, and *two* films—one occasionally in technicolour—and the news and sometimes a Donald Duck cartoon.

When the film broke, as it often did, everybody whistled and stamped and then cheered when it got going again. Going to the pictures was an event. Most of all, the cinema was a place you went with your parents—an adult pleasure which you were allowed to share from time to time. Later

"He keeps offering me 1s 9d."

when you went alone or with friends you felt on the verge of being grown up yourself.

I was so imbued with the magic of the cinema when I was a lad that it's not surprising (to me at any rate) that for the year or so when I was in the no man's land between school and National Service, I got a job at the Gaumont Palace in Wood Green as a projectionist. I felt like a novice in a religious order about to be initiated into the mysteries of the temple and, of course, my first job was to get the ''tea'' for the senior projectionists. The restaurant which was part of the cinema provided meals at specially low prices for the staff, but it was war time and my only clear memory of what we ate was something described optimistically as Welsh rarebit and which appeared to be an ingenious combination of felt and rubber.

The films we showed were a mixed lot but I remember *Dead Of Night* particularly. It was a collection of five short mystery cum horror stories by various authors, linked by most inventive and spine chilling narration involving a man's recurring dream. It starred, among others, Mervyn Johns, Roland Culver, Googie Withers, Michael Redgrave as a berserk ventriloquist, and the marvellous Frederick Valk. It was brilliant, British and, it's almost unnecessary to add, produced at Ealing by Michael Balcon.

In those days the programme ran from Monday to Saturday with three showings a day (with a complete change on Sunday) and the projectors with their carbon arcs and the films themselves with the occasional shaky joins needed constant supervision. Even with your day off you'd have seen the film over a dozen times before it was packed back into its tins (ten reels for a feature, eight reels for a second feature) and sent off to its next destination.

When you see them that often the majority of films become tedious, but once in a while there was one of outstanding quality that you were sorry to see go. *The Picture of Dorian Gray* starring George Sanders and Hurd Hatfield was one such, mainly because the

bit where you actually saw the hideous portrait was shot in colour in an otherwise black and white film—a piece of theatricality that was amazingly effective. I hadn't read any Oscar Wilde before seeing the film but did so immediately afterwards, and became a devotee. Years later, Marty Feldman and I wrote a parody of Dorian Gray for the radio show *Round The Horne*—and were able to do it without referring to the book so powerful were our memories of the original. Come to think of it, Dorian Gray would make a good story for a new Marty Feldman film with Marty as Dorian Gray and the portrait in the attic getting handsomer and handsomer. (Remember, you read it here first!)

Another film I remember but with less affection from those days was *A Song To Remember,* the story of Chopin's love for George Sanders, sorry, George Sand, and which in spite of starring Merle Oberon set my teeth on edge so much that I cannot listen to Chopin nowadays without breaking into a rash. And talking of Poles, two Polish servicemen, Marek and Rojak, joined our little team in the projection box at the Wood Green Gaumont in 1945. They'd had the most extraordinary adventures in the war, being overrun by the Russians in 1939, drifting through Russia in a labour battalion after the Germans invaded in '40, joining up with the Polish division in the Middle East, fighting with the 8th Army in the desert and in Italy. They'd been wounded in action at Monte Cassino and were being retrained in civilian occupations before going back to Poland. I had my first lessons in political reality from those two splendid young Poles. Wherever they are now I hope they're thriving.

During the week we were showing *A Song To Remember*, Marek came up to me and said, ''Excuse me, I know the music from this picture but what is the story?'' I told him but he didn't believe me.

Our chief was a dour man who'd been a projectionist from the days of silent films from the time in fact when projectors were handcranked. ''Ah,'' he'd say, ''in those days you could get home early if you wanted—You just cranked a bit faster.'' He'd shown the first talkie in Britain when the sound came from large discs that had to be synchronised with the film. His great ambition was to become the manager of a shoe shop. I know it doesn't sound all that strange an ambition but it seemed odd to me at the time to want to swap the airy fantasy of Garbo, Dietrich, Hayworth and Jinx Falconburg for the grim reality of the hammer toe, the bunion and the fallen arch. He used to read books on salesmanship and busi-ness efficiency and dream of prize winning displays of bootlaces and dubbin and left us younger chaps to see to showing the films, spot-lighting the organist and flashing on the advertising slides for Miners Liquid Make Up, Bronx cigarettes, Kolynos toothpaste and the rest in the interval between programmes.

From time to time we'd put the reels on in the wrong order, (boos and stamping feet) miss the changeover from one reel to the next, and there'd be an em-barrassing pause as the second machine was started and the dreaded 10, 9, 8, 7, 6 flashed up on the screen—and the assistant manager rushed, white faced, into the box and abused everybody in sight while the Poles cursed him back in Lower Silesian and the chief lingered on in the rest room, his head full of Phillips stick-a-soles and blakies.

Sometimes we forgot to re-wind the film and showed chunks of it backwards and upside down (boos to crescendo and threats of mass sackings). It was a relief when my call up papers arrived and I exchanged the silver screen for air force blue. I've never hankered to repeat the experience of projecting movies—but one strange side effect that brief episode in my life has left me with is that having seen *Topper*, *Mr Smith Goes To Washington*, *The Mark of Zorro*, *Tales Of Manhattan*, *Heaven Can Wait*, and *Step Lively*, many many times, I can (when I've had a couple) give an extremely accurate impersonation of the late Eugene Pallette . . . and good though Margaret Hinxman is, I bet she can't do that.

My Years with Marilyn

As the Monroe bandwagon rolls on, lovely (but temperamental) **Keith Waterhouse** grabs his scrapbook and scrambles aboard

The enigma that was Marilyn Monroe will intrigue me all my life, or at least all the way through a full-length biographical investi-gation, serialisation of same, a TV documentary, and half a dozen one-off articles explaining how the enigma came my way.

My fascination with Marilyn goes back to a chilly December dawn in 1959, the year of *Some Like It Hot.* It was 10.37 p.m. Pacific Time, 6.42 a.m. by my bedroom clock (I kept it five minutes fast and still do: a reminder, now, of Marilyn). My phone shrilled. It was Ziggy Tannenbaum, then head of production at Unilateral, speaking from Beverly Hills. He was planning an updated remake of *The Fall of the House of Usher*, but with lotsa laughs.

He saw Marilyn as the goil. The property was a very deep and very beautiful and very moving exploration of humanity trapped in its own consciousness, and there was already a screenplay by Hermann (*Cry, My Darling*) Pastrami which was truly a work of art. All it needed was the yoks. Given carte blanche to throw Hermann's script out the window, would I work on the re-writes?

I said I would be delighted.

''I had a feeling, Terry. I had a feeling this was your kind of movie. Like I was saying to my very beautiful wife Wanda who loves your work, with Marilyn as the goil all right I'm happy, but with Terry's name on the credits I'm twice as happy. Now lemme ask you this, Terry. How soon can you get off your ass and come over here?''

I said I could come on the next plane, but why was he calling me Terry?

''Isn't this Mr. Terence Rattigan, the English writer?''

''No,'' I said. ''You must have the wrong number.''

''Chee! Telephone operators!'' said Ziggy, and hung up.

So, in the end, I was never to meet Marilyn. I was never to meet Ziggy either, but I read in a fan magazine that the remake of *Fall* had been shelved. Marilyn was already on location for *The Misfits* and she had sent back Hermann's first draft unread. It was endearingly, infuriatingly, typical.

Marilyn was not the kind of girl you forgot, or ever wanted to. If she ever did stray from my mind for a moment, a glance at my bedroom clock, five minutes fast, would bring me back to cloud seven. The clock now stands on my desk as I write. It shows 4.58. It will be 4.53 in Newton Abbott . . .

A blazing afternoon in the autumn of 1973. I am standing on

the up platform at Newton Abbott station, and I have just learned that the 4.53 to Paddington runs only on Fridays. I have forty minutes to kill before the 5.30. (Funny how Marilyn, so crazily unpunctual, is forever linked in my mind with time.)

Browsing at the station bookstall, I picked up a newspaper. I don't know, will never know, why I should have chosen that particular paper but my instincts were right for it contained a full-page article on Marilyn. So, I think, did every other newspaper and magazine on the stall, so maybe it was not such a hunch at that.

Most of the stuff was old hat—the Monroe "legend" reworked by someone who had never even known her—but there was one story new to me, that throws some light on the secret of Marilyn's charisma.

In 1953, when she was working on *How to Marry a Millionaire*, the girls in the commissary had clubbed together and bought her a birthday present—a tiny dime-store wristwatch. Some of Marilyn's "friends" thought it was a heavy hint to stop arriving for breakfast during the second lunch setting. Maybe it was. But Marilyn, with her heartbreaking naivety, was as delighted as a little girl with her first doll. She promised to wear the watch next to her wrist.

Her notorious unpunctuality had long been noticed on the *Millionaire* set. The morning after the presentation she had been running a temperature of 214°F, two degrees above boiling point. On top of that her studio car had been involved in a minor collison on Ventura Boulevard. She arrived on the lot, white and tense, an hour and twenty minutes late.

One of the extras, who had been hoping to get away earlier to keep a dental appointment, muttered, "What the hell time does she call this?"

Nobody heard him except Marilyn. Forcing a dazzling smile, she looked at the cheap little watch on her left wrist and pouted: "Twenty after nine."

Recalling that story now, it seems to me there is something missing—a haunting punchline, perhaps, some elusive piece that will never be fitted into the jigsaw that was Marilyn Monroe. Was the point, perhaps, that she kept her dime-store watch five minutes fast, like my bedroom clock? I like to think so.

I haven't explained what I was doing in Newton Abbott that day. It doesn't seem important any more.

The story of Marilyn and the motorcycle is maybe apocryphal, maybe not. Perhaps, as with so many of the legends that began to cling like barnacles to her siren personality, the truth lies somewhere between fact and fancy. For what it is worth, it was told o me by Bobby Avocado. He had heard it on a TV chat programme.

Bobby was a sometime partner of mine in a publishing project we had tried to put together in the spring of 1972. It was going to be a monthly pocket magazine called *Marilyn Monroe Digest*, reprinting the best of all that was being written about Marilyn. If we had waited another eighteen months we would have made a killing, but we were ahead of the market. The first and only print of *Marilyn Monroe Digest* went for pulp.

But Bobby and I kept in touch when we could, and one autumn evening in 1973 he arrived at my house unheralded. It transpired that he had been in the neighbourhood and thought he would drop in for a drink.

Over a JB (straight, with a twist of lemon), Bobby asked—abruptly, I thought—"Did you see A——— C——— (a well-known writer) on the box last night? I couldn't understand a word he said."

I'd missed the programme. I remembered that the previous night I'd been playing squash.

"He started to tell some rambling, pointless story about Marilyn Monroe and a motor bike, then he broke off in the middle and said, 'No, I tell a lie, it wasn't Marilyn Monroe, it was Betty Grable.' Pie-eyed, completely."

"Marilyn? She was never a drinker."

"No, not Marilyn. A——— C———. Tight as an owl, if you ask me.

No studio that she ever worked for would have allowed Marilyn to ride a motor bike. Yet the legend persists. Was it, like her friendship with Kennedy, one of Marilyn's "open secrets"? We shall never know.

In 1950 Marilyn made *Love Happy*, followed by *The Asphalt Jungle* and *All About Eve*. In 1951, *Love Nest* and *Let's Make It Legal*. The pace was fast and dangerous—five movies in two years; three of them in one year, two in the other. Two of them had two-word titles, one had a three-word title, and another no fewer than four. Any analyst of her mood at that time, who wanted to fill up space, could go on to point out that three of these titles began with the letter "L", of which two were the same word—"Love". No wonder the girl who had been born Norma Jean Baker was confused.

Early in 1952 she spoke to a visitor from Denver, G. G. Potboil, who was on a conducted tour of the set. Potboil was fooling around with a "prop" stethoscope, and Marilyn thought he was a doctor.

"I feel dizzy," said Marilyn.

Potboil, who recalls the encounter in his book, *The Marilyn I Knew*, retorted: "Boy, you sure as all hell look dizzy!" He was escorte' from the set.

"The tip of the iceberg" is the wrong expression maybe, but I feel that in setting down these memories I have only brushed fingers with the real Marilyn Monroe. Maybe there was too much to say, and too little space to say it in. She remains, as I said a hundred thousand words back, an enigma. Maybe the key to the Chinese box of emotions that was Marilyn Monroe lies in a very long narrative concerning a visit to her dentist in 1955, the year of *The Seven-Year Itch.* But that is another story, and another book.

Screen Caption. "THIS DREADFUL SILENCE! WHAT WOULD I NOT GIVE FOR THE SOUND OF A HUMAN VOICE?"

As
Stanley Reynolds
rides away into
the sunset, he has
just one
complaint

They Don't Make Endings Like They Used To

Happiness may after all be egg shaped, a warm puppy, the light shining in my sweetie's eyes or, like the old song says, a thing called Joe. The difficulty in defining it may perhaps come from the fact that when you loom at one of·the traditional places for finding it, it just ain't there no more. I refer, of course, to endings, Happy Endings. *Three dozen Busby Berkeley Girls and Dick Powell singing in the middle of them . . . Do you see those Spitfires up there Miranda, well, that's where I belong, up there making sure Nosher and Pongo didn't die in vain . . . Wipe your tears, my dear, there's a clinic in Zurich that can . . . And so Tom Sawyer and me was home again with Aunt Polly and the reward money . . . I can (see) (walk) (talk) (dance) (sing) (love) (live) again . . .*

Is it, I ask myself lying awake at night, blinking in the darkness, waiting for that spark of inspiration like Don Ameche had when he played Alexander Graham Bell or Cornell Wilde had as Liszt, some kind of a goddam plot or something? Some vast conspiracy perhaps on the part of the entertainment industry to keep us all in our ordinary little places by showing us, on stage, screen, and printed page that not only does life no longer have the possibility of a happy ending, but also it often has no ending at all, merely a finish of the whimpering just before the credits roll. The consumer of the mass produced dream life sits huddled before television, silver screen, or over the printed page eager to be carried away on fantasy's winsome wings and inevitably as the play, film, or novel closes he is smacked in the face with the flannel of damp apathy when he is not sloshed over the head with a bucket of icy despair. It was not, I hasten to add, always so. *Betty Hutton marrying Eddie Bracken . . . Dick Powell marrying Mary Martin . . . Jimmy Stewart falling into the arms of June Allyson . . . You remember those old stocks and shares Uncle Albert left in his trunk, well they're worth a cool . . . Ziegfeld was out front tonight and he's coming backstage to . . . It is a far, far better thing I do . . . I'm saving these last bullets for Effie and the kids, if those murderin' devils—hey! is that the sound of a bugle? . . . But it was you I really always loved, Margie . . . And Scrooge was as good as his word . . . Gad, Holmes, you've done it again . . .*

Your average TV play comprises, in these days of tightened production budgets, maybe four characters. If two of them are male, two female, or anything closely resembling either, and the play is going out in one of the prestige drama spots, you can bet your hard-back copy of *A Christmas Carol* that if relationships all around don't break up before the sixty minutes are done your set must have broken down or maybe you dozed off and who can blame you. The only thing looking like an optimistic sign that I can make out on the mist shrouded horizon of TV drama is the modern alternative to the miserable ending which is, of course, *no ending at all.* You know the sort of thing. After some poor wretch has been through everything hellish that the modern mind can devise—lack of communications, his secretary sniggering at his new flared bell-bottoms—the play will end with him staring or walking into the distance with the theme music slamming home the message about how uncertain this whole life business is. Gone is the definite finish, the real end that we grew up with in the older more stable world of depression,

189

"I 'VE SEEN IT—'TAIN'T NO GOOD."
"'E GETS 'UNG, DON'T 'E?"
"YUS, BUT THEY DON'T SHOW YER THAT."

As far as the reader or viewer is concerned, the non-end is perhaps more satisfactory because he is able, with a little imagination, to provide his own happy finale as he drifts off in the arms of nembutal. The writer may have shunned anything as nastily bourgeois as a funeral, a wedding, a birth, or a volcanic eruption to put paid to his puppets but the imaginative consumer of today's packaged dream life can change all that, imagining for instance that the sinister man who came in to read the gas meter was in reality a long lost uncle who has made a fortune in Australia and has come back disguised as a sinister meter reader just to see if that niece of his has real character. "Wipe your tears, my dear," the sinister meter reader says, suddenly changing into Charles Coburn who made a fortune in Hollywood in the old days playing these parts, "we'll get Tiny Tim a new crutch; and there is a clinic in Zurich, and if they can't cure you—what the hell! Heroin grows on trees when you've got the kind of money I've got."

With your actual miserable and unhappy ending, however, there is no such escape. The consumer of the sorry dream life is stuck. Grim and dreary shades haunt him as he climbs the stairs to bed or puts aside the bedside book and blows out the lantern. The best advice here is to stop reading or viewing at that point where a happy ending looks at all possible. It is not much of a suggestion, but it may bring some relief to fellow escapists who are sick and tired of being left with a sinking, if not decidedly sunken, feeling at the end of a work of contemporary fiction, left miserable and wondering what ever happened to the supply of happy ends. *I thought, Belinda, if you knew that I were a King, you wouldn't... And I saw J.B. this morning, Sue, and he did... Free, free from the terrible curse of that monster my father, the Baron, created... And we'll be known as the folks who live on the hill... And there's four or five million more little people out there, Mayor McGinty, who are sick of being taken for suckers by political bums like you... And on the third day He... And then maybe Europe will be*

hunger marches, world wars, and no drip dry stay-pressed lightweight fabrics. *Free, free at last of this terrible curse of turning into a wolfman every time the moon is full... Dead, yes, but his (music) (poetry) (painting) (books) (electric light bulb) will shine forever... He was yellow, the dirty stinking rat was yellow ... Gosh, Mickey, you do... Perhaps it is old fashioned and stuffy of me, Miriam, but I think that England, and the ordinary men and* *women of England, stand for something bigger than Herr Hitler and Il Duce and their... The moon belongs to everyone, Eddie... So, obviously it could not have been Cartwright, and Lady De Villiers says she saw Dr. Jergens in the conservatory at nine o'clock, and so the murderer is... I do... And that is how Nicely Nicely Johnson is squaring it with the bookmaker, plus throwing a little something in the way of the old doll's home... It's ours boys! It's one of ours!...*

safe for free men to . . . It's oil, oil, oil, Miss Charlotte, gushin' up black and beautiful . . . OK copper, you got me dead to rights . . . And Yes, I said, Yes . . . And now maybe Dodge City will be a safe place for a . . . And just as soon as your leg is better, Dad, and you're out of hospital, Mr. Green wants to see you back at the plant . . . You do, Ginny, you really do? Sure, silly, I always have . . . That is the Zulu warriors tribute to brave men . . .

The trouble with modern fiction, however, is that the characters just seem to amble along, veering from apathy to boredom with only the occasional outburst of anger and tears to punctuate the disillusion and world weariness. What can you do with or for characters like that? They aren't vampires, they don't get attacked by Red Indians, they aren't trying to invent the electric light bulb like Spencer Tracy or ride the winning horse in the Grand National like twelve-year-old Elizabeth Taylor. The psychotic plots they are wriggled through are all neuroses and nothing money can cure. In fact, somewhere writers have picked up the idea that money doesn't solve anything. Where they got this idea I don't know, unless it drifted in along with the tax demands on the fat fees they earn. Now, unfortunately, all the most miserable people in novels or big or little screen dramas are miserable in the highest style of comfort, with wall to wall carpets, central heating, dream kitchens, and the latest in fashionable clothes. They are even all healthy. Just ask yourself, when was the last time you saw a character whose old mother needed an operation or whose kid brother would never play the violin again? Or, for that matter, whose little stockholders would all lose their life savings? Whose daughter was being forced into a loveless marriage? Whose son had let the regiment down? Whose great uncle, the Baron, had unleashed a monster on Transylvania or even the North Riding? Yes, there's the nub. It isn't so much the demise of the happy ending, it's just that they don't make misery like they used to. *Dead, dead, and never called me mother . . . Atlanta's burnin' Miss Scarlet . . . This is ruin, United Consolidated down another five points . . . All these years I've secretly hated you . . . So you von't talk, eh? . . . My God! The Thing! It's eaten Professor Charters . . . It's every man for himself now . . . I give up . . . I'll never (laugh) (love) (dance) (play) (sing) (walk) (write) (invent) again . . . ARGGGH! This is poisoned . . .*

"Hold it, I said!"

INDEX
OF
ARTISTS

'Brief Encounters,

Betty Grable
'My Blue Heaven,

Cécile Aubry -
'Manon,

Michel Auclain -
'Manon

Linda Darnell -
'No Way Out'

Sydney
Poitier -
'No Way Out'

Roger Blin -
'Passionelle,

Man's
Head
'Passionelle,

Odette
Joyeux -
'Passionelle,

Richard Widmark -
'No Way Out'

Stephen McNally -
'No Way Out,

Dan
Dailey
'My Blue Heaven,